500 DREAMS Interpreted

Helen Bertrand

WEST
SIDE
PUBLISHING

Writer: Helen Bertrand is a pseudonym used by an avid lucid dreamer who has been involved in dream research for more than 20 years. She has authored and coauthored several books and articles on the topics of dream interpretation, sleep paralysis, and lucid dreaming.

Fact Checker: Keith Potempa

Illustrators: Joan Falquet, Jessica Sporn

West Side Publishing is a division of Publications International, Ltd.

ISBN-13: 978-1-4127-7796-4
ISBN-10: 1-4127-7796-8

Manufactured in U.S.A.

8 7 6 5 4 3

CONTENTS

Introduction
DARE TO DREAM

—⟨⊙⊙⟩—

DO YOU REALIZE THAT YOU HAVE THE POWER
TO TRANSFORM YOUR LIFE OVERNIGHT? WHILE YOU
SLEEP, YOU HAVE ACCESS TO A VAST STOREHOUSE
OF KNOWLEDGE AND GUIDANCE—INFORMATION THAT
IS EXPRESSED THROUGH YOUR DREAMS, AVAILABLE
AND PERSONALIZED JUST FOR YOU.

—⟨⊙⊙⟩—

Dreams are a symbolic language designed to communicate
your inner wisdom to you while you sleep. The part of your
subconscious that processes dreams—your dream self—sends
messages as symbols and images, which in turn convey ideas
or situations in a visual language. Your dream symbols are not
meaningless, nor are they sent to confuse you. These messages
are always for your benefit: They are your mind's way of helping
you evaluate and improve various areas of your life.

Because your dream self is trying to communicate with you,
it strives to get its messages across in ways you can relate to
personally. Dreams are made up of elements of your everyday
experiences. Your dream self draws upon
your memories, beliefs, expectations,
fears, hopes—even your private
inner world of fantasies and
daydreams. Using this vast
amount of information, your
dream self creates a distinct,
symbolic language just for you.

When you learn the unique language of your dreams and discover how your mind uses associations, images, and figures of speech, you can discover the meanings behind the messages that your dream self sends you every night. In the process, you will become your own best dream interpreter. But if you aren't familiar with your dream language, it's like watching a foreign film without subtitles. You may get a vague idea of the movie's theme from the images you see, but the overall message will likely be unclear or confusing.

There is no such thing as "just a dream." Every dream you have carries a message to your waking self. Even if you think a particular dream means nothing—or if you cannot remember your dreams at all—your dream self makes every effort to support and guide you. With practice, you can learn how to fully explore your dreams and apply their symbolism to all

> *A dream which is not understood is like a letter which is not opened.*
> —The Talmud

aspects of your life, using them as a source of advice, encouragement, and inspiration.

A PICTURE IS WORTH A THOUSAND WORDS

The key to unlocking the meanings of your dreams is the realization that they are not one-way experiences in which your dream self simply bombards you with information. Dreams are not lectures or emotional forecasts; rather, they are cooperative endeavors and dialogues between your conscious and subconscious minds—between your waking and dreaming selves. Your part of the dialogue is generated by your thoughts, emotions, and experiences—in addition to how you communicate with people. Your dream self uses this information to create visual pictures that show you what you feel and how you see things in your world. In turn, these pictures assist you in living a more fulfilled and balanced life.

A FRIENDSHIP WITH BENEFITS

If you demonstrate an interest in learning your personal dream language, and if you respect your dreams and place value on them, you will be rewarded. Your dream self is like an acquaintance you occasionally converse with. If you are attentive to the conversations, they will become more engaging, and your acquaintance will offer more details and information. But why not take that relationship one step further? Make your dream self more than an acquaintance—make it a close friend. You will be amazed at how your inner world of dreams will respond to your efforts as you begin to tap its vast potential.

Your dream self can help you discover talents and abilities you may not know you possess. You can reduce everyday stress; gain insight into personal conflicts; find clarity in confusing professional situations; and discover ways to solve problems, improve skills, and develop and enhance your creative capabilities. In working with your dreams, you will gain confidence and a sense of control as you discover more about yourself.

As you learn how to interpret your dreams, you will also begin to recognize attitudes and habits that may not be serving you in a positive way. You can face fears and overcome personal challenges in a safe and private environment. You will start to welcome and embrace happiness, prosperity, and success in your life. With practice, you will learn to program or "incubate" a dream so you can address a specific problem, experience a dream adventure, or indulge in a dream fantasy. And because dreams often have several "levels" of meaning, the more dream work you do, the better perspective you'll have on your life.

THE KEYS TO SUCCESS

Throughout history, information acquired through dreams has been the source of prophetic warnings and predictions, as well as the inspiration behind significant sociological and scientific breakthroughs. Harriet Tubman credited her dreams with giving her the insight and courage to provide safe passage to fugitive slaves, and Albert Einstein claimed that a dream inspired his theory of relativity. But dream discoveries are not just for a chosen few, and you don't have to be an activist or a genius to profit from their wisdom. Everyone has the ability and potential to tap into the power of their dreams.

Becoming actively engaged with your dream self will open up a whole new world of understanding and empowerment. Are you ready to embark upon an exciting nocturnal journey of self-discovery? Go on, dare to dream, and unlock the treasures of your mind!

Lifesaving Sleep

Canadian physician Frederick Banting had a dream that led to a breakthrough in diabetes research. One night he woke from a dream and wrote down three lines of instructions for an experimental procedure. Banter and his colleagues subsequently performed the experiment and, as a result, discovered insulin.

Chapter One
WHAT HAPPENS BEHIND CLOSED EYES

Your subconscious mind is like a warehouse of personal history, a huge database filled with intimate details. If you are flexible in your attitude toward dreams, your dream self will be able to convey more information to you.

WHY DO WE DREAM?

This question, which has been asked since the dawn of time, has no definitive answer. Although it is not entirely clear why people dream, most experts believe that it is to assist the body with rest, repair, and rejuvenation. Others speculate that we dream for psychological reasons: to reexamine the day's events, to reduce and relieve stress, and to provide an outlet for pent-up emotions. Here are some widely recognized explanations for why we dream.

Compensation. Famed psychologist Carl Jung believed that we dream in order to compensate for underdeveloped parts of our personali-

> *Since everything living strives for wholeness, the inevitable one-sidedness of our conscious life is continually being corrected and compensated by the universal human being in us, whose goal is the ultimate integration of conscious and unconscious.*
>
> —Carl Jung

ties. This may explain why the dream behavior of some people is markedly different from the way they act in their waking lives.

Information Processing. This interpretation suggests that dreams help the brain process and organize the conscious and unconscious stimuli it receives during the day, which serves to refresh the mind. In this way, dreams are the brain's way of "rebooting the system."

Coping Mechanism. Psychiatry professor Ernest Hartmann proposes that dreams are directed by particular emotions, and new material is constantly "weaved" into the memory of the dreamer in ways that help him or her cope with stress, trauma, and other types of psychological anxiety.

Activation Synthesis. This theory, put forth by neurophysiologists J. Allan Hobson and Robert McCarley, suggests that dreams are the result of sensory-motor signals, which activate areas of the brain that deal with emotions, memory, and sensation. The brain creates dreams as it tries to give meaning to these signals.

Resolution. Some scientists believe that dreaming is a problem-solving function. They propose that while we sleep, our brains continue to process issues of concern in our waking lives and constantly attempt to come up with answers and solutions.

Wish Fulfillment. In 1899, Sigmund Freud wrote *The Interpretation of Dreams*, in which he suggests (among other things) that dreams are the result of repressed emotions and may represent unconscious thoughts, wishes, and desires.

To date, there has been no solid scientific evidence to prove or disprove any of these theories. But given the discoveries, inspirations, and innovations brought about by dreams, it is certain that they serve a multitude of purposes and are valuable and essential to our psychological and physical well being.

A Science in Its Infancy

Although dreams have fascinated humankind for millennia, the science of dream interpretation is just over a half century old. Sleep patterns were first discovered in 1935, but it wasn't until the early 1950s that dreaming sleep was more accurately evaluated, identified, and explained.

In 1953, Eugene Aserinsky—a graduate student performing research with professor Nathaniel Kleitman at the University of Chicago—was examining the eye movements of infants as they fell asleep. He noticed that the slow, rolling motions of their closed eyes sometimes became rapid, as though the babies were awake and watching something in motion.

While conducting subsequent experiments with sleeping adults, Aserinsky and Kleitman observed similar eye movement. The subjects were awakened at the point when their closed eyes started moving rapidly, and they were asked what they had just experienced. Most replied that they had been dreaming. Subjects who were awakened when their eyes were not moving rapidly often had no such memories. This rapid eye movement (REM) state became associated with dreaming, and the non-REM, or NREM, state was characterized by dreamless sleep. This groundbreaking discovery gave rise to the scientific study of dreams.

Your Nightly Roller Coaster Ride

When you lie down to sleep, you are usually alert because your brain is still producing small, rapid beta waves. But as you begin to relax and feel drowsy, the beta waves slow down and become alpha waves. At this point, you may experience a phenomenon called hypnagogia, which is characterized by visual and auditory hallucinations that could make it difficult for you to fall into a deep sleep. You may think you hear someone calling your name, or you may "see" random geometric patterns. Many people report sensations of falling, accompanied by sudden body movements (referred to as myo-clonic jerks). With all this activity, it's almost as if your body were fighting to stay awake. In fact, though, you are entering the first of several stages of sleep.

Each night, your body begins a cycle that alternates between REM and NREM states. Every 90 minutes or so, you go from light sleep to deep sleep and back to light sleep in a pattern that repeats four to six times (depending on the number of hours you sleep). With the use of an electroencephalograph (EEG), scientists have been able to identify and monitor the distinct stages of REM and NREM sleep, which are characterized by changes in brain-wave activity, heart rate, muscle tension, respiration, and body temperature.

That's Some Catnap!

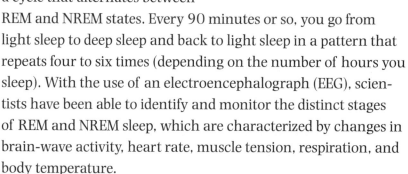

Researchers who have recorded EEG patterns among mammals, birds, and reptiles reveal that different animals need varying amounts of sleep. Bats and opossums are the sleepiest creatures, requiring approximately 20 hours of sleep in a 24-hour period. The typical house cat naps at least 12 hours per day, and most dogs doze for 10 hours. At the other end of the spectrum is the giraffe, which sleeps only 5 or 10 minutes at a time for an average of just 2 hours per day.

NREM Sleep

Stage 1: As you enter this stage of transition, you begin to drift off. Your muscles relax, your body temperature and blood pressure decrease slightly, and your breathing begins to slow. As your brain's production of alpha waves decreases, your awareness of extraneous noise and light begins to fade, and your eyes exhibit slow, rolling movements. This phase lasts only 5 or 10 minutes, and you can be awakened from it easily.

Stage 2: After an undisturbed period in Stage 1, you will descend to Stage 2 and begin to experience a deeper relaxation. You may not feel deeply asleep, but you are well on your way. Your body temperature decreases further and your heart rate slows. Your brain produces slower theta waves, which are accompanied by higher peaks of activity called sleep spindles. You remain in this state for 10 to 20 minutes.

Stage 3: You are now in a deeper sleep, and you can't be roused easily. Your body temperature continues to drop, as do your heart rate and breathing. Your brain is still producing theta waves, which will gradually change to larger, lower-frequency delta waves.

Stage 4: You are sleeping deeply now but not yet dreaming, and it is difficult for you to be awakened because your body's sensitivity to its surroundings is diminished. Brain activity consists mostly of delta waves.

Resurfacing to REM Sleep

After about 20 minutes in Stage 4 NREM sleep, you begin to cycle back up through Stages 3 and 2. But instead of returning to Stage 1 and then waking, your body enters its REM-sleep state. You are now in prime dream mode. The electrical activity in your brain is similar to when you are awake (characterized by beta waves), and your eyes move back and forth quickly beneath your lids. It's as if you were awake and concentrating on something. Some researchers believe that your brain is focusing intently on your dreams.

In this phase, your heart rate and breathing speed up, your temperature rises, and oxygen flow to your brain increases. During REM, your body also undergoes what is referred to as sleep paralysis, in which your muscles (except those in the eyes) are essentially immobilized. Some scientists believe sleep paralysis occurs to prevent us from "acting out" our dreams and possibly hurting ourselves.

Up and Down, Round and Round

During the first part of the night, you will spend the majority of your time in Stage 4 sleep, which allows your body to rest and rejuvenate. Consequently, if you don't get enough Stage 4 sleep, you wake up tired. The time you spend in Stages 3 and 4 decreases as you continue sleeping, allowing you more time in REM, or dreaming, sleep. Early-morning dreams are longer and more vivid than dreams you have earlier in the night because each new cycle through REM sleep lasts a little longer than the previous one. During the early-morning hours after a good night's rest, REM sleep lasts from 25 to 45 minutes each cycle.

End of the Ride

When you begin to wake up, you might experience a sensation referred to as hypnopompia, which is similar to hypnagogia (the mild hallucinations typical of Stage 1 sleep). You could feel momentarily disoriented, as if you were getting off an actual roller coaster. You may feel as if there is great pressure on your chest or that you are underwater. Sometimes it feels and sounds as if someone has entered the room and is sitting on the bed beside you. You may also wake with a jerk or feel like you are falling. During hypnopompia, your mind wakes up before your

body does; your body is still "paralyzed" from the REM stage of sleep. Many people fall asleep and awaken without incident, and even if they have episodes of hypnagogia or hypnopompia, they don't remember them. But people who do recall these feelings often describe them as disturbing or frightening. If you experience hypnopompia when you are trying to wake up, remain calm and relaxed, and soon your body will be fully awake and you will be able to move.

Don't Deprive Yourself!

If you were to become sleep-deprived, and therefore REM-deprived, you would not dream. You would experience fatigue, irritability, loss of memory, and difficulty concentrating, in addition to a host of other symptoms. Research has shown that extreme sleep deprivation can cause people to enter the REM stage while awake, inducing hallucinations and sleep paralysis. In effect, they start to have waking "nightmares," which is the body's response to needing sleep. Other unpleasant effects of sleep and dream deprivation include blurred vision, muscle aches, depression, delirium, paranoia, headaches, weight fluctuations, and a weakened immune system. The long-term effects of sleep deprivation (particularly symptoms of depression) can last as long as six months. Recent studies even suggest that there is a link between sleep deprivation and diabetes and obesity.

So not only is dreaming an essential part of maintaining good physical health, but mining the wisdom of your dreams can greatly improve your mental health as well.

If You Don't Snooze, You Lose

Many people have attempted to set records for time spent without sleep. In 1964, California high school student Randy Gardner stayed awake for 11 days under the supervision of researchers at Stanford University. Other sources cite subjects who have gone as long as 18 days without sleep, though there is insufficient evidence to back these claims. Because of the extreme dangers associated with prolonged sleep deprivation, *The Guinness Book of World Records* no longer recognizes the category.

Chapter Two
REV UP YOUR DREAM RECALL

IT'S A SCIENTIFIC FACT THAT EVERYONE DREAMS.
EVEN PEOPLE WHO SWEAR THEY DON'T ACTUALLY
DO—THEY SIMPLY CAN'T REMEMBER THEIR DREAMS.
BUT DREAMS ARE ACCESSIBLE TO EVERYONE.
ALMOST ANYONE WHO DOES NOT RECALL DREAMS
CAN LEARN TO REMEMBER THEM.

START PLAYING MIND GAMES

The first step to good dream recall is keeping the visual images fresh in your mind. What's more, you'll want to remember as many details as possible so you can get the most out of the messages sent from your dream self. Whether you remember fragments of your dreams or you think you don't remember them at all, you can activate or improve your recall by doing some interesting—and fun—dream work.

Window of Opportunity

This visual exercise is designed to develop your observational skills, which will, in turn, enhance your dream experiences every night.

Pick a comfortable place to sit near a window. Take a few moments to relax and then let your gaze wander outside. Observe as much detail as you can while staying focused but

receptive—you should not feel as though you are preparing for a test.

Let's say the window overlooks a park. Take in the various colors you see in the sky and in the different trees, grasses, flowers, etc. Identify as many species of plant life as you can. Are the walkways similar to well-worn garden paths, or are they paved or gravel-lined? Study any benches, monuments, or other decorative features. Notice any wildlife present or passing through: ducks, birds, butterflies, squirrels. Do you see a lake, pond, or brook? If there are adults in the park, are they walking, jogging, pushing baby strollers? Watch how the children are playing—on swings or slides, or perhaps with toys such as balls or kites. Make note of any vehicles or buildings.

After you have thoroughly observed the scene, turn away from the window and take out a notebook or a sheet of paper. Write down the date and time, and then begin to write, in the present tense, what you have just observed. Write as though you are reliving the scene. It doesn't matter the order in which you record things, nor is it necessary to remember everything. Just be sure to include the obvious details of whatever comes to mind, and note the emotions you felt while looking at and contemplating the view.

If you have an artistic nature, you may want to try sketching the scene or some element of it that made an impression on you—perhaps a water fountain, tree, or a particular person. Sometimes, this approach enables you to include details that you may have missed in a written recollection, and often, these images are more compelling and thought-provoking than simple words.

Take It to Another Dimension

After doing this exercise several times (preferably while look-ing at the same scene from different vantage points), you may

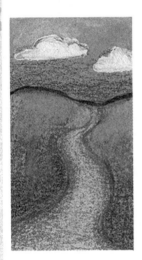

want to enhance the experience by adding imagination to observational recall. This time, try to be more creative by making the scene "dreamier." Pretend you are actually in the park smelling the flowers, stroll-ing along a path, or feeding the ducks. To make it even more dreamlike, you may want to include something out of the ordi-nary, such as visualizing yourself walking on the surface of the pond or meeting up with a friendly extraterrestrial. Take it a step further and give him or her a detailed, guided tour of a typical Earth park!

After you have finished (as you did the first time), turn your attention away from the window and jot down, in the present tense, what you observed. Write out the details of the "real" view as well as your participation and any additional elements that you imagined in your scene.

To get even more from this dream-recall exercise, choose two or three objects from your window scene that stand out for you and reference their general meanings in the dream diction-ary in Chapter 6. But keep in mind that this is simply a practice exercise, and there is more information in the coming chapters concerning the interpretation of symbols. At this point, you just want to get a feel for the potential meanings of dreams.

Rewrite Recent History

If gazing out a window is not practical or convenient, another way to help stimulate or enhance your dream recall is to choose an event that occurred during your day and pretend it was a dream. Write it down in the present tense, reliving it as you write. For example, you could

> The past is all of one texture—whether feigned or suffered—whether acted out in three dimensions or only witnessed in that small theatre of the brain which stays brightly lit all night long.
>
> —Robert Louis Stevenson, *Across the Plains*

write about your morning commute to work, or how you spent your lunch break. You could begin by asking yourself these questions:

★ What time do I leave and arrive?

★ What am I wearing?

★ What's the weather like?

★ What day of the week is it?

★ What is my mood?

★ Do I speak with anyone?

★ How do I travel?

★ Am I alone?

You can extend the exercise for as long as you want while including as much detail as you can. Recalling, considering, and recording these real-life details as though they took place in a dream helps train your mind to remember your dreams, and writing out an event mimics writing in a dream journal—an extremely important tool in dream work.

The Power of Suggestion

Another effective approach is to frequently suggest to yourself that you will remember your dreams. Select a short, positive phrase such as, "I remember my dreams easily." Rather than implying success at some point in the future, you will achieve better results if the statement is in the present tense.

You may want to choose a "suggestion trigger" to remind you to repeat your phrase throughout your day. For instance, every time you look at your watch or at a clock, repeat the phrase (either aloud or in your mind) as though it is an established fact. While doing so, visualize yourself writing out or sketching the details of your dreams.

You could also post reminder notes wherever you will notice them often, such as on your bathroom mirror, someplace in your car, or on your computer at work. It doesn't matter if you write your phrase on the notes or leave them blank, as long as they serve to remind you of your intent.

All of these playful but powerful exercises will alert your mind to the fact that you are serious about wanting to remember your dreams. You will be communicating visual images to your dream self, just as it does for you. The more you practice these exercises, the greater your recall—and its benefits—will be.

An Alarming Dream Exercise

Renowned science fiction author A. E. van Vogt devised a method to make creative use of his dreaming mind. Before falling asleep, he placed a card with the title and theme of a story-in-progress on his bedside table. Then he set his alarm clock to wake him every 90 minutes. He referred to this process as "an organized dreaming approach to writing." During the next seven years, the alarm went off every hour and a half, 4 times a night, about 300 nights a year.

Chapter Three
THE DREAM JOURNAL

ONCE YOU GET USED TO CONTEMPLATING
AND RECORDING YOUR EVERYDAY EXPERIENCES,
YOU CAN START A JOURNAL OF YOUR DREAM
MEMORIES. JOURNALING IS AN ESSENTIAL TOOL
IN DREAM INTERPRETATION BECAUSE IT OFFERS
PROOF TO YOUR DREAM SELF THAT YOU ARE
COMMITTED TO LEARNING FROM IT.

A SLEEPER'S BEST FRIEND

There is no right or wrong way to keep a dream journal—it is
your own personal account of what you experience as you sleep.
The most important thing is that the process feels comfortable,
which will help you record your dreams in a consistent fashion.
This way, you will quickly become familiar with your unique
dream language and how it relates to your waking life. Here are
a few suggestions that will help you get started on your quest to
master dream interpretation.

Choose a journal that suits you. Although some
dream journals are sold specifically as such,
with elaborate designs meant to inspire
you and spark your memory, these may
not be the right types for you. Some
people prefer more formal, hardcover
books. Others use a plain notebook or

loose pages that can be inserted into a binder. Whichever kind of journal you choose, leave a few blank pages at the beginning so you can create a table of contents. This will make it easy for you to scan your entries when you're looking for a particular dream or recurring themes and symbols.

Prepare yourself and your sleep environment. Avoid strenuous exercise and too much alcohol or food before you retire, as each can disrupt the sleep cycle and, in turn, affect your ability to dream. If you are the type of person who can't concentrate in a messy room, tidy up before you lie down. Then fluff your pillows, adjust your covers, and put on comfortable sleepwear. Also be sure that the room temperature is the way you like it. These simple steps will help ensure that you will not be distracted by small annoyances as you sleep.

> ### Dear Old Diary
>
> The first dream diary, or dream journal, dates to about 500 B.C. and belonged to the Greek rhetorician Aristides. Much of it has been lost, but what remains is in five volumes of what he called *Sacred Teachings*.

Place your dream journal close to your bed. Also keep a pen or pencil and a small flashlight handy (or use a penlight) in case you wake in the middle of the night and want to record a dream. (It will be easier to fall back asleep if you don't have to get up to turn on a light.)

Before you close your eyes, open your journal to a fresh page. First, note the city you are in (particularly if you travel a lot), the date, and the time. Leave space at the top of the page so you can title your dreams the next morning. Summarize the day's events (they may influence dream content), and be sure to jot down your reminder phrase. If you want, include other notes, such as the mood you are in as you get ready for bed or the state of your health. As you drift off to sleep, gently repeat your suggestion to yourself several times.

Rise and Shine!

Set your clock so that you'll awaken about 15 minutes earlier than usual—this will give you time to write out the details of the dream in your journal. If possible, wake to gentle music or talk radio instead of an alarm. Sometimes, being startled awake can cause a dream memory to fade and vanish. On the other hand, if you rely on a loud alarm to wake you, you can still train your mind to remember your dreams. Simply suggest to your- 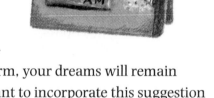 self that when you hear the alarm, your dreams will remain fresh in your mind (you may want to incorporate this suggestion in your reminder phrase).

As you begin to awaken, lie still and keep your eyes closed (this will help "cement" the details in your subconscious). Without attempting to manipulate your thoughts in any way, carefully consider the night's dreams. When you are satisfied with what you have recalled, start writing immediately. Write in the present tense, reliving the dreams as you record them. You can start at the beginning or middle—you can even work your way backward. The important thing is to get the dreams on paper. Alternately, you can record the details on tape, but be sure to write them out in your journal later. It's more helpful to read your dreams on paper than it is to hear them.

Every Scribble Counts

Include as many details as possible (people, places, colors, actions, animals, symbols, and emotions), but don't be discouraged if you can't recall every aspect of your dreams at that moment. Even fragments are important to note, and more information may come as you write. If you can't recall any details but have an idea of the general themes, write those down. And if you don't remember dreaming anything at all, note how you felt about that when you woke. The important thing is that you write something—anything!—to reinforce the significance of recording dreams. Finally, save room on the page (or follow it with a blank page) for interpretation and comments. Events throughout the day may trigger more memory of the dreams. If this happens, make a note of what you've just recalled and add it to your journal later.

When you have finished recording what you can, write the time you woke and choose appropriate titles for the dreams (or the emotion you felt if you couldn't recall one). Assigning titles (and creating a list of them in a table of contents) can enhance your ability to make connections and identify recurring patterns, themes, symbols, or characters. Titles can also help summarize dreams or reveal more meaning to you.

Throughout the day, repeat your reminder phrase frequently and give thought to the benefits you will derive from keeping a dream journal. At night as you prepare for bed, reconnect with your dream self by reading over the previous night's notes and remembering details as vividly as you can. Also, briefly review your day. Did any of your dream symbols turn up? If so, make brief notes of those before you drift off to sleep.

Daytime Dreamwork

If you weren't able to recall a dream, take some time during your day to write about that as though it were a dream. You might include the time you woke and whether it was dark or light out, what you were wearing, or what was playing on the radio. Be sure to include the title you assigned to your emotion (for example, "Close, but No Cigar"). Then enhance the exercise by imagining that you did recall something. For example, you could write, "I awake with a vague feeling of having been in a sunny place. There is brightness and warmth," which you could title "No Cigar, but Getting Warmer!"

In Your Ancient Dreams

Early dream records were found on clay tablets in King Ashurbanipal's library in Assyria, dating from approximately the seventh century B.C. Dream interpretation was also featured in a poem from ancient Mesopotamia known as *The Epic of Gilgamesh,* in which Gilgamesh, the hero-king of the city of Uruk, considered his dreams to be cryptic omens and guidance from the gods.

Practice, Practice, Practice!

To get the most out of your dream journal, it is important to make entries as consistently as possible. However, if your lifestyle is not one that can accommodate daily dream recording, choose days that are better for writing and stick to that routine, even if it is only one or two times a week. Finally, don't feel discouraged if you do not get immediate results. As with learning any skill, dream recall takes time and patience. If you persist, you will soon discover that the rewards are well worth the effort!

Chapter Four
THE ART OF DREAM INCUBATION

—◦◦◦◦◦—

DREAM INCUBATION IS THE PRACTICE
OF "PROGRAMMING" YOURSELF TO HAVE A
PARTICULAR KIND OF DREAM, PERHAPS FOR
PERSONAL GUIDANCE OR TO FIND A SOLUTION TO
A PROBLEM. IN ANCIENT TIMES, PEOPLE OFTEN
REQUESTED HEALING DREAMS FROM THE GODS IN
AN ATTEMPT TO CURE ILLNESSES.

—◦◦◦◦◦—

IN THE TEMPLE OF DREAMS

Throughout the world, elaborate dream temples have been
erected for the purpose of inducing and incubating dreams, and
some have been in use for almost 1,000 years. In ancient Greece,
hundreds of dream temples were built in honor of Asklepios,
the god of healing. Nonvenomous snakes were allowed to slither
freely among the sleeping chambers
because people believed snakes were
sacred symbols that evoked the power of
many gods. As a dream symbol,
snakes still represent physical or
emotional healing and are part
of a widely recognized symbol of
modern medicine, the caduceus

(two serpents entwined around a staff).

Egyptians, Romans, Greeks, Assyrians, Chinese, Japanese, and Indians are just a few of the ancient cultures that commonly practiced dream incubation. Dream temples were often situated in pleasant rural settings, away from city noise and distractions. People traveled long distances to spend one or several nights in a dream temple in order to obtain

The Healing Power of Asklepios

The most venerated dream temple dedicated to the healing god Asklepios was built in the fourth century B.C. in the ancient Greek city Epidaurus. Inscribed stones discovered there refer to more than 40 "patients," their diseases, and the curative dreams they received while sleeping in the temple. The remains of the temple can be seen today along with other ancient buildings, which include an excavation museum and an amphitheater—all are popular tourist attractions. The Sanctuary of Asklepios at Epidaurus is a World Heritage Site.

answers, cures, or enlightenment from the gods. These ancient temples provided a structure in which seekers could clarify their intent and concentrate on the outcome they desired. Because this intense focus also encouraged the power of suggestion on the dreaming mind, it was not unusual that people received the specific message they were looking for.

A Night in a Temple

Ancient dream seekers prepared for their journey to a temple by abstaining from sex and alcohol for several days and were also required to fast for a period of time (fasting continued within the temple). Highly esteemed dream interpreters, referred to as priests or "Masters of the Secret Things," attended to them during their stay. Under the guidance of these men, the dreamers participated in elaborate physical and psychological rituals that prepared them to receive their desired message.

Prior to entering the sacred grounds (usually early in the morning), a priest assisted the dreamers in taking a purifying bath and provided them with fresh garments. The dreamers then made offerings to the temple god—perhaps an animal, currency, or food—and were required to pray with the priest at specified periods throughout the day.

Other rituals included singing hymns, reciting incantations, and burning incense. Dreamers spent considerable time in solitude in an effort to clarify and reflect on their requests. When the priest felt they were ready, he led them to an inner sanctum—the sacred, noise-free chamber in which they were to sleep and receive their dream messages.

The next morning, after the priest listened carefully as they described the details of their dreams, he helped them interpret the symbols and suggested ways in which they might derive the most benefit from them. Before their departures, the dreamers documented the dreams by engraving their statements into plaques or writing them on scrolls. To this day, there are many such representations that depict the names of supplicants who traveled to the temples, as well as their particular ailments and what healing images they contemplated and received. Some records date back thousands of years and are housed in museums—lasting testimonials to the power of dreams!

The Many Roads to Dream Incubation

Rituals and rites varied among different cultures, and some dream temples were used for purposes other than healing. The ancient Chinese, for example, used them in conjunction with political functions. Government leaders and other officials were required to periodically spend nights in dream temples in the hope that they would acquire the insight and fortitude to help them rule and legislate in a just manner.

Not all cultures had access to these special temples, but that didn't stop them from incubating their dreams. Some ancient Egyptians wrote their questions or requests, as well as a prayer and the name of a god, on scraps of linen. They meditated on their desired dream with the linen tied to their wrist, or they soaked the cloth in oil and burned it with incense while reciting prayers. Then they peacefully drifted off to sleep, fully expecting that their god would bring them the solution they desired in their dreams.

These days, temples and elaborate rituals are seldom used to facilitate beneficial dreaming, but the practice of incubation is not uncommon. People continue to program their dreams for a variety of reasons, whether to solve problems, seek enlightenment, or simply enjoy the wonderment of it.

A Temple to Call Your Own

Your dream incubation procedure can resemble those used in ancient times, with practices rich in detail and ritual, or it can be much simpler. But as it was with ancient dream seekers, it is important that you focus on your desired message as intently as possible. You will notice that the following steps are similar to those used to promote good dream recall.

Choose your phrase. Be sure to use your suggestion in the present tense, and keep it brief but firm and always positive (for example, "Tonight I fly to the moon"). Several times during the day and just before you fall asleep, repeat the phrase to yourself or visualize an image that represents your dream desire. Consider writing it out on a piece of paper (or

creating a drawing), and then place it under your pillow or on your nightstand. Remember to record it in your dream journal when you are preparing for sleep.

Form a clear intention. Closely examine your reasons for incubating a particular dream. Even if you have several things you want to dream about or questions you would like answered, it is best to pick only one topic on which to concentrate. Too many desires could cause your dream self to send confusing messages. And don't forget the importance of being sincere in your belief about the power of dreams. Otherwise, you will inhibit or distort the information you receive. If you really are unsure of how you feel, try taking a playful "What if?" attitude. Suspend disbelief and see what happens.

Prepare your mind. If possible, spend some time that day in a place you find particularly peaceful, where you can carefully consider your request. It may be a quiet table at your favorite cafe, the walking path in a forest preserve, or a secluded spot on a beach. Even a corner in your public library will suffice if it feels right to you. If a place away from home isn't practical or desired, choose an area in your home where you can relax and focus without being disturbed.

Get comfortable. To facilitate the dream incubation process, you will want to make your nighttime ritual as tranquil as possible. It could be a simple gesture, such as meditating, or you could do something more elaborate, such as taking a bath in a room filled with candlelight. While relaxing in the warm water, concentrate on and repeat your dream request. Pretend you are participating in a cleansing and purification ritual before entering your personal dream temple—your bedroom. The romantic notion of proceeding through ancient rituals and rites can make you feel "dreamy" and put you in a positive, receptive mood.

Release tension. To encourage refreshing and peaceful sleep, you may want to practice some relaxation techniques in bed. Many people find yoga or similar deep-breathing exercises to be highly effective, while others

> *He who has learned aright about the signs that come in sleep will find that they have an important influence over all things.*
> —Hippocrates

prefer to concentrate on relaxing each muscle group, starting at the feet and slowly working upward. To enhance your experience, repeat your suggestive phrase as you do this.

Visualize the dream's solution. Focused visualization can prepare you to accept advice from your dream self. Imagine a general version of what your dream will be like—for example, you could envision a dream character who either offers you direct advice or points to an object that suggests a solution. Consider these scenarios:

★ Opening a door and finding a package that contains your answer

★ Reading a line of advice in a book

★ Picking up a phone and hearing your answer

★ Having the advice handed to you on a silver platter

★ Seeing the answer acted out in your personal "dream drama"

Be receptive to the many ways your answers can be revealed, but don't get bogged down in too much detail and don't try to tell your dream self which dream symbols to send you.

Contemplate your reaction to the message. It is also helpful to consider how you hope and expect to feel after you have awakened with an awareness of possible solutions. For example, if your desire is to improve your golf swing, picture yourself on a course later that day, recalling the advice you got in your dream. Envision yourself taking a technically accurate swing and landing an excellent shot. Imagine the satisfaction and enthusiasm you will feel about the improvement.

EMBARK ON A DREAM-INCUBATING VACATION

There's no need to cash in your frequent-flyer miles for this trip! Incubating a dream vacation to solve problems and access advice can greatly improve your life. If you're lethargic and depressed, for example, you can boost your energy and elevate your mood by having a fun, exhilarating dream adventure. On the other hand, if you're feeling panicked and overwhelmed, imagine the benefits you will derive from a calm, pleasant dream experience. Incubating dream vacations will provide you with a break from your daily routine and give you a fresh, positive outlook.

Preflight Instructions

When you really want to get away from it all and enjoy a dream vacation, it is important that you choose a night when you're not overly tired or have urgent commitments the following day. If you were to try to incubate a dream the night before an important meeting, for example, your dream would likely end up having a work-related theme.

Choose a place you would like to visit, whether real or imaginary. You might consider a part of the world you have never been to but have always wanted to see. You can use your dreams much like a time machine: Try traveling to another planet or a mythological place—go wherever your heart desires.

Once you have chosen a destination, consider symbols that represent it. For example, suppose you want to go to Hawaii. Invest in travel books or brochures, pick out pleasant scenes and images, and then post them where you will see them often. Also, keep a symbol—maybe a kitschy figurine of a hula dancer—on your nightstand to remind you of your dream intent.

Whenever you glance at the images of your destination, visualize yourself there. Engage as many of your senses as you can. Imagine yourself in Hawaii feeling the warm sand under your feet as you stroll the beaches, gazing upon the beautiful sapphire water, and hiking the majestic green mountains. Anticipate eating local foods, smelling exotic flowers, or attending an authentic luau. Choose a simple phrase to accompany your visualizations, such as, "Tonight I travel to Hawaii."

Proceed as you would when encouraging any other type of dream: Repeat your phrase often, focus on your images, and engage in your preferred rituals. Spend some time reflecting on how relaxed and peaceful you will feel upon waking from this overnight dream journey. In the morning, record your dream as usual. But because you are simply programming a dream vacation, there may not be much, if any, interpretation to do. Be attentive nonetheless: Your dream self may take this particular opportunity to slip in a message to you.

THE BENEFITS OF INCUBATING DREAMS

As many people in ancient times did, you can use your dreams simply for advice or guidance. But remember that as you explore your unique dreaming mind, you are limited only by your imagination. Consider these additional benefits of dream incubation:

Know yourself better. When you incubate a dream, you specifically address your dream state, and in so doing, you take an active and conscious role in building a bond with your dream self. When you keep the goal of dream incubation firmly in mind, you offer a clearer picture of what you desire. This, in turn, will enable you to learn more about your personal dream language and strengthen your dream-interpreting skills.

Enhance your creativity. You can better access your creative side by suggesting dreams that will bring inspiration. Authors, artists, and other accomplished individuals often look to their dreams for ideas and insight. Some writers dream entire stories, whereas others dream particular scenes, plots, or themes. Some even dream through the eyes of their characters and then use the information they receive in their work.

Improve your performance. Many athletes who "practice" sports in their dreams by trying new techniques or approaches often see pronounced improvements in their game. Some politicians rehearse speeches in their dreams to help them remember key points—and the same exercise can help people

Dali and Dreams

Salvador Dali believed that the greatest potential for inspiration lay in dreams. He developed a technique he referred to as "slumber with a key" to capture dream visions, which he then used in his surrealistic paintings. When teaching this technique to students, he instructed them to sit in a comfortable chair, hold a heavy key between the thumb and forefinger of the left hand (which was suspended over a ceramic plate on the floor), and then drift off to sleep. When the key slipped from the fingers and landed on the plate, the noise would awaken the sleeper, who would then capture his or her immediate dream image on canvas.

overcome anxieties about speaking in public. Why not ask your dream self to reveal talents or special abilities that you are not aware you have? You may be surprised to find a whole new side of yourself.

Obtain solutions to problems. Dreams provide us with an outlet through which we can express our deepest emotions without being judged. Through "dream dramas," we can experiment with ideas or behaviors that we wouldn't consider in our waking lives. Try acting out a particular situation or scenario in a dream, and upon waking you will better understand the "moral of the story." Similarly, this type of rehearsal can shorten the time it normally takes to find a solution.

For example, say you are having difficulty in a relationship, but a confrontation will only exacerbate the problem. Why not use your dreams as a testing ground for other approaches? Incubate a dream in which you resolve the conflict peacefully, or program several dreams so you can compare different outcomes. Sometimes our dreams will point out that we haven't been seeing someone or something in a realistic light.

Challenge yourself. Let's say you are afraid of heights. You could incubate a dream in which you practice climbing ladders of various sizes, or you could imagine being a trapeze performer who doesn't give heights a second thought. Breaking free from fears in your dreams could reduce anxiety in your waking life, even if only temporarily. Perhaps you would like to try something you have never done before because you've been too afraid. Set your adventurous spirit free. Imagine yourself bungee jumping, rafting down a raging river, or even playing the lead in a sold-out Broadway show. Your choices are endless.

Get healthier. Like the dream incubators of long ago, you can program dreams to improve your health. Because the body rejuvenates during sleep, these types of dreams may encourage and improve your natural healing functions. Some people believe that symbols in incubated healing dreams can point to undisclosed health issues, whether physical or psychological.

Dream On

The more you work and play with your dreams and the more familiar you become with your personal dream language, the more you will learn about yourself. Your dreams are like a magic mirror that reflects not only your outward appearance but, more important, what lies within.

Your sense of empowerment will increase as you become aware of such things as why you make certain choices, how well you deal with conflict, and how your beliefs direct your thoughts and actions. In turn, this knowledge will give you the confidence to reach beyond self-imposed boundaries that may be holding you back in life. Working with your dreams in such a way frees your creative spirit and allows you to flourish and grow into the best person you can be.

Chapter Five
LUCID DREAMING

As you begin to understand your dream language and how to interpret your personal symbols, you will notice that your dreams are changing. In fact, you may become so observant that you will, on occasion, realize that you are dreaming while you are dreaming. This is referred to as "lucid dreaming," and it can have a great impact on your waking life.

AWAKE IN YOUR DREAMS

Lucid dreaming has been documented since the fourth century B.C., when Aristotle wrote his work *On Dreams*: "For often, when one is asleep, there is something in consciousness which declares that what then presents itself is but a dream." In 1867, French professor Hervey de Saint-Denys published the book *Dreams and How to Guide Them*, in which he describes techniques to achieve a state of realization while dreaming. But in 1913, Dutch psychiatrist Frederik Willem van Eeden actually coined the phrase *lucid dream* in a study presented to the Society for Psychical Research. In it he explained that "the reintegration of the psychic functions is so complete that the sleeper reaches a state of perfect awareness and is able to direct his attention and to attempt different acts of free volition. Yet the sleep, as I am able confidently to state, is undisturbed, deep, and refreshing."

Proving the Validity of Lucidity

Until the 1970s, few psychologists believed in the phenomenon of lucid dreams and instead thought that people who claimed to have them were experiencing nothing more than the vivid dreams that occur during REM sleep. But unlike the rest of the body, eye muscles are not immobilized during this phase of the sleep cycle, so researchers began to monitor and record the eye movements of lucid dreamers in REM sleep. Chief among their findings was a consistent correlation between the activity of the patients' "dream eyes" and their actual eyes.

At the University of Hull in England, researcher Keith Hearne used this information to explore the concept of "ocular signaling," in which patients indicate the onset of lucid dreams with specific eye movements. Working with Hearne in 1978, lucid dreamer Alan Worsley was the first person to move his eyes in a predetermined pattern when he became aware that he was dreaming. Meanwhile, at the Stanford Sleep Research Center in California, Dr. Stephen LaBerge employed similar techniques with lucid dreamers and achieved equally successful results.

LaBerge went on to demonstrate that physical actions intentionally performed in a lucid dream state could have an effect on the body. He used a variety of monitoring devices to show that when lucid dreamers attempt to manipulate respiration, muscle tension, and heart rate, analogous changes occur in the body.

According to LaBerge in his book *Lucid Dreaming*: "Our work at

Frederik van Eeden

In 1913, Frederik van Eeden first presented his work and experiences with lucid dreaming in a fictional novel called *The Bride of Dreams*. He chose this format so he could freely express what he thought were "rather unusual ideas in a less aggressive way—esoterically, so to speak."

Stanford has amassed strong laboratory evidence indicating that what happens in the inner world of dreams—and lucid dreams, especially—can produce physical effects on the dreamer's brain no less real than those produced by corresponding events happening in the external world. The results of the experiments . . . show that the impact of certain dream behaviors on brain and body can be fully equivalent to the impact produced by corresponding actual behaviors."

Perchance to Dream Lucidly

There are many advantages to lucid dreaming. In this state of consciousness, you are able to experience an extraordinary kind of freedom. When you become lucid, you are in a position to direct your dreams in any way you wish—in fact, you can turn almost any dream into something entirely different if you so choose. You have the ability to perform any number of supernatural feats: You can walk on water or through walls; you can fly around or make things appear or disappear. You can engage in "forbidden" romantic affairs or eat all the chocolate you want—you won't be blamed for your behavior, and you will pay no "price." Consider this example of a lucid dream:

I am driving along smoothly in traffic, heading for an important meeting across town, when the car in front of me begins to slow and then stops. There is a long line of cars ahead; we are caught in a traffic jam. Frustrated at the thought of being late, I wish I could just fly over all the cars and proceed on my way.
Suddenly, I feel the car rise into the air and begin to fly over the vehicles below. I am elated but soon think to myself, "Wait a minute, cars don't fly. I must be dreaming!" Because I know I'm dreaming, I decide to fly off into outer space instead. I look up to the clouds and soar toward them.

The benefits of dreams in general include improved decision-making and problem-solving skills and better access to advice, inspiration, and revelation. With lucid dreams, these benefits are enhanced because you are consciously participating in them. Many people report that their lucid dreams are richer and more vibrant than their nonlucid dreams. Some even claim that their lucid dreaming experiences seem more intense, or more "real," than their waking reality.

When lucid, you can basically do as you please *at the moment you realize you are dreaming.* You don't have to wait until you have a specific dream. Many lucid dreamers engage in playful experiments and report that the invigoration, excitement, and happiness they feel in this state often stays with them after they awaken, sometimes lasting for days. Besides an increased sense of well-being, lucid dreaming offers these benefits:

★ **Better dream interpretation.** Being consciously aware in your dream can take you a step further in the process of understanding and interpreting your dream messages. You can ask your dream characters what they represent or what the entire dream symbolizes. If a symbol's definition is not immediately obvious, you can ask your dream self to offer another one or to provide clarity in some way that will help you understand the overall message. (As with dream incubation, it is best if you have your questions firmly in mind before you sleep, so your dream self realizes what is foremost on your mind.)

★ **Richer incubated dreams.** When you are lucid during an incubated dream, you are aware of what is happening as it happens and not after the fact. You can direct the dream from the inside, alter it if you desire, or just see how it unfolds. Consider the incubated dream vacation to Hawaii described in Chapter 4. If you are lucid during that dream, not only will you "gaze upon the beautiful sapphire water," you can swim through it with the speed and skill of a porpoise and explore the underwater world of mermaids. Because the experience of the dream is immediate, you will feel as if you are doing those very things, and the impact will be stronger than that of a nonlucid dream.

★ **Honed performance.** German sports psychologist and researcher Paul Tholey found that once a particular skill is learned in the waking state, it can be enhanced through lucid dreaming. Athletes, for example, can substantially improve their sensory-motor reactions by repeatedly manipulating their body movements in lucid dreams. In the same way, performers (actors, musicians, dancers) can gain confidence by rehearsing in a lucid dream state.

★ **Physical improvement.** People have attempted to rid themselves of illnesses during lucid dreams and claim to have accelerated the process by doing so. Although this is often dismissed as "the power of positive thinking" as it relates to health, studies indicate that it could be a valid approach. Experiments in which lucid dreamers sing and count have shown brain-wave activity identical to that in the waking state, and if brain functions such as these can be influenced by a lucid dreamer's intentions, some speculate that cellular activity can be as well.

★ **Nightmare control.** One of the greatest advantages of lucid dreaming is that it provides you with the ability to cope with, and even reduce the frequency of, nightmares. When you become lucid, you are aware that you are in a dream environment and can't actually be hurt by anyone or anything. The understanding that frightening images are not "real" can eliminate the anxiety and fear you feel in the dream. You can  confront your dream monsters and ask them what they represent, or you can embrace them in a symbolic gesture that shows you aren't threatened or afraid. Many people report that in doing so, their dream monsters become friendly or disappear altogether.

12 Common Nightmares

For the rare person who has never experienced a nightmare, here is a basic explanation: It is a distressing dream that provokes emotions that range from mild anxiety to paralyzing fear. Other feelings can include guilt, anger, and extreme sadness. According to renowned dream researcher Patricia Garfield, these are the 12 most common nightmares:

1. Being chased or attacked
2. Being injured, ill, or dying
3. Car trouble
4. House or property loss or damage
5. Poor test performance
6. Falling or drowning
7. Being naked or inappropriately dressed in public
8. Missing a boat or other form of transport
9. Machine or telephone malfunction
10. Natural or human-caused disasters
11. Being lost or trapped
12. Being menaced by a spirit

Learn a New Way to Dream

Some people are born with the ability to dream lucidly, but research has shown that it is a skill anyone can learn. Those who have never had a lucid dream (or don't think they have) may find it hard to imagine what it feels like to become consciously aware in a dream state, but using these basic techniques, you can train yourself to have lucid dreams. It may take some time to learn lucidity, but keep in mind that these steps are the same as or similar to those you use to enhance your dream recall and to practice dream incubation.

Remember to record it. As with any type of dreaming, your dream journal is your best tool, and good dream recall is essential to having lucid dreams. If you make a concerted effort to remember and record your dreams, you will be able to recognize changes in the way you feel while dreaming. With practice, it will soon become obvious when you achieve lucidity, and from there, you can even increase its frequency.

Tap the power of suggestion. Simply telling yourself that you will become lucid in your next dream can be enough to make it happen. Use a phrase such as, "I recognize that I'm dreaming." Repeat this throughout the day and at bedtime.

Check your reality. A favored technique among lucid dreamers is "reality testing," which requires that you closely observe your surroundings and activities and then ask yourself whether or not they are real. Performing frequent reality tests increases the chances that you will make the same observations in your dreams. If you notice something that seems implausible, carefully consider why. You may conclude that what you have observed is actually possible, but there could be other signs that will make it clear that you are, in fact, dreaming.

Recognize inconsistencies. It has been found that certain things do not remain stable in dreams. For example, if you are reading something, then look away and find that the text has changed when you try to reread it, you are obviously dreaming. Also pay attention to mechanical devices—light switches, digital watches, or telephones—that malfunction or stop working altogether, as this frequently happens in dreams. Make these observations an integral part of your reality checks (and rechecks) throughout the day. Then, as you sleep, notice if lights turn themselves on and off, or if your phone makes a barking sound when it should be ringing. Because these things can't actually happen, you will instantly know you are dreaming.

Pull the trigger. Be sure to test your reality regularly by establishing predetermined "triggers" that remind you of your task. For example, whenever a clock chimes, stop and think about what just happened. If you are sure it's approximately six o'clock in the evening, and the clock chimed just three times, make a mental note of that. Or if you habitually eat each meal at a certain time and you're suddenly eating lunch in the middle of the night, you will know that you are dreaming. In the same way, it is a good idea to perform reality tests whenever something unusual appears in your environment.

Let's say you are sitting in a park, and a clown suddenly walks past. Perhaps he or she is performing in a circus nearby, but don't let the observation end there. You then notice that the clown is walking a two-inch-tall horse on a leash. Now, circus or no circus, that just isn't possible.

For further practice, you can even attempt to do something humans can't do in waking reality, such as levitating or outrunning a speeding train. All of these activities will encourage and enhance your ability to have lucid dreams and help you appreciate their advantages.

Take Charge of Your Dreams!

Once you practice and become comfortable with these techniques, you can increase the frequency and duration of your lucid dreams. Better yet, you can start to play around with them.

Start by recalling a sad or frustrating dream (include as much detail as possible) and changing a particular scene or the outcome. For example, say you had a dream in which you went to see a favorite performer but were turned away at the ticket counter because the show was sold out. You felt dejected and disappointed, especially because you were alone and had nothing to do but return to an empty house.

Now, here's where you can turn things around: You are once again at the counter, but instead of being turned away and leaving, envision yourself *intentionally* making a ticket appear. It can materialize out of thin air and land in your hand or, more subtly, you can slowly pull it out of your pocket. Feel yourself strolling past the counter and into the venue, where you sit amid a group of friends (who you also "willed" to be there). This sense of confidence and control is what you will feel when you become lucid.

The Green Dream Goddess

Theater critic, playwright, and journalist William Archer was known for his interest in—and playful attitude toward—dreams, and for years he maintained a journal of his own "nighttime journeys." He often referred to a particularly poignant dream that occurred in September 1919, in which he envisioned that he and a group of friends were kidnapped in India by a band of barbarians led by a woman. Archer's critically acclaimed stage play "The Green Goddess" was based on that dream based on this dream.

Dream While You Are Awake

Another way to practice and encourage lucidity is to visualize your waking life as if it were a dream. Convince yourself that even the oddest things you may imagine are possible.

At some point during your day, stop whatever you're doing, look around, and pretend you are in the middle of a dream. Believe that you can change the situation in whatever way you want. Consider this scenario: You are working in the yard on a sunny summer afternoon. Perhaps you stroll into your garden and cut some beautiful flowers. You take them inside, arrange them in the nicest vase you have, and then present them as a gift to the attractive person who just moved in next door. Imagine engaging in a long and interesting conversation with that person and realizing that he or she is the soulmate you have been searching for.

Why not go a little further and envision the two of you flying out of the window, hand-in-hand, and landing at a cozy sidewalk cafe in Paris just minutes later? You can take the fantasy as far as you want. And while you may not be able to fly on a whim in real life, this imagintion exercise can help you develop your ability to have lucid dreams, which in turn can help you become more clear-thinking and observant in your waking life. This will enable you to make better conscious choices and decisions. When you wake up in your dreams, you can change your life while you sleep!

Chapter Six
DEFINITIONS OF COMMON DREAM SYMBOLS

—◦⟨⟨⟩⟩◦—

NOT ALL SYMBOLS HAVE THE SAME MEANING FOR EVERYONE. USE THIS DICTIONARY AS A BASIC GUIDE TO HELP YOU INTERPRET YOUR DREAMS.

—◦⟨⟨⟩⟩◦—

T he definitions in this dream dictionary (especially those referred to as "archetypes") are common among people of diverse backgrounds, ages, and attitudes. But because your personal dream symbols are created by your dream self, they hold meaning that is specific and unique to you.

Think of each symbol within the context of its particular dream. How or where a symbol appears is just as important as the symbol itself. Furthermore, a certain definition may take on a different meaning in conjunction with other symbols.

If a symbol in a dream has no immediate or apparent personal meaning for you, check this dictionary for a general definition and consider the ways in which it might apply to you. Rely on your intuition, and when you experience strong feelings of recognition or resonance with a certain meaning, you will know that the interpretation is the right one for you.

A

abandonment

If you have never experienced real abandonment, this dream feeling suggests that you rely too heavily on someone and should look to your own strengths. To abandon someone points to personal burdens. *See also* **stranded.**

abbey

An abbey is a place of solitude, peace of mind, and freedom from worries. Entering an abbey in a dream indicates that you need to take time for yourself.

abduction

If you are the abductor, you may envy someone's situation in life or desire a certain quality (or object) a person possesses. If you are abducted, you distrust others but feel controlled by them. *See also* **captivity, kidnap.**

above

Reaching upward indicates that you are ready to move outside your comfort zone and will benefit from doing so. The higher you reach, the better.

absorption

If you see something that is being absorbed, you likely need time to assimilate recent events or new information. To absorb something yourself emphasizes your ability to accept and adapt to change. *See also* **sponge.**

abstinence

Abstinence is symbolic of cleansing, repentance, or releasing yourself from a habit. To dream about abstaining from sex may indicate your desire to be left alone or to do something without input or interference from another.

abuse

To witness physical or verbal abuse is to be warned of someone's misuse of power or influence. To endure abuse is to feel helpless.

abyss

Looking into an abyss generally means you are examining empty areas of your life, whether at home or in the workplace. Falling into an abyss may be a sign of depression, loneliness, or a lack of direction. *See also* **canyon, hole.**

accident

Dreams that involve accidents are often acknowledgements or premonitions of troubling situations. If you witness an accident, you likely feel unable to fix a waking-life problem. If you cause or are involved in an accident, pay close attention to important issues to avoid making dire mistakes.

accordion

If you hear music from an accordion, you will soon enjoy a celebration. An accordion that is not being played suggests that you make an effort to enjoy yourself more. *See also individual musical instruments.*

ace

An ace card face reveals the following: An ace of hearts foretells a new romantic relationship; ace of diamonds is a good omen for money matters; ace of clubs foretells success after a minor setback; and an ace of spades warns of disappointment.

achievement

This dream theme is often contrary: reevaluate plans or projects to make sure you are taking the right steps toward your goal.

acid

Consider this an omen of an unpleasant encounter in which harsh words will be exchanged. *See also* **poison.**

acorn

This dream image implies that you have great potential

The Daring Young Man

In 1974, trapeze artist Tito Gaona revealed to an interviewer that he often dreamed about his airborne maneuvers and then mastered them while awake. He was the first person to perform the "double-double"— a double twist while doing a double somersault—after he envisioned doing it in a dream. It was considered the greatest gymnastic feat at the time. Gaona went on to found the Tito Gaona Flying Trapeze Academy and Tito Gaona's Flying Fantasy Circus. In 2001, he was inducted into the World Acrobatics Society's Hall of Fame.

for personal or professional growth. Be careful that you don't overlook an opportunity. *See also* **plants, trees.**

acrobat

To dream of watching or being an acrobat means that you should be flexible in dealing with business partners or significant others in order to achieve harmony. *See also* **gymnast.**

acting

If you dream that you are an actor, consider whether you're portraying your true self to others in your waking life. It would serve you well to view others with the same scrutiny. Always look beyond the surface. *See also* **performance.**

acupuncture

You are looking for balance and peace of mind and will soon find it, though it may be through unusual means.

addiction

Addiction in dreams often symbolizes a refusal to give up negative or outdated ideas. It can also indicate loss of control. *See also* **alcohol, drinking.**

addition

Adding figures in a dream portends an increase in some area of your life. It could refer to family, perhaps because of a marriage or birth, or you could see financial gains due to a work promotion. *See also* **subtraction.**

adolescence

To dream that you are an adolescent implies that you are naïve regarding a serious situation and would do well to take a more mature view of matters. *See also* **age, childhood.**

adrift

To be adrift in a dream points to feelings of being lost or cut off from something. To set something adrift is a positive sign of releasing a burden or negative emotion. You will soon feel a sense of freedom or relief. *See also* **boats.**

adultery

This can symbolize any breach of faith. To dream of committing adultery indicates that you are betraying your ideals in some way, though it may or may not be related to romance. To dream that another person commits adultery is a sign that someone is trying to take credit for something that is not rightfully theirs.

advertisement

An advertisement may be your dream self's way of getting your attention or of pointing out a specific message. Carefully consider the symbolism in what is being advertised. *See also* **alarm, siren.**

aerobics

If you are doing aerobics, you have the ability to handle many situations at once. If watching the activity, you are procrastinating and work is piling up.

affair

To experience a dream love affair is actually a sign of a promising new business partnership; expect the opposite if it is an adulterous affair.

> *Take, if you must,*
> *this little bag of dreams,*
> *unloose the cord,*
> *and they will wrap*
> *you round.*
> —William Butler Yeats

affection

Showing or receiving affection in a dream may be an omen of a new relationship or enhanced feelings in an existing relationship. Conversely, it could indicate that a current romance is losing its appeal.

affluence

To be surrounded by affluence is to be reminded of your personal achievements and status. To see the affluence of others is a warning not to compare yourself with people or sell yourself short. *See also* **wealth.**

age

Your age in a dream can indicate your mental or emotional state. If you are young, you may be holding on to hurtful experiences from your past. If you are older, consider it an omen to seek advice from a respected friend or mentor.

aggression

Aggressive behavior is often viewed as hostility or assertiveness and usually indicates your state of mind. For more insight, try to identify the reason for the aggression. *See also* **anger, attack.**

air

When you notice the air in a dream, consider its quality. Fresh, cool air signifies clear-headed thinking and good focus, whereas dirty air points to a lack of perspective. *See also* **pollution.**

airplane

Dreams in which you are a passenger on a plane imply that you have high expectations of yourself. To dream that you are piloting the plane warns that those expectations may be unrealistic. An airplane that crashes foretells disappointment. Boarding and disembarking a plane have implications of new experiences or abandoned dreams. *See also* **climbing, flying.**

aisle

If you are walking down a church aisle, you likely desire a commitment, though not necessarily a romantic one. To walk down other kinds of aisles indicates that you will be recognized for your efforts to reach your goals.

alarm

Hearing any sort of alarm in a dream serves to draw your attention to an issue or situation in your waking life that could potentially cause you anxiety. *See also* **advertisement, siren.**

alcohol

Clouded thinking is distorting your perception and judgment with regard to a social matter. *See also* **drinking.**

aliens

Dreams of aliens can point to insecurities about fitting in or appearing different. On the other hand, consider whether you are feeling rejected or ignored (or perhaps you're alienating someone else).

alligator

An alligator in water suggests that lurking problems will surface quickly. If the alligator moves onto land, the situation will be addressed and resolved to your satisfaction.

altar

This dream symbol implies that you seek redemption for an act or comment you now regret. Also, consider the play on words: Perhaps you should consider changing (altering) your behavior.

amber

This gemstone portends a gift of money or real estate.

ambulance

A problematic personal situation will soon be resolved with the assistance of others—possibly strangers.

amethyst

Seeing or wearing amethyst indicates that you will enjoy financial security and contentment in old age.

amputation

A dream that involves amputation is an obvious symbol of sacrifice. You may feel the need to give up something important to you, but think carefully before taking action. It may also refer to feelings of loss or helplessness. *See also* **castration, separation.**

amulet

Traditionally, an amulet is a sign of protection and positive intuition. This dream symbol is telling you to trust your instincts.

amusement park

To dream that you are at an amusement park symbolizes your need for unpredictable fun. Break away from your mundane routine and enjoy yourself. *See also* **carnival.**

anchor

As a dream symbol, an anchor suggests that you are firmly attached to certain ideas or convictions that may not serve your best interests. If the anchor is being lowered, you will suffer consequences. If the anchor is being raised, you are ready to open your mind in a way that may change the course of your life.

angel

This is most often an omen of protection, security, and guidance. The angel archetype represents spiritual ideals and wisdom of the inner self, but it can also warn of paths best avoided.

anger

To express anger in a dream implies that you have difficulty releasing tension in your everyday life. Repressed feelings are causing you undue stress. *See also* **aggression, attack.**

animals

These common dream symbols usually reflect how you feel about or react to them in your waking life. An aggressive animal can be a general representation of your fears or insecurities, whereas an affectionate animal signifies your loyalty and ability to express love. *See also individual animal listings.*

antiques

To dream of antiques often points to your unconscious mind and how you might tap into it. This can help

Animals in Our Dreams

Many ancient dream documents depict animals as primary symbols—and they continue to be central to the human dreamscape. The animals that appear in our dreams often represent such basic instincts as our "fight or flight" response and emotional issues such as the desire to nurture or be nurtured. How you interpret a specific animal image depends on your personal experiences with that animal. For example, if you have ever loved and cared for a dog as a pet but dream of being chased or attacked by one, consider whether someone close to you currently presents a physical or emotional threat. How you respond to the attack in your dream will instinctively guide you in dealing with the person in your waking life.

Here are some animals that commonly show up in our dreams and how they represent our behavioral traits (both positive and negative):

Bears: wisdom; aggression
Birds: freedom; predation
Cats: independence; indifference
Dogs: loyalty; unpredictability
Lions: power; intimidation
Mice: diligence; timidity
Pigs: intelligence; sloth

you differentiate between what holds value for you and what doesn't. Try to let go of outdated ideals or attitudes that prevent you from living in the present. *See also* **ruins.**

anxiety

If you frequently feel anxious in your dreams, you should make an effort to be more accepting of what you cannot change in your waking life. For further clues, consider who or what provokes the anxiety.

apartment

This symbol indicates that you feel isolated or separated from those you care about. Alternately, it can point to your independence and self-reliance.

appearance

How you project yourself to others is often displayed by your appearance in dreams. How others appear can give you a clue as to how they are feeling. *See also* **mirror, reflection.**

applause

To hear applause implies that you are seeking recognition for efforts that have thus far gone unnoticed. To applaud someone is a gesture of appreciation.

apple

Traditionally, this fruit is associated with temptation. The quality of the apple (fresh or bruised) indicates whether you should give in to your desires. A shriveled apple means an opportunity has passed you by.

apron

Wearing an apron often points to contentment among family members. To see an apron on another person implies that you are neglecting obligations around the house. Try to strike a balance between your career and home life.

arch

This dream image symbolizes stability and support. To dream of walking under an arch is an omen of a long and happy marriage.

architect

If you dream that you are an architect, you are in charge of shaping your life. If working with plans, are you pleased with the design you have created, or could it benefit from changes?

arctic

To dream that you live in an arctic environment means you feel that your waking life is dull and uneventful. But the real problem may be your attitude: If you warm up to people, you will likely see an immediate change. *See also* **ice**.

argument

If you get into an argument in a dream, you are likely facing a challenging decision that only you can make. Closely examine your feelings after such a dream to help clarify your options.

arms

Dreams that feature your arms indicate that you should welcome and embrace new ideas. But if your arms are folded, your tendency to be close-minded will cause you to lose the respect of coworkers, family, or friends.

arrow

An arrow in flight is an omen of a romantic relationship, but note the direction in which it travels (up, down, or straight) and whether it falls short or goes too far. If you shoot the arrow, be sure to aim well.

arthritis

To dream that you suffer from arthritis represents something that hinders you in your waking life. This could refer to physical or emotional blocks but can also point to unbending attitudes or beliefs.

ashes

This image often symbolizes images or memories lost to time. It can also represent things burned, which indicates an ending. If the ashes are glowing, however, anticipate a heated encounter over a problem that has been smoldering for a long time. *See also* **burn, fire**.

aspen tree

Consider the quivering limbs of this tree. As a dream symbol, an aspen warns that someone close to you who displays nervous behavior should not be trusted. *See also* **trees**.

asteroid

Be prepared for an interesting event or piece of news. Dreams of asteroids can also precede periods of great creativity or productivity.

atlas

To dream of scanning an atlas foretells opportunities for exploration beyond your typical boundaries. Alternately, this image can mean that you have lost your way in life and are trying to get back on track. *See also* **globe, map.**

attack

If you attack someone in a dream you are either releasing pent-up anger or you are trying to make your feelings clear. Consider the person (or object) under attack. If you dream of being attacked, you likely feel vulnerable or insecure about a relationship or situation. *See also* **aggression, anger.**

attic

This dream symbol represents your mind and imagination.

Consider whether the image makes you feel bored or inspired. *See also* **basement.**

audience

If you're a member of the audience, are you comfortable just watching the show, or would you rather be on stage? To perform before an audience symbolizes your extroverted personality and, often, a need for attention. *See also* **performance.**

autumn

Dreams involving this season reflect a peaceful period, or one of quiet introspection.

avalanche

To dream of being caught in an avalanche indicates that you are finally ready to release negative emotions that you have been holding back for too long. *See also* **landslide.**

Go with the Flow

Dreaming of something that moves or flows by means of its own force (e.g., a stream or river, lava, or an avalanche) reflects your emotional and/or physical energy. Does the movement of any of these dream symbols coincide with your efforts to do what you want in life?

---

avoidance

Dreams in which you avoid a person or situation often point to low self-esteem. What you are really trying to avoid are negative aspects of yourself.

Go Away, Gorilla!

In her book *It's All in the Playing,* actor Shirley MacLaine tells of a recurring dream she had as a child, in which a gorilla chases her to the edge of an abyss. Usually, she would awaken at that point, but one night, as she approached the edge, she decided to confront the gorilla. She turned to face him and asked, "What do I do now?" Throwing up his hands in exasperation, the gorilla replied, "I don't know, kid, it's your dream!"

B

baby

In its most literal form, this dream symbol reflects a desire for, or thoughts about, offspring. Other interpretations involve new beginnings, potential, and a desire for growth. It can also represent a need to nurture or to be nurtured. To dream of a baby who cries indicates feelings of vulnerability or neglect—most likely from your own childhood. *See also* **childhood, pregnancy.**

babysitting

Are you spending a lot of time assisting someone (it could be a child, parent, friend, or co-worker) who requires your help? If dreams about babysitting cause you stress, you should pull back and spend more time tending to your own needs.

back

To dream of your own back suggests that you have shunned or neglected someone close to you. Alternately, something may be going on that you are not aware of. If you are sitting or standing in the back of a room, you should analyze a problematic situation before you attempt to intervene.

back door

If you dream of leaving through a back door, you may be harboring guilt over something that could potentially cause you embarrassment. A back door also implies that you don't necessarily have to go through official channels or routine procedures to get to your desired goal or location—consider alternatives.

backward

If you dream that you are moving backward, you may need to examine your approach to a situation and take it in a different direction. What you are currently doing is getting you nowhere and may even be counterproductive.

badge

To display a badge indicates that you are misusing your authority in some way. If you receive a badge, you likely desire to be part of a group that you hold in high esteem. A badge on its own symbolizes your desire for a different identity.

badger

Someone who seems to be annoying or pestering you is actually in need of your attention and advice.

bag

Dreams in which you are carrying a bag or bags imply that you feel burdened by something or someone. If you carry the bag close to your body, you may be harboring secrets and are afraid of being exposed. *See also* **luggage.**

bagpipes

To see bagpipes is a sign that you may receive assistance from an unconventional source. The sound of bagpipes foretells an unfortunate event.

baking

If you dream of baking, you could be caring for someone who is taking you for granted. On the other hand, baking can represent your patience in dealing with situations that would frustrate others. *See also* **cooking.**

balcony

A balcony reflects your desire for advancement in the workplace or a higher social status. If you are standing on a balcony, you want to be recognized for your achievements. If you are waving or speaking from a balcony, you are trying to get the attention of someone in your waking life.

bald

This common dream image often represents personal insecurities and a fear of being exposed. To dream that you are slowly going bald indicates anxieties about getting older. *See also* **hair.**

ball

An opportunity is in your court; take advantage of it. This symbol also implies that you should be more assertive in going after what you want. It's time to get in the game!

ballet

To dream that you are attending or dancing in a ballet is a warning to stay on your toes, particularly in the workplace. It also suggests that you tread lightly around a sensitive situation or person.

balloons

This image can represent either realized or unfulfilled dreams. Are the balloons in flight or deflated? To see or hear balloons popping foretells a stressful situation that will bring disappointment. If you see a bunch of balloons, you will soon receive more than you wished for.

bamboo

To dream of constructing something out of bamboo indicates that you are strong-willed but can be flexible when necessary.

bananas

If you are eating ripe bananas, expect a period of hard work that will bring prosperity. Green bananas warn against planning too far in advance.

bandage

This dream symbol represents a temporary solution to a problem. Rather than covering up hurt feelings, get them out into the open so they can begin to heal. *See also* **blister.**

banjo

To hear someone playing a banjo warns that a forthcoming celebration will be far less exciting than you expected.

bank

This image represents your storehouse of emotional riches. You are secure with yourself and have a lot to offer others. Alternately, to dream of a bank can point to impending financial difficulties. *See also* **money.**

bankruptcy

If you are at a loss and feel like giving up, a dream involving bankruptcy is often a good omen: It represents a fresh start and severed ties to an unfavorable person or situation. *See also* **money.**

banquet

A banquet that is abundant and enjoyable indicates that you are personally fulfilled. To be at a solemn or poorly attended banquet foretells disharmony among family members.

baptism

A baptism represents purification and initiation. Regardless of your religion (and even if you aren't religious), to be baptized in a dream is a sign that you are ready to let go of fear and negativity and are about to embark upon a more rewarding journey. *See also* **bath, shower.**

bar

Dreams of a dark, rundown bar reflect a similar state of mind or health. Make an effort to break out of your rut and engage in some fun physical activities.

barbarian

This image refers to someone who is brusque in manner or speech. It also represents an idea, plan, or project that is in a primitive, or early, stage.

barefoot

Dreams in which you are barefoot have varying meanings. They can represent your sense of freedom and independence, or they can warn against self-sabotage that may have personal, legal, or

Dream Charades

The Native American Iroquois once celebrated an annual dream-sharing festival called "Ononharoia." Also known as the Feast of Fools, "Ononharoia" translates as "turning the brain upside down." During the festival, villagers acted out their dreams and encouraged others to guess their meaning, much like a game of charades. According to James R. Lewis, author of *The Dream Encyclopedia*, this practice "could be characterized as community psychotherapy."

financial consequences. *See also* **feet, shoes.**

barking

If you hear barking in a dream, consider the way you communicate with work associates or family members. People will be more receptive to your ideas or requests if you are polite and tactful in your approach.

barn

A barn full of animals symbolizes abundance and pride, whereas an empty barn implies that you should put more thought into your future.

barnacles

To see barnacles on something points to your tendency to take advantage of the generosity of others. Alternately, it warns that you should end relationships that are inhibiting your freedom. *See also* **leeches.**

baseball

See **ball, sports.**

baseball bat

Swinging a baseball bat is equivalent to throwing a temper tantrum. Examine other symbols in the dream: who or what you are swinging at, and whether you make contact or "strike out." *See also* **bowling.**

basement

This symbol reflects your state of mind. Consider the condition of the basement. Is the space full of cherished mementos, or a dark, dank depository for junk? *See also* **attic.**

basketball

See **ball, sports.**

bath

If you dream of taking a bath, you have a need to cleanse yourself, physically and emotionally. Sitting in an empty bathtub points to a lack of personal awareness. *See also* **baptism, shower.**

bats

Flying bats connote conflicting or confusing thoughts. Rely on your intuition when making plans or coordinating projects. *See also* **birds.**

battery

This symbol emphasizes the fact that you need to boost your energy before you take on an important project at home or at work.

> But I, being poor, have only my dreams;
> I have spread my dreams under your
> feet; Tread softly because you tread on
> my dreams.
> —William Butler Yeats

battle

To dream of watching or engaging in battle is often a literal image that reflects a personal dilemma or conflict of beliefs. *See also* **war.**

beach

Beach scenes represent the connection between your unconscious and conscious thoughts. Therefore, soothing images (clean sand, warm water) reflect a similar state of mind. On the other hand, if you dream about a hot, crowded, littered, or inaccessible beach, plan a nice vacation and get away from it all.

beans

If you are cooking or eating beans, your financial difficulties will soon pass. To grow beans indicates that something thought to be worthless may turn out to be valuable.

bear

This image symbolizes the wisdom derived from a spiritual awakening. Being chased by a bear represents your relationship with a domineering individual. *See also sidebar on page 54,* **hibernation.**

beard

To dream of a bearded person implies that you will acquire knowledge or insight from someone older. If you suddenly grow a beard (whether you are a woman or a man), determine if there is something in your waking life that you are trying to cover up. *See also* **disguise, hair.**

beaver

This animal represents the determined effort you put into your home and work lives. Don't feel guilty about asking the same of others.

bed

Literal interpretations of this image relate to comfort and security. To make a bed is to tidy up your personal life. If you are lying in a bed, consider whether you require more rest or if laziness is preventing you from achieving your goals.

bedroom

To dream of a bedroom (whether or not it's yours) points to a need to examine your intimate thoughts in a secure, private environment.

beehive

A beehive is a place of cooperative activity. If you have this dream image, you will soon work with others toward a common goal. Expect success.

bees

A swarm of bees portends success in collaborative financial pursuits. If you hear bees buzzing or are stung by a bee, you are likely the subject of hurtful gossip.

beets

The interpretation of cooking or eating beets is that you are keeping a potentially embarrassing secret. If you choose to reveal it, use discretion.

begging

If you dream of being a beggar, you may need to ask someone for assistance but are reluctant to do so. Your troubles will linger unless you swallow your pride and accept help.

behind

You should quicken your pace if you want to achieve the results you are hoping for. Alternately, consider the benefits of hindsight when obstacles are behind you.

bell

If you hear bells in a dream, expect cheerful news. Church bells foretell a profitable union, either in a business endeavor or personal relationship.

below

This position implies that you have trouble reaching your goals, most likely because of insecurities or low self-esteem.

belt

A belt can represent your attitude toward personal relationships. If you are wearing a belt, does it fit comfortably, or have you outgrown it to the point that you feel constricted? Also consider idiomatic expressions such as belting someone or belting out a song.

berries

To dream of foraging wild berries portends a new acquaintance who will prove to be deceptive. Picking and eating fresh, ripe berries predicts a romantic encounter that will leave a lasting impression.

bicycle

Dreams in which you are riding a bike indicate that you are trying to balance your life. Consider whether you are riding uphill, downhill, or on a straight path. To dream of a bicycle by itself predicts travel, but the journey won't take you far or last long.

binoculars

This symbol indicates that you should focus on something that you feel is beyond your reach.

Keep in mind that it is closer than you think.

birdcage

An empty birdcage suggests that you are feeling trapped or have limited freedom. It can also indicate that you are restless and bored and have an urge to "spread your wings." *See also* **cage, imprisonment.**

birds

Birds are most often symbols of inspiration and positive messages. However, a flock of birds represents the fact that too many thoughts are inhibiting your ability to make a decision. *See also* **bats.**

birth

As a literal symbol, this image implies a desire for offspring. It also recommends the initiation of work projects, because you are formulating creative and innovative ideas. Alternately, to dream of being born may represent a desire for the security and safety of the womb, or your need for a fresh perspective on life.

birthday

Dreams pertaining to this personal milestone can be

examples of positive self-recognition. To dream that someone has forgotten your birthday indicates that you feel insignificant in that person's life.

biting

If you are bitten by anything, expect to be betrayed. To dream of biting someone or something is a warning that you have taken on (bitten off) more responsibilities than you can handle. *See also* **sting.**

black

This color symbolizes the unknown, malevolence, and power. It can also represent dark thoughts or even depression. *See also sidebar on page 85.*

blame

To place blame on someone means that you are ignoring or rejecting your own responsibilities. To be the one blamed is a sign that you are taking on unnecessary duties or worries.

blanket

This can be a symbol of your ability to nurture and provide security, or it can represent concealment or secrecy. Examine what or who the blanket covers for further clues.

bleach

If you are using bleach to disinfect or remove stains, there is likely a troubling issue or situation that you can't get off your mind.

blindness

Dreams in which you are blind indicate that there is something you have lost sight of or are refusing to see. To dream of a blind person suggests that you are keeping potentially hurtful information from someone in an effort to protect him or her. *See also* **eyes.**

blister

This symbol usually represents a sore spot or a sensitive issue. To pop a blister will provide relief, but the issue will eventually surface again—and may be worse when it does. *See also* **bandage.**

Half-Brained Sleeping

Research has shown that a bird can sleep while half of its brain is awake. According to several studies, a duck is able to keep one half of its brain awake, and one eye open and alert, while the other half of the brain sleeps. This phenomenon, called unihemispheric sleep, is believed to be a survival mechanism. A similar ability enables whales, dolphins, manatees, and seals, which sleep underwater, to rise to the surface to breathe without waking up.

blood

Dreams involving blood can have a variety of meanings. To bleed reflects feelings of depletion, whether physical, emotional, or financial. If you see a person bleeding, you may feel incapable of assisting someone in your waking life.

blossom

To see a flower blossom is most often an omen of pride, contentment, and personal growth. *See also* **flowers.**

blue

This color symbolizes devotion, loyalty, and sometimes sadness. *See also sidebar on page 85.*

board games

To dream of playing board games emphasizes your competitive spirit and desire to get ahead in life. Alternately, it suggests that you are wasting your time and energy pursuing goals that others see as frivolous or meaningless.

boats

In general, dreams involving boats represent your current emotions and expectations. Examine the type of boat (e.g., rowboat, speedboat, yacht) and its overall condition. Are you at the helm? Is it docked, adrift, or sinking? Boats also reflect your journey through life. Consider whether you are on course or have lost your sense of direction.

bones

Seeing random, scattered bones reflects your inherent strength but also indicates that you are unsure of how to use it to your advantage. Similarly, bones can signify a personal or professional hunger or desire. *See also* **skeleton.**

books

Reading a book means you appreciate the power of knowledge and will benefit from it. An unopened book represents closed or repressed chapters of your life. *See also* **library, reading.**

boomerang

Something you tossed out will soon return to you, whether it was a comment (compliment or gossip), a relationship, or even someone you have been neglecting.

boots

To dream of someone who is wearing boots indicates that you will be rejected. If you are wearing boots in an inappropriate situation, you are misusing your authority. *See also* **shoes.**

border

Crossing any kind of border can mean you are on the verge of a significant discovery or achievement. However, this image can also indicate separation or alienation.

boss

This dream often has negative connotations, regardless of your relationship with that person. It can mean that you feel inadequate or pressured in the workplace, or that you consider yourself undervalued or unappreciated. If you dream of being a boss, you have a desire to take control of a stalled situation.

bottle

A full bottle reflects courage and/or bravado. An empty bottle represents a lack of passion or ambition.

bowling

Bowling is a good indication of your success in life. Are you throwing strikes or gutter balls? If your average is high, you could be in for a big surprise— prepare to be knocked over! *See also* **baseball bat, sports.**

box

Consider the emotional symbolism of this image. Are the contents visible to all, or is the box taped shut? If you dream of opening a box, you

Blake's Muse

Artist William Blake claimed to have been frequently visited in his dreams by a man who would show him images to paint as well as offer him advice regarding various painting techniques. Blake based many of his paintings on his dreams and, in 1819, produced a portrait of his nocturnal instructor, aptly titling it *The Man Who Taught Blake Painting in His Dreams.*

may soon discover something about yourself.

bracelet

To dream of wearing a bracelet portends a new friendship. To lose a bracelet is a warning of an argument that could strain a close relationship.

braces

See **legs, teeth.**

brakes

When you apply your brakes, how well they function corresponds to the control you have in your life. The simple act of stepping on a brake pedal suggests that you approach a certain situation cautiously.

brambles

If you see brambles, you may encounter a few snags in a project or business deal.

If you are entangled in the brambles, you feel trapped in a relationship or situation.

bread

To dream of baking bread reflects your desire for a more simple, down-to-earth lifestyle. On the other hand, considering that the word is slang for money, you could soon receive good news about your finances.

breathing

Breath symbolizes life force, and the way you are breathing reflects your physical and mental state and the pace at which you live your life. Labored or rapid breathing can signify either anxiety or excitement, and to dream that you are unable to breathe is a warning of a potential health problem. *See also* **strangulation, suffocation.**

bribery

If you dream of being bribed, you are likely feeling pressured into doing something in your waking life. Bribery can also refer to someone who can be bought and is therefore not trustworthy.

bricks

This symbol represents emotional blocks. To dream of a solid brick wall with no windows or doors indicates that you have run out of ideas, energy, or resources and are unsure of where to turn for help. Other symbols in the vicinity of the wall may be clues to a different direction or solution.

bride/bridegroom

Aside from the obvious association with a wedding (or the desire for marriage), these dream images generally mean that you are about to embark on a life adventure that may or may not include a romantic relationship.

bridge

This is a common symbol of transitions and possibilities. If you cross a bridge, you will overcome difficulties. Building a bridge portends favorable opportunities, whereas the image of a collapsed (or burned) bridge warns against taking advantage of people for your personal gain.

bronze

This metal indicates development and progress. You are meeting and overcoming challenges.

broom

You should make a clean sweep of things: Either tidy up your physical environment or come clean in a relationship.

brother

This archetype represents intellect and strength of character. It could reflect your relationship with an actual brother or someone with similar traits. *See also* **family.**

brown

The color brown symbolizes the earth, family matters, and feeling grounded. *See also sidebar on page 85.*

bruise

If you are bruised in a dream, you are taking comments made by others too personally. If you see a bruise on another person, your words or actions have been misunderstood. *See also* **blister, sting.**

brush

This symbol indicates that you are either disregarding (brushing off) something important or that you need to let go of insignificant negative emotions.

bubbles

To see or blow bubbles implies that fun and relaxation will help ease your tension. However, if the bubbles pop, you will face disappointments.

buckle

This dream image encourages you to persevere under pressure. If the buckle is damaged, you will be let down by a broken promise.

buds

To see buds on a tree means that a new development will result in a pleasant surprise. Alternately, it can suggest that long-held hopes will never be realized.

bugs

See **insects.**

bull

The presence of a bull can have quite different meanings, all of which reflect character traits: Consider whether you are stubborn and quick-tempered, too easily manipulated (bullied), or often untruthful. A white bull is an omen of good luck.

burial

To witness a burial in a dream indicates your need to put a troubling matter to rest. If you

A Mid-Night Solution

When bestselling author Sue Grafton has difficulty solving something, she suggests to herself, while going to sleep, that a solution will come. While writing *B Is for Burglar,* she came to a point where she suffered writer's block. But then she woke in the middle of the night and knew how to solve the problem: She would tell the story from a different angle. According to Grafton, the idea didn't come out of a specific dream but did originate from the same REM sleep state that creates dreams.

dream of being buried alive, consider what or whom in your waking life overwhelms you. *See also* **casket, digging, funeral.**

burn

If you burn something, your deep-seated anger too often causes heated arguments. To be burned portends that you will encounter mistreatment or deception. *See also* **ashes, fire.**

bus

This dream image indicates the route your life is taking. Are you on the wrong bus, or have you missed it entirely? To dream of waiting at a bus stop or station represents a stalemate. Don't rely on others to get you where you want to be.

butter

You likely feel the desire to splurge on something. If you dream of spreading butter, there is someone with whom you are trying to gain favor.

butterfly

This symbol of transformation suggests that you are entering a new phase in life

that will bring satisfaction and freedom. *See also* **caterpillar.**

buttons

If you lose a button, you should pay close attention to how you behave in social situations, particularly if they are formal gatherings. To dream that you are have trouble buttoning your clothes signifies that you will have difficulty closing a business deal.

buying

Dreams in which you buy something usually reflect your self-esteem. Purchases that are beyond your means suggest that you are insecure about (or unsure of) your future. Buying items at a sale price indicates confidence and discretion.

bystander

You are missing opportunities, and life is passing you by.

C

cabin

Building or living in a log cabin reflects anxiety over the condition of your current home and your ability to "keep up with the Joneses." Alternately, it points to a need for isolation or reflection.

cactus

As a dream image, a cactus represents defensiveness and rejection. You should consider letting down your guard and allowing people to get closer to the "real" you.

caddy

If you are carrying someone's golf clubs, you are placing the needs of others before your own, or someone may be taking advantage of you. If you are assisted by a caddy, expect easier financial times.

caduceus

The symbol of two snakes entwined around a staff represents the medical profession and is a good omen if you are incubating dreams for healing. *See also* **serpent, snake.**

cage

If you dream of being confined to a cage, you are feeling inhibited or restricted on a personal or professional level. Alternately, a cage can represent pent-up emotions. *See also* **birdcage, imprisonment.**

cake

This is often a sign of forthcoming fulfillment and satisfaction, but it can also suggest that you are expecting more of something than you deserve.

calculator

Your financial worries will be alleviated through careful planning, perhaps with the help of a professional.

calendar

The obvious interpretation of a calendar is that it is a reminder to make arrangements for an important event or trip. It can also represent anxieties about meeting deadlines or making appointments. *See also* **schedule.**

A Great Dreamer

When Alexander the Great campaigned throughout the Persian Empire, he employed soothsayer Aristander of Telmessos, who had written a book on dreams, as his personal dream interpreter.

---

camel

Are you carrying an emotional burden? This dream symbol also refers to stored resources, so rest assured that whatever you need to lighten your load is easily accessible.

camera

Using a camera represents important memories and links to the past. If you are taking photographs with a camera, pay close attention to what you are trying to capture and preserve—a photo can frame a message or detail that should be attended to.

camping

If you dream of sleeping peacefully beneath a star-lit sky, you likely have a need to get away from the daily hustle and bustle (you might even consider a change of residence).

If the dream is of a more rugged nature, you are striving to achieve self-reliance and independence.

cancer

This image is often a warning of toxic influences in your life. Examine your personal and professional relationships to determine the source of negative energy. At the same time, don't disregard the literal message regarding the state of your health or that of someone close to you.

candle

A burning candle reflects wisdom and can also foretell a revelation or inspiration. An unlit candle signifies unfulfilled promises, whereas

One Poet's Climb to the Top

For more than 20 years, poet and author Maya Angelou has had a recurring dream that reassures her that her writing is going well: "There is a dream which I delight in and long for when I'm writing. It means to me that the work is going well. I dream of a very tall building, and I'm climbing it with alacrity and joy and laughter. I have no sense of dizziness or discomfort or vertigo. I'm just climbing. I can't tell you how delicious that is!"

a candle that has burned out represents low energy or a loss of perspective.

cane

If you see a cane in a dream, you will receive much-needed support from a friend or family member. If you are using the cane for assistance, you may be relying too heavily on someone. *See also* **crutches.**

canoe

If you are paddling a canoe alone, you enjoy self-reliance and independence. On the other hand, paddling out of sync with another person will get you nowhere. *See also* **boats**.

canyon

There is a gap in your life that is making you feel empty or trapped—or both. Alternately, you could be dividing your attention among too many things. *See also* **abyss, hole.**

cape

See **coat.**

captain

If you dream of being a captain, you are in control of your destiny and are clear about your direction. Consider whether someone else would benefit from your guidance.

captivity

Being held captive suggests that you feel you must keep your ideas to yourself. You may also think you are being controlled or scrutinized. Be mindful of any thoughts or plans of escape. *See also* **abduction, imprisonment, kidnap.**

car

Vehicles such as cars often represent the physical body. A car in good running order is a reflection of your health. On the other hand, is it in need of repairs or refueling? The symbol has emotional implications as well. If you are driving the car, do you know where you are going? If you're a passenger, are you silent, helpful, or critical?

cards

If you dream about playing a game of cards, you are ready to take a risk in life. Just be prepared to accept the hand you are dealt. *See also* **gambling.**

caricature

This symbol represents a distorted opinion. You have an unfair view of someone or something without knowing all the facts.

carnations

To dream of receiving carnations is a general omen of a platonic and long-lasting friendship.

carnival

This carefree and casual atmosphere is in stark contrast to your strict or overly serious demeanor. If you loosen up and enjoy yourself more, others will enjoy you, too. *See also* **amusement park.**

caroling

See **singing.**

carpentry

You are trying to build a solid foundation for personal and financial growth. Skillful work is an omen of steady improvements and rewards, but shoddy construction will cost you in the long run.

carrot

If you dream of eating a carrot, you may soon be tempted by an alluring but questionable offer. Also consider the homonym *carat*—that offer may be of a romantic nature.

cartoon

To dream that you are a cartoon character indicates that a silly misunderstanding is causing you embarrassment. To dream of others in a cartoon suggests a lack of respect.

casket

Aside from its obvious association with death (or the fear of it), this dream symbol represents a cessation or completion of a project or

---

A Dream for Some, a Nightmare for Others!

Russian chemist Dmitri Mendeleev had been struggling for years to find an orderly way to classify the chemical elements. One night in 1869, he dreamed he saw a table "where all the elements fell into place as required." When he woke, he immediately sketched the table. That dream brought to the world the Periodic Table of the Elements, which remains one of the most important frameworks in chemistry, physics, biology, and engineering.

relationship that you found wearisome. Now it's time to rest. *See also* **burial, funeral.**

castle

This image foretells a happy marriage and family life. If you see a moat around the castle, you will provide well for those you love.

castration

You feel impotent in a situation, unable to exert control or influence. Dreams involving castration can also represent loss or sacrifice. *See also* **amputation, impotence.**

cat

This dream symbol can have a variety of meanings but usually points to self-reliance, independence, and good instincts. Negative symbolism can include lack of trust, insensitivity, and isolation. *See also sidebar on page 54.*

catalog

Whether you dream of looking through a catalog or of cataloguing items, you are faced with many options regarding an important decision. Keep your priorities straight and choose carefully.

catch

Depending on the context of the dream, there are several metaphorical interpretations. To catch an object such as a ball can represent understanding, as in "catching on." To catch someone after a chase means you consider the person a romantic prospect, or a "good catch." Catch can also refer to a hidden agenda or something that has strings attached, so be sure to read the fine print before closing a deal.

caterpillar

Life seems to be inching along, but your patience will be rewarded in the form of a positive transformation. *See also* **butterfly.**

cattle

To dream of cattle represents contentment and prosperity. If you are driving a herd of cattle, you are starting to bring all of your resources together.

cauliflower

Although an odd symbol, dreams that feature this vegetable (which resembles a brain) often serve as reminders to think with your head and not your heart.

cave

Hiding in a cave implies that you are avoiding painful issues. If you are emerging from a cave into bright daylight, you have examined your problems and will overcome them.

ceiling

This dream symbol represents limitations. Examine other images in the dream (people and objects) for clues that will help you overcome personal or professional obstacles.

celebration

If attending a celebration, expect to receive recognition for a recent accomplishment. If you are watching others celebrate but are not included, you may feel that you have fallen short of your goals.

celebrities

Dreams that feature celebrities emphasize your desire for success. If you dream that you are a celebrity, you are lacking attention from someone important to you.

celery

This vegetable symbolizes your mental health and physical vitality; consider whether the stalks are green and crisp or brown and rubbery.

cellar

Seeking shelter in a storm cellar represents a need for security in a personal relationship. If you are hiding in a dark cellar in a house, it reflects fears of being emotionally exposed. *See also* **basement.**

cemetery

Walking through a cemetery is a clear sign that you are ready to accept the losses in your life and move forward.

center

Being in this position reflects either an inflated ego and a need for attention or low self-esteem that makes you shun the spotlight. Alternately, you feel comfortably centered at this point in your life.

centipede

This symbol warns you to walk away from trouble or temptation; take advantage of your ability to do so.

chains

You are in some way an important link, a connecting factor. If you dream that you are bound in chains, consider what or who is keeping you from achieving your goals.

chair

This often symbolizes your position in the workplace. If the chair is empty, you should be more assertive in offering your opinions. If you are sitting in the chair, expect sudden changes around the office.

chameleon

Depending on the context of the dream, this image can have several meanings. Do you adapt well to fluctuating circumstances? Or perhaps you try to hide your true colors to please others or to gain their favor and praise. Keep in mind that some things are not how they first appear.

chandelier

A lit chandelier is an omen of social advancement. An unlit chandelier means it may take time for others to accept your bright ideas. To dream of swinging from a chandelier is a sign of luck and happiness.

chariot

If you dream of driving or riding in a chariot, consider it a warning to slow the pace of your life and take an easier and less hazardous route.

chasing

Chasing something or someone indicates that you are actively pursuing your goals. But the object or person you are chasing doesn't necessarily represent those goals. To be chased suggests feelings of inadequacy or vulnerability.

cherries

This symbol foretells temptations in love and romance. To see cherries on a tree indicates that your desires are well within your reach.

chess

Chess is a game that emphasizes strategy. If you are playing chess in a dream, plan carefully before you make a move in your waking life.

chickens

Don't forget the adage about not counting on something before you know it exists. Patience now will prevent disappointment later.

childhood

If you dream of a friend or family member as a child, you have a desire for that person to view you the way he or she did at that phase in your life. Perhaps you have felt less important over time, or you feel guilty about something that has transpired since then. *See also* **adolescence.**

childhood home

The interpretation of this image depends on your experiences in that home (or homes). If you have fond memories, you likely have a desire to return to a time when you had fewer responsibilities. Unfavorable recollections may actually foretell positive changes in your life. You are moving on.

chill

If you feel chilled in a dream, you will soon realize that something once frightening is ultimately harmless. Also consider the slang use of the word—adopt a more relaxed attitude. *See* **heat, warmth.**

chiropractor

To perform the duties of a chiropractor indicates that something in your life is out of alignment and needs adjusting. If a chiropractor is working on you, it is a sign that you feel manipulated by someone.

chocolate

This is a universal symbol of indulgence and luxury. Have you been doing something in excess, or do you need to pamper yourself more?

choking

The feeling that you are choking or being choked indicates oversensitivity to concerns that most others shrug off. It can also reveal that you find a recent revelation hard to accept or swallow.

church

This image represents your attitude toward or belief in organized religion or spirituality in general. The dream of sitting in an empty church suggests a need for reflection without judgment. *See also* **abbey, religion, temple.**

cider

This is a traditional symbol of good fortune. Drink it, and watch how your life (particularly your health) improves.

cigar/cigarette

While often thought to reflect an oral fixation, these symbols have more to do with your dependence on an object or person that will ultimately cause you harm. Current feelings of pleasure or fulfillment will be short-lived. *See also* **addiction.**

circles

Dream images of anything circular can have contradictory meanings: Are you making the same mistakes over and over? Stop and examine pointless routines. Alternately, circles can indicate that you are living a complete, rewarding life.

circus

To perform in a circus means your life is too chaotic. Take this as a sign to slow down, take on fewer responsibilities, and finish one project at a time. If you are attending a circus, consider tapping into your under-utilized creative talents.

clams

There are different interpretations of this dream symbol. It could be telling you to stop digging into the personal lives of others or at least keep quiet (clam up) about what you know. It may also suggest that you come out of your shell and reveal your emotions.

classroom

The general message of this common dream is that in order to achieve your goals, you should make an effort to learn something new or improve your current skills. Be alert to the details and activity in the classroom, as they may offer more specific advice. *See also sidebar on page 240,* **school.**

claws

To see or be grabbed by claws indicates that you are envious of or threatened by someone and are holding tightly to feelings of jealousy or vulnerability. If you have claws instead of hands, think twice before grasping at the first opportunity that comes along.

clay

This dream image symbolizes your malleability. You can change a situation for the better simply by changing your attitude, but don't be too easily influenced by others.

clean

To clean your house or other personal object indicates that it is time to clean up your act or come clean with information or feelings you have been withholding. *See also* **bath, shower.**

cliff

A cliff is a sign of forthcoming changes. To be pushed off a cliff warns against making hasty decisions, but if you jump off a cliff, you are ready to face any challenges that come your way. *See also* **abyss, canyon.**

climbing

You are striving to achieve something. Whether you're climbing with ease or with difficulty indicates your confidence in achieving your goal. *See also* **hill, mountain.**

cloak

See **coat, disguise.**

clock

This symbol reflects your awareness of or anxiety over the passing of time. A ticking clock indicates that your life may be progressing at too fast a pace, whereas a cuckoo clock represents a nagging reminder of repetitious behaviors or stagnancy. *See also* **watch.**

closet

First, examine the contents of the closet relative to the purpose it is intended to serve. For example, a clothes closet full of only linens means you are confused about how to organize your life. An empty closet can point to depleted emotions or the possibility of a fresh start. A full or overfilled closet is a warning to not take on more than you can manage. A closed or open closet door signifies shame or self-affirmation— consider the association with personal issues.

clothing

Clothing is one of the most common dream symbols, and it invariably reflects how you perceive yourself. To wear ripped, soiled, or inappropriate clothes points to issues of self-esteem, and the interpretation depends on your state of mind. For example, to proudly wear clothes that set you apart from others is a reflection of your individuality and creativity. (Conversely, shame or self-consciousness represents insecurities.) Tailored or designer clothes that are admired by others imply ambition and egotism, but to dream of wearing ill-fitting or poorly constructed clothes reflects uncertainty about your social or professional standing. *See also* **coat, disguise.**

clouds

White, billowy clouds connote creative reflection. Storm clouds portend a temporary period of anger or anxiety. Overcast skies reflect a lack of clear thinking. *See also* **sky, weather.**

clover

Traditionally considered a symbol of luck (particularly a four-leaf clover), the image can also warn against spending too much time striving for something that is likely to be unattainable.

clown

The interpretation of this image depends on your childhood experiences with clowns. If you have a positive view of them, your dream suggests that you lighten up and express your silly side. If you fear the image of a clown, consider whether you are trying to project yourself in a way that will please others— or perhaps you are afraid of making a fool of yourself.

clutter

This is most often a literal symbol: To dream that you are surrounded by clutter indicates that you are overworked or have too much on your mind. Make an effort to prioritize and bring order to the chaos.

coat

To see a coat on a hanger portends an unfortunate, unplanned situation, but the well-being of those close to you will be protected. Wearing a coat suggests that you are trying to conceal something about yourself. *See also* **clothing, disguise.**

cobweb

Brushing away cobwebs means you should clear your mind of tangled thoughts before making an important decision. Fear of cobwebs implies a denial or suppression of painful memories. *See also* **spider.**

coins

If someone gives you coins, expect a downturn in your financial situation. If you find coins, anticipate good luck with new investments. To search for change on the street indicates indecision regarding your profession.

collar

Any sort of collar (e.g., shirt collar, dog collar) implies that you are being coerced into a situation. Ask yourself if you really want to follow this lead before you go any further.

colors

To see a multitude of colors suggests variety and diversity. Many choices or opportunities are available. *See also sidebar on page 85 and individual colors.*

computer

If you are unaccustomed to using a computer, this dream reflects legitimate anxiety about unfamiliar technology. But if you use a computer frequently, the symbol reveals how you program your thoughts. Using a computer with dexterity indicates clear thinking; if it malfunctions, you may feel overburdened; if you are unable to type properly, you are likely overwhelmed with work-related responsibilities.

concave

Something concave, or curved inward, is a symbol of need or want. Dreams of a concave mirror warn of distorted perception—because everything is minimized, you may not be giving people or situations adequate attention. *See also* **convex, mirror.**

contest

To dream of winning a contest implies that you desire recognition. To dream of losing a contest is an indication that you have significant competition in the workplace.

convent

If you enter a convent, you have a need to explore your spirituality. To see a convent represents a restriction that's being imposed on you. *See also* **abbey, church.**

convex

Something convex, or bulging outward, symbolizes abundance, or perhaps a

Dreaming in Color

In the 1950s, with the widespread popularity of black-and-white television, scientists debated whether or not people were starting to dream in black and white. However, the consensus among researchers and dream interpretation experts is that many dreams occur "in color" (that is, we recall dream symbols or entire scenarios in different hues). The explanation is that our daily waking-life visual experiences are represented in a variety of colors, which ultimately show up in our dreams.

Still, there are people who swear they do not perceive colors in their dreams, and one reason is that dreams often fade when we wake up. The parts we manage to recall are in a blurry tone of gray, which often makes it difficult to identify symbols. But when a color shows up in a dream—especially in a black-and-white dream—it is most often a reflection of our emotions or overall state of mind. When recalling your dreams, pay particular attention to symbols with inappropriate or contradictory colors (e.g., a blue bear or a black lemon), as these give further meaning to the symbols themselves.

Here are some common meanings of the colors that are most prevalent in our dreams:

Black: power, the unknown, mourning
Blue: spirituality, intuition, sadness
Brown: nature, practicality, illness
Gray: humility, neutrality, indifference
Green: fertility, tranquility, jealousy
Orange: balance, warmth, deception
Pink: romance, compassion, passivity
Purple: royalty, wisdom, injury
Red: passion, embarrassment, anger
White: purity, enlightenment, naïvete
Yellow: hope, intelligence, cowardice

pregnancy. A convex mirror alters your perception— consider the warning "objects in mirror are closer than they appear." *See also* **concave, mirror.**

cooking

Dreams in which you are alone and cooking for a group (family, friends, etc.) point to issues of control: You prefer to be in charge of the menu, so to speak. If cooking cooperatively with others, do you feel comfortable, or does the adage "too many cooks in the kitchen" come to mind? Alternately, cooking highlights your creative and nurturing personality. *See also* **baking, kitchen.**

coral

Exploring a coral reef reflects your curiosity with inner beauty, which may not be obvious in those you meet for the first time. Alternately, to hold a piece of coral portends an encounter or entanglement with a thorny character. *See also* **rose.**

corner

To dream of a corner in a room signifies guilt or a fear of embarrassment. If you have your back to a corner, you are being restricted or perhaps coerced. To turn a street corner foretells a pleasant surprise.

corridor

See **hallway.**

cotton

One interpretation could relate to how content you are with your lifestyle. For example, if your bed clothes or linens are made of cotton, would you prefer satin or silk? On the other hand, this dream image often reflects a comfortable, peaceful state of mind.

couch

As a piece of furniture, this image can have opposite meanings: You need to either get off it or spend more time on it, whichever will bring you the most benefit. Also consider the word as a verb that relates to how information is conveyed: Make sure you are straightforward in your communications.

counting

Counting things is common when one is trying to fall asleep: Consider what you are counting (Sheep? Days before a deadline?

Money in your bank account?).
Note the number you reach, as
it could indicate a goal or desire.
If you are in a tranquil state of
mind, perhaps you are simply
counting your blessings. *See also
sidebar on page 175,* **numbers.**

court jester

This symbol can represent one
who is wiser than he or she
appears, or it can refer to one
who enjoys playing the fool. A
court jester can also imply that
you are being distracted from
more serious matters.

courtroom

Seeing or sitting in a courtroom
means you feel the need to
justify your actions or those
of people close to you. *See also*
judgment, jury.

cow

A cow in a field is a reflection
of domestic comfort and
nurturing. A cow in a barn
portends hard work that will be
rewarding. *See also* **cattle.**

coyote

One howling coyote portends
a plea for help, whereas a pack
warns of bad news. *See also*
dog, howl, wolf.

cradle

The general interpretations
point to either desires or avoided
responsibilities. An empty
cradle represents unfulfilled
wishes. A baby in a cradle
suggests that you will soon have
to juggle many tasks.

craving

To crave something indicates
that your talents have not been
fully recognized. Put yourself
in the spotlight to receive the
attention you deserve.

crawling

This image reflects the fact that
things may not be happening as
fast as you would like. Examine
other symbols in the dream to
identify possible obstacles. To
view someone else crawling is a
sign of impatience.

credit card

Using a credit card warns that
you don't have the means
(financial, emotional, or
physical) to do as you please
and that you will eventually
have to pay up if you try to.
Pace yourself accordingly.

crescent

A crescent-shaped image often reflects phases of the moon and may be pointing to a specific and significant time in the month. A crescent is also a symbol of arcane knowledge. *See also* **moon.**

cross/crucifix

You may feel that a personal sacrifice is necessary before you can reach a goal. These symbols also have religious connotations that represent your spiritual nature.

crossroads

You will soon face a difficult decision.

crow

To see one crow implies that you have been boasting about your achievements. If you see a flock of crows, you should avoid people who have been known to gossip behind your back.

crowds

Feeling uncomfortable in a crowd shows that you are easily distracted by the judgments of others. Spending time alone will help you formulate your own opinions.

> *One can write, think and pray exclusively of others; dreams are all egocentric.*
> —Evelyn Waugh

crown

This is a sign of reverence and authority. If you dream of wearing a crown, you have earned the respect of your peers. *See also* **royalty.**

crusade

Are you on a mission? A crusade may indicate aggressive negotiations: Perhaps you are forcing your ideas on someone. It can also mean that you are a single-minded individual who is passionate about your work or personal interests.

crutches

Examine a dream in which you are using crutches: Are you indeed injured and need them for support, or do you just rely on them out of habit? Crutches most often symbolize dependence on a person or a substance. *See also* **addiction, cane.**

crying

This is a significant dream feeling in that it represents an intense release of emotions that you suppress in your everyday life. If you actually wake yourself because you are crying, you have an urgent need to express and let go of painful thoughts or memories. To watch someone crying can reflect your desire to transfer those feelings rather than deal with them. To hear a baby cry points to insecurities you may have had as a small child.

cuddle

This is a literal sign of affection or fondness. It can also indicate that you are embracing a new idea, or it may foretell a new romance.

curtain

Closed curtains suggest that there is more to a story than what you are being told, or that you are withholding information. If the curtains are open, you have an opportunity for advancement in the workplace. *See also* **door.**

cut

To dream that you have cut yourself suggests that you desire to sever ties to something or someone. If you are cutting fabric, paper, etc., you are

attempting to see aspects of a situation in a different light.

D

daisy

A daisy signifies simplicity, innocence, and affection. To dream of receiving a bouquet of daisies foretells a close friend-ship. *See also sidebar on page 115.*

dam

To dream of seeing a dam suggests that you have pent-up or repressed emotions that should be released with caution. If you dream that the dam breaks, someone close to you will feel sorrow and shame. *See also* **avalanche, landslide.**

dance

To dance in a dream can represent a happy, carefree state of mind. If you are dancing with a partner, consider whether you are in step with each other, as this could point to the state of your relationship with a significant other. Alternately, dancing in a dream can suggest that you are sidestepping an issue or situation that you need to face.

dandelion

A field of dandelions foretells the wedding of a close friend. If you are gathering dandelions, you will soon receive word of a broken relationship. To dream of weeding dandelions from your lawn suggests that you are dealing with a seemingly endless problem.

dandruff

If you notice in a dream that you or someone else has dandruff, there is likely a physical or emotional problem (probably yours) that you are brushing aside. *See also* **hair.**

danger

To face danger indicates that you must be vigilant in avoiding negative or threatening people or circumstances. Who or what in the dream do you consider dangerous?

darkness

A dark dream atmosphere represents a lack of knowledge or understanding. If you are unable to find your way out of darkness, someone may be keeping something from you. To willingly step into darkness is to face the unknown: Proceed with caution.

darts

Playing darts implies that you are trying to achieve a goal and will succeed only with determination and focus. *See also* **arrow, target.**

daughter

The archetypal daughter can represent any young female who is close to you. Also consider the word offspring; she may symbolize a creative project or pursuit. *See also* **family.**

dawn

To dream of the dawning of a day means that you will soon gain the emotional strength to bring you out of a dark period.

deadline

Images of looming deadlines usually accompany a period of stress, whether at home or at work. If you miss a deadline, you are concerned about a lost opportunity. *See also* **calendar.**

deafness

This is an obvious sign of communication problems. If you dream that you are deaf, you are refusing to acknowledge a negative situation. If you dream of someone who is deaf, your advice is being ignored.

Think of a better way to get your point across. *See also* **ears.**

death

Dreams of death indicate the end of a stage in life and a time of positive or negative change. To dream that you have died suggests that you are no longer able to cope with a troubling situation and should seek the help or advice of others.

deer

This symbol represents your gentle, intuitive spirit but can also warn against placing yourself in vulnerable situations. *See also sidebar on page 54.*

deformity

A dream in which you have a deformity reflects a battered ego but also foretells a chance for personal growth. To point out someone with a deformity highlights your tendency to ignore the positive side of things.

deluge

See **avalanche, dam, landslide.**

demon

This image represents things that you find unsettling in your waking life, and it often has to do with your character. Take clues from a demon's prevailing attitude (e.g., hostile, guilty, withdrawn). *See also* **devil, evil.**

dentist

For many people, a dentist elicits fear. As a dream image, a dentist often represents a fear of hurting someone if you speak your mind (or reveal the truth) about a touchy subject. To maintain a clear conscience, be certain of

Sledding Under the Stars

When Albert Einstein was a young man, he dreamed he was sledding with friends at night. His sled began to slide so fast that he realized he was approaching the speed of light. Looking up at the stars, he saw them being refracted into colors he had never seen before. He knew that he was looking at "the most important meaning" in his life:

"I knew I had to understand that dream and you could say, and I would say, that my entire scientific career has been a meditation on my dream."

the facts before you say anything.

departure

While often suggestive of an impending trip, this image can also point to your need to free yourself from negative relationships or circumstances. *See also* **travel.**

depression

Whether or not you suffer from depression, this dream feeling reflects overwhelming sadness in your waking life. *See also* **crying.**

descent

This is often a symbol of emotional or physical decline. To descend into darkness warns that your brave and adventurous spirit could get you into trouble.

desert

To dream that you are wandering through a desert points to depleted creativity. Alternately, consider the use of the word as it relates to being abandoned.

detective

Are you in search of vital information? This symbol can also reflect a desire to know yourself better or a fear of revealing too much about yourself.

detour

Taking a detour foretells a career change. If you see an unfamiliar detour sign, you are on the wrong track but will be guided by a mentor.

devil

This archetype represents negative aspects of the self.

The Devil Made Me Do It!

When he was only 21 years old, 17th-century Italian composer Giuseppe Tartini dreamed that the devil was sitting at the foot of his bed. When Tartini handed him his violin and challenged him to play, the devil performed the most exquisite piece that Tartini had ever heard. Upon awakening, Tartini tried to play the music from his dream but was never able to reproduce it. All he could remember was a very distinctive double-stop trill, and it was around those notes that he composed his renowned "Devil's Trill Sonata."

It suggests that you explore conflicts in your personality. *See also* **demon, evil.**

dew

Consider it a sign of encouragement and hope. To see dew drops on flowers means that you will have a fresh start in life. *See also* **dawn.**

diamond

You will be repaid a debt faster than you expected. Diamond jewelry symbolizes a commitment, but not necessarily one of romance.

diary

To dream of making an entry in a diary shows that you are contemplating the wisdom of recent words or actions. For guidance, examine what you have written on the page.

diet

Dreams of dieting don't always pertain to food or weight. They can also indicate that discipline is required where finances or emotions are concerned. You may feel deprived temporarily, but your restraint will pay off in the end.

digging

If you dig a hole to bury something, what are you trying to hide or dispose of? Digging for something represents a desire to find more meaning in life. If you are digging in order to plant vegetation, expect a new business opportunity. *See also* **burial, shovel.**

dining room

This particular room symbolizes sustenance and nurturing. If the room is empty, you find a personal relationship to be lacking. A dining room full of people suggests that you are comfortable and satisfied with life. *See also* **kitchen.**

dinner bell

To hear a dinner bell is an omen that someone will soon ask you for a favor, and there is something you can gain by granting it.

dinosaur

Don't let outdated ideas hold you back. Opening yourself to

> ## A Lifetime of Dreams
> You will spend as much as one third of your life asleep. If you were to sleep 8 hours a day for your entire life, by the time you reached the age of 80, you would have spent more than 25 years in quiet slumber. Approximately 5 years of that time you were dreaming, which amounts to more than 100,000 dreams.

new experiences and opinions will invite success.

directions

To dream of giving or asking for directions is a good indication that you are questioning the path you are on. Do you feel you have wandered off course, or are you considering an entirely different journey?

dirt

Are you trying to unearth scandalous information about someone? Dreams of having a dirty appearance can point to low self-esteem, while wiping dirt from something can reflect the need for a fresh start. *See also* **clean.**

disappearance

If things or people disappear in a dream, it is a sign that you are losing interest in them or no longer have use for them. Alternately, you may be feeling anxious about recent or potential losses in your life.

disappointment

Feelings of disappointment imply that you are putting too much emphasis on a work- or home-related issue. You would benefit by keeping things in perspective.

disapproval

Whether you express or receive disapproval, you are harboring guilt over something you have recently said or done.

discovery

To discover an object in a dream frequently hints at hidden creative talents. If you uncover a secret, you will learn a valuable lesson that enhances your personal growth.

disease

A dream that you or someone else has contracted a disease

can mean you have uncomfortable feelings about your physical or spiritual well-being. It can also suggest uncertainty where business is concerned. *See also* **illness**.

disguise

Dreams in which you appear in disguise can represent a fear that others will catch a glimpse of the real you. Alternately, you may feel a need to change some aspect of your personality. Are only certain parts of you disguised? *See also* **clothing**.

disoriented

You are facing an unfamiliar situation or receiving conflicting information. You might also take it as a warning to get your thoughts or personal effects in order—something is missing or out of place.

ditch

This symbol indicates that you need to get rid of (ditch) negative influences. If you fall into a ditch, you could face embarrassment or personal loss. *See also* **hole**.

diving

Diving in a dream reflects an intrepid spirit and the onset of new adventures. Plunge in headfirst—but only if the water is clear.

divorce

You should anticipate some sort of emotional or physical separation. Alternately, business contracts or personal promises will be broken.

dizziness

To experience dizziness in a dream implies that you are having trouble balancing your life. You may have too much going on at home or at work—though, more likely, it's both.

doctor

This common dream image symbolizes a need for self-healing. If you are seeing a doctor, what are you being examined for? Another interpretation is that you will be called upon to help someone through a time of crisis.

> *All human beings are also dream beings. Dreaming ties all mankind together.*
> —Jack Kerouac

dog

A dog often represents your own trustworthiness, loyalty, and friendship, but be mindful of aggressive behavior. To be growled at or chased by a dog is a sign that you feel unappreciated or unfairly criticized by someone close to you. *See also sidebar on page 54.*

doll/doll house

Don't idealize people or relationships. Take a closer look at someone who appears (or claims) to have it all. If you dream of arranging dolls in a doll house, you have unrealistic expectations of family members and how they interact.

dolphin

As a dream image, a dolphin symbolizes a release of tension; one that jumps out of the water represents an intuitive leap in thought that will provide clarity and potential resolution. *See also sidebar on page 54.*

dome

View this image within the context of the dream. If you see a dome in the distance, you will fail to reach short-term goals. If you are standing in a dome, expect overdue recognition for your achievements.

donkey

Your work ethic needs improvement. If you are riding a donkey, you will encounter difficulties with a stubborn person or be forced to address a persistent problem.

door

An open door is a sign of new opportunities. A closed door means you have missed your chance and should move on. A locked door represents barriers. *See also* **gate.**

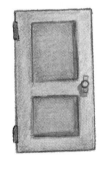

dove

A lone dove indicates emotional emptiness and a desire to be loved, whereas a pair of doves portends tranquility and happiness in the home.

dragging

Anything that you drag behind you in a dream represents a burden that prevents you from progressing. On the other hand, if you are dragging your heels about something, make up your mind and move on.

dragon

A dragon is a traditional symbol of force and power. It is a good omen for those on a spiritual quest.

dragonfly

Expect a sudden change in your routine, most likely a short but enjoyable trip.

drinking

The interpretation depends on what you are drinking. Water means you are taking in all life has to offer, whereas milk points to a need to be mothered. Drinking wine or spirits foretells new social connections that should be scrutinized. *See also* **alcohol.**

driving

This common dream theme represents a quest to reach your goals. If you are driving in control, you have a firm grasp of how to achieve success.

Careless driving reflects an indifferent or imprudent attitude. Also note the speed at which you are moving relative to other drivers: If it's noticeably slower, pick up the pace!

drowning

Do you feel that you are in over your head? Dreams about drowning reflect the anxiety and stress in your waking life. *See also* **swimming, water.**

drumming

If the rhythm of the beat is pleasant, you are following your heart and will make the right decisions. If the beat is disagreeable, your timing is off with regard to a plan or project.

drunkenness

Unless it reflects an actual addiction, this dream feeling often indicates a rebellious rejection of what is conventionally acceptable or desirable. It can also point to an attempt to fill an inner emptiness. *See also* **addiction, alcohol.**

duck

To dream of seeing a duck suggests avoidance. Are you dodging your responsibilities?

Face challenging and awkward situations head on. Alternately, if the duck is with a drake, you will enjoy a happy marriage.

duel

The meaning of a dream duel is the same as an argument: You are facing a challenging decision and question your judgment. But because dueling is an old-fashioned way to settle matters, you should address the antiquated thoughts that are preventing a resolution. *See also* **argument, enemy.**

dummy

If you dream that you are a ventriloquist's dummy, someone speaks too often on your behalf or puts words in your mouth (vice versa if you are the ventriloquist). Forming and expressing your own opinions will serve your interests better. This symbol can also reflect a lack of emotion or energy.

dump

To be in or near a garbage dump implies that you don't appreciate or are ashamed of your lifestyle. It can also point to emotional trash that continues to accumulate. Consider any relevance to the slang terms "getting dumped" (being rejected) or feeling "dumped on" (disrespected or overburdened). *See also* **garbage.**

dusk

This image could foretell a period of respite after a hectic time, but it is also a possible reference to an increasingly dark state of mind.

dust

Dreams in which you see an accumulation of dust indicate that you no longer find something appealing and are inadvertently neglecting it (that something can easily be

---

Wake Up, Sleepyhead!

Rip Van Winkle is a fictional character who fell asleep as a young man and woke many years later as an old man. The "Rip Van Winkle Effect" is a term that refers to excessive sleep. According to research, getting too much sleep—even an hour more than is needed—can be almost as debilitating as sleep deprivation.

a person). The symbolism of both dust and dirt warn against procrastination: Neglected problems are ultimately harder to brush off. *See also* **dirt.**

E

eagle

As a dream image, an eagle represents confidence in your ability to soar to greater heights (loftier goals). It also highlights keen eye for detail. Alternately, this is a symbol of predation: You may be feeling vulnerable or threatened.

earrings

Whether your are a man or a woman, to dream of wearing earrings (or an earring) indicates that you will soon meet a charming and attractive person. If you lose an earring, you fear that people are making thoughtless judgments of you.

ears

To dream of your ears can mean you are open to new ideas and are respectful of others' opinions. Alternately, this symbol suggests that you listen more carefully to the advice someone is trying to give you—it is more important than you think. *See also* **deafness.**

earth

Dreams that feature earth indicate that you have been reflecting on your sense of being, your heritage or background, and your ideals. If you see damage to or destruction of the planet Earth, contemplate how your everyday actions affect your quality of life (and that of others) and make necessary changes. *See also* **end of the world.**

earthquake

This dream symbol has different meanings. It can reflect the fact that you have experienced a big change and are operating on shaky ground because of it. On the other hand, this change may have taken the excitement out of life. Try to shake things up a bit.

eating

Eating in a dream corres-ponds to understanding or comprehending something (taking it in). Eating also reflects how well you nourish and sustain all aspects of yourself. Overeating or refusing to eat indicates emotional emptiness. *See also sidebar on page 101,* **food.**

eavesdropping

Despite the negative connotation, eavesdropping in a dream reflects simple curiosity or a greater quest for knowledge. Don't be afraid to ask questions, but at the same time, don't believe everything you hear.

ebb

See **tide.**

echo

Be cautious when relaying information to people you don't know well. Your words may be repeated and could come back to haunt you.

eclipse

Something is obscured from your view. Wait until you can see it more clearly before you form an opinion or take action. This dream can also imply that you are feeling overshadowed or minimized on a personal level. *See also* **sun.**

edge

To stand at the edge of something signifies that you are on the verge of a realization that could change your life. To notice objects with sharp edges indicates that you are too sensitive to what people say or how they behave. Finally, consider whether phrases such as "feeling edgy" or "being edged out" have relevance to your life. *See also* **abyss, cliff.**

eel

To see or handle an eel warns that a golden opportunity could slip through your fingers if you don't act quickly.

egg

This symbol has several meanings. Gathering eggs from a nest predicts financial success over time, and eating eggs symbolizes new beginnings. Broken eggs indicate that you are coming out of your shell, whereas eggshells that are cracked suggest that you tread lightly around someone who is feeling fragile. *See also sidebar on page 101,* **embryo.**

elbow

To dream of your elbow usually means that you are

I Dream of Eating

The universal dream symbol of eating represents the basic human need for physical, emotional, and spiritual nourishment. For most people, eating provides a sense of comfort and satisfaction, but for others it can be a meaningless but necessary act of survival.

To accurately interpret dreams that involve eating, first consider with whom, if anyone, you are dining. In general, eating alone foretells the loss of a loved one or a lowered social status, while dining in the company of others (particularly family and friends) is an omen of abundance in personal and financial matters. Also examine the atmosphere in which you are eating—is it cheerful or peaceful, or do disharmony and strife prevail?

Central to your interpretation are the quality and types of foods you are eating and your personal associations with them. If you consider this in relation to other symbols in the dream (people, places, attitudes), you should come away with a satisfactory explanation.

Here are the symbolic meanings of foods that commonly appear in our dreams:

Apples: knowledge, good health, temptation

Berries: wealth, truthfulness, indiscretion

Bread: patience, resourcefulness, poverty

Cake: luck, satisfaction, selfishness

Chocolate: contentment, sensuality, indulgence

Eggs: creativity, hope, disappointment

Grapes: wisdom, romance, frivolity

Lemons: popularity, optimism, embarrassment

Meat: strength, prosperity, aggression

Onions: reliability, complexity, deception

Oranges: vibrancy, frugality, naïvete

Pasta: wholesomeness, intuition, deprivation

Peppers: excitement, stimulation, irritability

Pickles: patience, satisfaction, indecision

Pizza: generosity, abundance, impulsivity

Potatoes: serenity, fortitude, laziness

bending to the will of someone. Other interpretations point to your flexibility in handling complicated situations or your need for more freedom (elbow room) in a relationship. *See also* **arms.**

election

Are you feeling judged by others? You could be asked to take on more responsibilities, but you should also consider the possibility of an emotional letdown.

electricity

To dream of electricity foretells a surge in your creative or physical energy. However, electrical faults or short circuits could cause you to lose your drive and focus. If you employ an electrician, your energy and drive need a boost. A dream in which you are electrocuted forecasts startling news. *See also* **engine.**

elephants

This is a powerful symbol that indicates your strong character and thick skin will help you endure impending criticism. It can also serve to remind you of something important or to urge you to hold on to cherished

memories. *See also sidebar on page 54.*

elevator

If you are riding an elevator up, you are working to achieve your goals but too often take the easy way to get to the top. It may also signify a spiritual high. Riding an elevator down foretells discouragement or disappointment. Being trapped in an elevator signifies emotional frustration. *See also* **ladder, stairs.**

elf

Images of elves reflect how you perceive yourself relative to those around you (friends, co-workers, or family). Do you feel small and insignificant, or do you loom large in comparison? *See also* **giant.**

elope

To dream that someone elopes foretells the unpredictable, but not necessarily bad, marriage of a person close to you. If you dream of eloping but are already married, avoid making impulsive decisions.

embarrassment

If you feel embarrassed in a dream, you will soon be asked

to do something that you are unfamiliar with or that takes you out of your comfort zone. This emotion can also reflect guilt or a fear of being judged.

embryo

This is a common dream among women who are pregnant, but it can also represent the germ of an idea. An opportunity is developing that requires care and attention to reach its potential. *See also* **egg.**

emerald

This gemstone represents fertility, growth, and envy. If you receive emerald jewelry, you may soon face family strife regarding an inheritance.

empty

Empty objects or places (a jar, room, landscape, etc.) can represent either the potential for growth or lost opportunities. To feel emptiness reflects something lost or lacking in your waking life, usually spiritual, physical, or emotional energy. To empty an object of its contents is to discard something (or someone) that is no longer meaningful to you.

enamel

Smelling or applying enamel is a warning to closely examine problematic financial or professional matters. Important issues that have been glossed over will bring resolution. *See also* **varnish.**

enclosure

Depending on the dream, an enclosure is a symbol of either protection or confinement. If you are in a small enclosure,

---

Hey, I'm Not Done with That!

Most people have had the experience of dining in a restaurant and having their food taken away before they are finished eating. Consider this old wives tale the next time that happens to you:

If a family member clears away the platter of food before you are done eating, it foretells that you will have domestic trouble and vexation from those dependent upon you. If a waitperson takes your plate away without your permission, you will encounter grave financial difficulties.

do you feel safe or trapped? Large enclosures foretell new endeavors or relationships, though you may encounter limitations. *See also* **cage, imprisonment.**

encyclopedia

Although you prefer to acquire wisdom through the written word, you need the insight offered by real-life experiences. This will provide the answers you are looking for.

end of the world

Frequently, such dreams are exaggerated symbols of despair over a change in life, but they can also point out the possibility of a fresh start. Alternately, this image is often reported by people with grave concerns about our planet's ability to sustain life. *See also* **earth.**

enemy

Dreams of confronting an enemy reflect issues of self-doubt. You should address inner conflicts or negative aspects of your personality. *See also* **argument, duel.**

engine

An engine symbolizes your driving force. If it is running smoothly, you should push forward with confidence to acquire what you want. A sluggish or malfunctioning engine will get you nowhere. *See also* **electricity.**

entry

Attempting to gain entry to something points to insecurity over being recognized or accepted. For example, waiting in line to get into an engagement or venue reflects a desire for increased social status. A blocked entryway may be daunting, but exploring what lays beyond brings validation.

envy

To experience envy highlights what you feel you need to make your life complete. Of whom are you envious and why? If someone is envious of you, be wary of projecting a boastful attitude.

eruption

See **explosion.**

In dreams, fantasy gets even with the shameless imp, Reason.

—German dramatist Friedrich Hebbel

A Cheesy Sleep Study

A study led by Nigel White, secretary of the British Cheese Board, set out to prove that, contrary to popular belief, eating cheese before bedtime does not cause nightmares. In this week-long experiment, 200 volunteers ate a small piece of cheese 30 minutes before they retired. Three-fourths of the group slept well every night, likely due to an amino acid in cheese called tryptophan, which facilitates good sleep. Furthermore, researchers found that the variety of cheeses the participants ate affected the kind of dreams they had. For example, those who ate Stilton reported having vivid but very strange dreams; volunteers who ate cheddar dreamed of celebrities; and those who ate Lancashire cheese had work-related dreams.

escape

A dream in which you escape (or plan to escape) can give you clues as to a way out of unfavorable circumstances. Examine the strategy you used. However, such a dream can suggest that you are unwittingly fleeing from a situation that could prove beneficial. *See also* **captivity, imprisonment.**

evil

An evil presence or atmosphere reflects a negative sense of self. Understanding why you perceive certain images as evil will help you address the character issues troubling you. Evil also indicates repressed rage. *See also* **demon, devil.**

exam

Doing poorly on (or failing) an exam or test means you feel inadequate (mentally, physically, or socially) compared with other people. To dream that you are unprepared for an exams foretells a challenging assignment or task. To dream of undergoing a physical exam can be a warning of a health problem. *See also* **school, test.**

excitement

Feeling excited in a dream is generally an omen that you will soon be involved in an interesting situation or

That Sinking Feeling

The night before the infamous sinking of the *Titanic,* a passenger aboard the ship woke her husband and told him that she'd just dreamed of the impending disaster. Although the husband dismissed her fears, the woman's dream haunted her throughout the next day. That night she put her children to bed in warm clothes and gathered some necessities "just in case." A few hours later, the Titanic struck an iceberg and began to sink. The woman and her children escaped and were rescued, but her husband was not so fortunate.

relationship. However, contemplate the type of excitement you felt (nervous? enthusiastic?) for a better sense of what interesting implies.

exercise

To exercise in a dream can be a literal message that you need more physical activity. It can also be telling you to exercise caution or exercise your rights when making personal or business decisions.

exhaust

The smell or sight of exhaust fumes is a warning to back away from a potentially unpleasant situation. It can also foretell an unexpected depletion of your finances. Finally, consider the word "exhaustion." Are you feeling worn out or unusually tired?

explosion

Dreams in which something explodes often represent anger that will cause a sensitive situation to blow up. If you dream of holding an explosive device, be careful expressing your feelings. Alternately, this symbol suggests that you will soon be the target of an outburst in which a damaging secret will be revealed.

eyebrows

Encountering a person with thick, dark eyebrows means you will meet a nefarious character. Arched eyebrows indicate a forthcoming surprise.

eyeglasses

If you dream of wearing glasses (whether or not you do in your waking life), how well you see through them represents your interpretation of a current situation. Eyeglasses that blur your vision indicate distorted thinking.

eyelashes

Seeing someone with unusually long eyelashes predicts that an attractive person will prove to be deceptive. Don't reveal confidential information.

eyes

As they do in everyday life, eyes that appear as a dream image reflect insight and awareness. Open eyes signify curiosity or a willingness to see things from different perspectives. But if they are closed, you are blind to a problematic issue that is obvious to others. One eye indicates a lack of intuition; more than two eyes reflects curiosity. *See also* **blindness.**

F

face

The expression on your dream face usually contradicts your waking life feelings or state of mind. For example, an exaggerated smile means that you are sad or depressed but are trying to put on a happy face for others. An angry expression represents confidence, self-respect, and contentment. And if your face is devoid of expression, you are dealing with a range of conflicting feelings that you are unwilling or unable to sort through. *See also* **mirror, reflection.**

face card

If you dream about playing cards and are holding the king, queen, or jack, expect success in a risky business venture. *See also* **cards.**

factory

A factory signifies routines, repetition, and predictability. If this is a common dream symbol for you, consider taking a break to do something that inspires you. Alternately, this image predicts that your hard work and dependability will enable you to advance.

failure

Although usually considered a reflection of low self-esteem, dreams of failure have other

Things that Go Bump in the Night

In 1816, the poet Lord Byron hosted several guests at his villa in Switzerland, one of whom was 19-year-old Mary Wollstonecraft Godwin (who later married the poet Percy Shelley). On stormy evenings, Lord Byron enjoyed reading to his friends, often from a book of ghost stories. On one such occasion, Byron challenged his guests to create and present their own tales of horror. That night, after Mary fell asleep thinking about what she would write, she dreamed of a wretched man kneeling beside a frightful creature he had just assembled. When the monster stirred to life, it glared at its maker with yellow, watery eyes. The vision so terrified Mary that she knew instantly that what she had seen in her dream would be the basis for her horror story. The next day she began to write the novel *Frankenstein*.

implications. A failed work project or business venture reveals that with perseverance, you will eventually succeed. If a relationship has failed, avoid making impassioned promises that you will later regret.

fairy

The image of a fairy (or pixie, gnome, etc.) reflects your feminine side and ability to make things happen when others cannot. It is also an omen that you will receive help from an unexpected source.

falling

This is one of the most common dream feelings, especially when you are just drifting off (hence the phrase "falling asleep"). But it also occurs later in the sleep cycle, and the emotions it evokes can range from fear to loss of control to exhilaration. Your specific reaction likely mirrors your reaction to a waking-life situation.

false teeth

As with any disguise or facade, this image represents an attempt to cover up something. False teeth warn of rumors and gossip, particularly from sources that you believe to be sound and reliable. *See also* **disguise, teeth.**

fame

As they say, "fame is fleeting," and to dream of achieving fame implies that you have not been sufficiently recognized at work or among your friends. Don't be afraid to remind people of your contributions. If you dream of associating with a famous person, you may covet their characteristics you admire.

family

Dreams that involve family members reflect your long-held, rich, and often complex relationships with them (whether harmonious or antagonistic). But a family doesn't have to consist of relatives. It can represent any group of people who are united by a common factor. *See also sidebar on page 119 and individual family members.*

fan

Fanning yourself means that an embarrassing situation will soon be forgotten or that you are reacting too intensely to something. To fan someone warns against fawning over people who don't deserve it.

farm

A well-maintained farm portends good health and prosperity. If the farm is run down, important business or personal matters need to be addressed. To dream of living on a farm highlights your desire for a simpler, more self-sufficient lifestyle.

fasting

This is typically a symbol of rejection—you are pushing away someone or ignoring what is considered socially acceptable. However, it can also be a positive sign of purification, an effort to cleanse yourself of negative influences or habits.

fat

Feeling fatter in a dream than you actually are can reflect guilt about myriad overindulgences in life that often have nothing to do with food (spending, sex,

> And all my days are trances,
> And all my nightly dreams
> Are where thy grey eye glances,
> And where thy footstep gleams—
> In what ethereal dances,
> By what eternal streams.
>
> —Edgar Allen Poe,
> "To One in Paradise"

drugs, or alcohol). Another common interpretation is that you are carrying a burden so large that it is weighing you down. *See also* **heavy.**

father

The archetype represents a male authority figure. Dreams of your own father usually highlight exaggerated images of his personality (good or bad) that reflect your perception of him. *See also* **family.**

faucet

This is a symbol of self-control, or your ability to turn your emotions on and off when necessary. A faucet that drips or runs dry reflects depleting or spent resources (emotional, financial, or physical).

fear

Fear reflects issues that you haven't been able to cope with, so it is important to recall the details of these dreams. The symbolism will enable you to see threats in proper

> *The future belongs to those who believe in the beauty of their dreams.*
> —Eleanor Roosevelt

perspective, and chances are they won't loom so large. *See also* **nightmare.**

feast

To attend or host a feast indicates that your life is abundant and you are confident in your ability to provide for those close to you. Alternately, this dream image can point to insecurities about your financial future.

feathers

This image has contrary interpretations: It can signify either luxury and glamour or need and frugality. Floating feathers foretell celebrations and fulfilled wishes.

feet

To dream of your own feet means you are questioning your independence and stability and how grounded you feel. If they appear out of proportion or injured, you will endure an arduous journey. Random feet foretell a personal or professional move forward.

female

The archetype represents intuition, nurturing, fertility, and vulnerability.

fence

Does the fence elicit feelings of safety or entrapment? A chain-link fence warns against taking the easy way out of problems, whereas a solid wood fence recommends forbearance and tenacity in confrontations. To dream of climbing a fence represents escape, but a fence wrapped in barbed wire means you will face impediments. *See also* **cage, wall.**

ferret

If you dream of this animal (especially if it is a pet), you will find what you are seeking—but only with perseverance and tenacity.

fever

It may be that your sleep environment is too warm, but if that isn't the case, feeling feverish can indicate health issues that range in severity. Other interpretations are that you are perceived as having a hotheaded temperament. Before matters get out of control, heed the adage "cooler heads prevail." *See also sidebar below.*

fiddle

The music of a fiddle can foretell a casual but meaningful celebration. Alternately, it can warn you of someone who will play (or fiddle) with your emotions.

field

Consider what is growing in the field and your reaction to that image. To some, a field in its wild state illustrates freedom

Hotheaded Dreaming

Fevers often bring on nightmares, but some nightmares that are not caused by a fever can evoke strange hallucinations commonly associated with being feverish. These include objects or people that are ridiculously smaller or larger than they are in real life and sounds or movements that are dramatically slower or faster than normal.

and independence; for others, it points to waste and lost opportunities. A field full of healthy crops reflects a positive state of mind, whereas a barren field connotes depleted energy.

fighting

Physical fights translate as aggression toward something or someone (whereas verbal arguments reflect internal conflicts). To fight in self-defense is to take a stand against a perceived threat. If you are watching a fight, you are afraid or unable to express your everyday frustrations.

fingernails

Nails are a sign of your physical or emotional state. Are yours healthy and groomed or discolored and broken? Nails that are excessively long reveal a need for attention, whereas bitten nails mean that something is gnawing at you. *See also* **hair.**

fingers

Each finger has a different connotation, but all of them represent nonverbal communication. To dream of your index finger indicates a need for emphasis (to what or whom are you pointing?); the pinky finger signifies the importance of your feminine side; the ring finger suggests issues of commitment; and your middle finger represents authority and assertiveness.

fire

The range of meanings behind this ancient image include power, transformation, destruction, purification, and renewal. If the fire is wildly ablaze, you may feel creatively inspired or angrily frustrated. A glowing fire represents repressed emotions. Standing in a fire can foretell a period of passion but may also point to self-destructive behavior. Putting out a smoldering fire portends the release of painful memories. *See also* **ashes, flames, smoke.**

firecrackers

To dream of setting off firecrackers means you are desperate for someone's attention but aren't being assertive or articulate enough to be heard. If you hear or see firecrackers going off, persistent but petty irritations will stop if you ignore them.

fired

Many dreams in which you are fired from a job have little to do with employment. Rather, they reflect personal issues of rejection or separation. Is your reaction to being fired one of remorse, shame, or surprise? Feeling relieved implies that you will figure out how to extricate yourself from a stagnant relationship.

fireflies

Pay attention to sudden or recurring ideas, as they point to a bright future. Alternately, be warned that shocking behavior will be noticed by everyone.

fireplace

A glowing fireplace predicts contentment in a romantic or familial relationship. Alternately, consider the implications of a cold fireplace, as it can point to your inability to "keep the fire lit."

fireworks

If you hear fireworks in the distance, you will attend a celebration in your honor. To set off fireworks indicates that you are blowing an issue way out of proportion.

fish

As a dream symbol, fish reflect the thoughts or emotions that you keep just below the surface. Also consider whether related idioms such as "a cold fish" or "a fish out of water" apply to you.

fishing

In general, to dream of fishing reflects a desire or need for information or knowledge, or that you are ready to access what you have pushed to the back of your mind. But fishing can also encourage you to pursue a romantic interest. Patience and perseverence will enable you to land your catch.

fist

A fist can represent either controlled or repressed anger. Shaking your fist at someone symbolizes determination. *See also* **hands.**

flames

Are you fanning the flames of an already heated situation?

Step back and let things cool down before they get out of control.

flies

See **insects.**

floating

Floating in air means you are going through life with your head in the clouds or that you are detached from people or responsibilities. What's more, floating on water warns that the imbalance between your physical and emotional selves will pull you under. *See also* **flying.**

flood

To dream that you are caught in a flood warns against being swept up in a potentially dangerous situation. To witness an approaching flood is a sign that you will receive news of a life-changing oppportunity.

floor

This image represents stability: Does the floor feel solid, uneven, or ready to collapse?

flour

Baking with flour is a good omen for long-term financial investments. An unopened sack of flour is a sign of wasted potential. If you are grinding your own flour, adopt a less materialistic lifestyle.

flowers

The symbolism of flowers varies widely. Receiving or sending flowers indicates a desire for attention or admiration. Planting or maintaining a flower bed foretells opportunities for change. If you pick fresh flowers, the excitement of a current romance will fade. A field of wild flowers encourages you to pursue unfamiliar avenues. *See also sidebar on page 115.*

flute

If you hear flute music, you are striving to achieve harmony and balance in your life. If you are playing a flute, you will accomplish that goal.

flying

Dream flight refers to that ethereal feeling of being transported by your own will out of a place or situation. The

A Rose by Any Other Name

As a prevalent image in our waking lives, flowers evoke feelings that range from sadness (illness, funerals) to love (celebrations of all kinds), and in this way they symbolize the complete cycle of life and death. As dream symbols, they reflect our emotional, physical, and spiritual well being, as well as our personal growth and creativity.

When flowers appear in your dreams, pay close attention to their color and vitality, as these provide clues as to their meanings. Healthy, vibrant flowers often reflect a similar state of mind, whereas wilted or faded flowers can point to depleted energy or emotions. Notice flowers that appear in atypical hues (e.g., dreams of blue roses could represent unrequited love) and whether the image is of a single bloom, a bouquet, or a resplendent garden.

Here are some common flowers and their corresponding dream meanings:

Flowers in Different Hues

Roses: Red roses represent passion and devotion; white: purity and innocence; pink: comfort and contentment; yellow: platonic friendship; black/purple: deception and illness

Tulips: Red tulips imply romantic promises; yellow: well wishes; white: forgiveness; purple: apologies and devotion

Carnations: Red carnations mean innocent affection; white: flirtation and admiration; pink: celebrations and well wishes

Individual Flowers

Daffodils: renewal, newfound happiness

Daisies: innocence, honesty

Lilies: humility, hope

Orchids: devotion, individuality

interpretation of this common but significant dream depends on your reason for taking flight. If you are flying toward or away from something or someone, what is the reason? Flying with ease reflects a desire for freedom, but if you encounter impediments, evaluate their symbolism. Finally, make note of the particular images you see from high above: Does rising above things give you better perspective?

fog

Don't judge what you can't clearly see. Fog often represents your unconscious: What is obscured by the fog is the self-awarenesss you seek. If you manage to identify objects or people in the fog, try to clarify your waking-life connections with related images. Finally, look for signs that the fog is lifting.

follow

See **behind.**

food

Many people dream of food, and its symbolism represents both physical and emotional sustenance. If you are eating and enjoying food, you are receiving positive input in your life. If you are serving food, how the recipient reacts indicates whether you are nurturing your relationships or merely feeding a problem. *See also* **eating.**

fool

The archetype represents self-sabotage that prevents you from gaining the respect of others and, thereby, accomplishing your goals.

footprints

To dream of seeing footprints indicates a lack of direction or originality. To see your own footprints represents loss or loneliness—perhaps you have been separated from a significant other or a child.

forest

Walking through or feeling lost in a forest means you are searching for answers that are right in front of you. Step back and view the bigger picture. *See also* **woods.**

forget-me-not

Consider the figure of speech. Someone wants your attention, or you have been neglecting some aspect of yourself.

forgetting

The common dream feeling that you have forgotten something points to general waking-life anxieties. But being forgetful in a dream often has the benefit of reminding you to do what needs to be done.

fork

If you dream of using a fork to eat, you are eager to obtain as much knowledge as possible. Using a bent fork portends a brief period of indecision; hold off on choosing the right path.

fossil

Take a fresh look at or a new approach to something you have considered set in stone. This symbol also indicates concerns about growing older. *See also* **antiques, ruins.**

fountain

A flowing fountain is a sign of creativity and generosity. To dream of a dry fountain indicates that you are thirsty for new friendships or a romantic relationship.

fox

Be upfront in your business dealings and recognize the difference between being shrewd and being deceptive. *See also sidebar on page 54.*

freckles

To dream that you have freckles indicates a yearning for the innocence of childhood. Freckles can also represent perceived imperfections and warn against making superficial judgments.

freezer

There are conflicting interpretations: Placing an object in a freezer can warn against putting off something that should be dealt with now. On the other hand, to freeze something represents foresight and preservation: You are prepared for difficult times.

friends

It is common to dream of friends—particularly those with whom you no longer have contact. Consider whether the character traits of each friend are admirable or not, as they often mirror your own.

frogs

Frogs symbolize transformation and ambition. Croaking frogs reflect stagnant or nagging thoughts. To see frogs jumping recommends that you stop hesitating and take a leap of faith.

fruit

To dream of eating ripe fruit foretells good fortune and health. Unripe fruit warns of premature decisions; rotten fruit signifies opportunities that have passed you by. *See also sidebar on page 101.*

funeral

Funeral images reflect fears of loss—whether they involve something or someone close to you or aspects of your personality. Watching your own funeral indicates that you are examining what you have accomplished in life. Make careful note of these dreams and take advantage of the messages they send.

gagging

To dream that you are gagging indicates incredulity, or that you find a certain idea hard to swallow. If you are wearing a gag, you feel either stifled or unable to express yourself.

gambling

Think twice before taking chances in business or personal matters. *See also* **cards, lottery.**

garage

A garage often symbolizes a place in which to escape, a private space where you can organize your thoughts or express your creativity. But it can also be a sign that you are storing too many emotions or isolating yourself.

garbage

The image of garbage represents what you need to prioritize and organize. But a more important message is: Your emotional "junk" is so old that it's starting to stink up the rest of your life. Address small or persistent issues now before they become overwhelming to you and obvious to everyone else. *See also* **clutter.**

Dream Archetypes

Archetypal dream symbols are also referred to as "universal symbols" because they hold similar general meanings for most cultures. They represent the emotional connections that people around the world have shared since the dawn of time—and are what influence our instinctual behavior. According to psychologist Carl Jung, archetypal images come from the "collective unconscious," which he describes as "the whole spiritual heritage of mankind's evolution born anew in the brain structure of every individual."

Archetypal dream images can have either positive or negative connotations, depending on your personal associations with them. The most common archetypal figures are:

★ **Child,** which can represent innocence, fear, or the need for unconditional love. Variations of the Child archetype include the Wonder Child, the Wounded Child, and the Eternal Child.

★ **Mother,** which can represent intuition, nurturing, or love. Variations include Earth Mother, Wise Old Woman, and the Black Madonna.

★ **Father,** which can represent protection, authority, or power. Variations include Hero Father, Wise Old Man, and Malevolent Father.

Dreams also consist of archetypal themes, which include birth, transformation, death, fear, and self-awareness. These themes primarily become evident in recurring dreams.

garden

A garden symbolizes the self—your state of mind and the fruits of your labor. A thriving garden reflects fulfillment in love or business. Tending a neglected garden predicts that your artistic creativity will bring you success.

garlic

To cultivate, cook, or smell garlic foretells a social exchange that seems pleasant at first but will end up leaving a bad impression. *See also* **onions.**

garnet

This gemstone emphasizes that affairs of the heart should have priority. Consider whether these "affairs of the heart" mean underlying health problems.

gate

This symbol represents opportunities. An open gate bodes well for your future. If the gate is closed, or if you have a hard time opening it, someone is preventing you from reaching your goals (and that someone is likely you). Be sure to note any symbols around or beyond the gate. If you dream that you are a gatekeeper, consider who you allow to pass through and why. *See also* **door, entry.**

gems

To dream of holding a variety or a large number of gems symbolizes options. Translated to your waking life: Choose carefully, because only one will bring you happiness. *See also individual gemstones.*

germs

A dream in which you are overly cautious about germs can point to rational health concerns, either for yourself or someone you have close contact with. It can also symbolize contamination and can warn against someone who is a bad influence.

ghost

First consider the form the ghost takes: If it is frightening, you are harboring guilt over an issue that you fear will never go away. A ghost that evokes little emotion means that you feel overlooked or invisible. If that's the case, being more expressive will get you the attention you seek. Alternately, dream ghosts represent patterns of thought that are preventing you from "living in the present."

See also **demon.**

giant

If you dream of being a giant, consider whether you are trying to wield (or want to wield) too much control or power over others. If you encounter a giant image, you feel inferior, out of place, or overwhelmed. This can represent problems that seem too big to handle, but it also points to a lack of perspective. *See also* **elf.**

gift

To be presented with a gift portends the awareness or awakening of latent talents or skills. If you are the one bearing a gift, you will help someone realize his or her potential.

Music to His Ears

In 1789, Ernst Chladni was experimenting with the acoustic properties of water-filled crystal glasses in an attempt to create a particular sound. One afternoon while napping, he dreamed of a new musical instrument and woke with a profound feeling that it would create the sound he was looking for. Based on that dream image, Chladni invented an instrument that he called a "euphonium." It was similar to what we now know as the tuba but produced a more mellow tone—precisely the one he'd been seeking. Chladni later became Europe's leading authority on acoustics.

giraffe

As a dream image, a giraffe can personify arrogance and superiority. Do you feel you are above someone? Or perhaps you feel that someone underestimates you. Alternately, the image implies that you perceive something differently from others.

glacier

Your career seems to be progressing slowly but will pick up force enough to draw attention. *See also* **avalanche.**

glass

Because this symbol represents your emotional state, consider the properties and condition of the glass. Is it delicate or sturdy, transparent or opaque, merely cracked, or is it broken into shards? If it is a drinking glass that contains liquid, do you see it as half empty or half full?

glasses

See **eyeglasses, goggles.**

globe

In general, a globe indicates that you are searching for ways to broaden your horizons, perhaps through travel or educational opportunities.

A spinning globe represents confusing issues that could affect a large number of people. *See also* **atlas, map.**

gloves

To wear gloves in a dream (unless they are for warmth) is a sign that you are distancing or protecting yourself from others. It also indicates that you are reluctant to get involved in a situation that could become messy. If you dream of taking off gloves, you are ready for new challenges or are open to new relationships. *See also* **clothing, disguise.**

glue

Working with glue points to your ability to hold things together when others can't. You will soon be called upon to do just that. However, glue can also mean that you are stuck in a situation or bound to a relationship that is not serving your best interests.

goat

This animal symbolizes either energy and determination or stubbornness and irrationality. *See also sidebar on page 54.*

god/goddess

As archetypes, these symbols represent a creator, masculine/feminine dominance, and control of destiny. The interpretation of dreams in which you see or speak with a god that represents a higher power vary widely and depend on your religious or spiritual beliefs. Consider the feelings that such an encounter evokes—anything from elation to enlightenment, to fear to guilt—and how they pertain to the way you live.

goggles

If worn underwater, goggles reflect clarity of purpose or an enhanced view of something obscured or unfamiliar. Make note of what you see or are trying to see. Alternately, goggles represent blinders. *See also* **eyeglasses, glass.**

> The dream is a little hidden door in the innermost and most secret recesses of the soul, opening into that cosmic night....
> —Carl Jung

gold

If you come upon gold in a dream, you will soon discover one of the most valued aspects of your character. This dream symbol also points to your desire to be the best in everythign you do, though be wary of the problems that come with perfectionism.

goose

The image of a single goose can represent frivolity and silliness, whereas a flock of geese can represent conformity and commitment. Geese in flight portend well-planned travel.

gossip

You should exercise caution when speaking with someone unfamiliar to you, as you may be misunderstood. To be the subject of gossip can point to your own guilt, vulnerability, or insecurity.

gown

A formal gown portends a social occasion or workplace situation that will require proper and appropriate behavior. To dream of yourself in a nightgown suggests that a break from your daily routine will benefit your mental and physical health.

graduation

To attend or participate in a graduation ceremony foretells a time of transition that will likely be confusing. It can also signify the completion of a cycle.

grain

A dream in which you are harvesting grain or cooking grains indicates that your health problems will improve with exercise and a diet that suits you better than your current one.

grandparents

These archetypes can represent either wisdom and experience or outdated attitudes. Consider your relationship with your own grandparents for further clarity. *See also* **family.**

grapes

Traditionally, grapes foretell a long and prosperous life. To make wine from grapes indicates your desire and ability to bring joy to others. Underripe or overripe grapes, however, warn of disappointments to come. *See also* **wine.**

grass

This symbol represents personal growth. Consider the condition of the grass: If it is green and lush, expect positive changes in your life (particularly if you are mowing the grass in your yard). Dried or weed-ridden grass indicates irresponsibility or a lack of commitment. *See also* **lawn.**

grasshopper

A single grasshopper foretells progress in a work project, though it will be in short bursts. A swarm of grasshoppers represents a confused or overwhelmed state of mind.

grave

The literal interpretation points to fears of death, but equally valid explanations reflect suppressed emotions or the end of a personal or professional relationship. Also consider the use of the word to describe a weighty or solemn matter. Are things really as bad as you perceive them to be? *See also* **burial, death, digging.**

gray

This color represents a transitional period in which things are not clearly defined. Important matters should be made obvious to everyone involved. Gray dream images can also signal depression or a lack of emotion. *See also sidebar on page 85.*

green

The color green has varying meanings that depend on the feelings it elicits in you. It is most often associated with growth and renewal, but it it can also point to envy or undetected illness. *See also sidebar on page 85,* **grass.**

grenade

A grenade represents a potentially explosive situation. To toss a grenade is to purposely stir up trouble. To throw yourself on a grenade is a symbol of great personal sacrifice. *See also* **explosion, fireworks.**

gridlock

See **traffic.**

grief

This common dream feeling is a sign that you do not want to give up (or give up on) something important to you. It can also be a positive release of any emotional stress in your waking life. To see someone else grieving suggests that sad news will arrive soon. *See also* **crying, depression, sadness.**

growth

To dream that something is growing usually portends a positive change. However, an overexaggerated growth of anything can point to anxiety or stress in your waking life.

guard

See **angel.**

guidebook

Reading through a travel-related book means you have been looking for solution to a nagging problem but can't find one. Skip the guidebook and trust your instincts or "inner guide." *See also* **atlas, calendar, map.**

guilt

To feel guilty in a dream is usually not so much a reflection of the same real-life emotion; rather, it often warns against becoming involved in a situation that you will regret.

If you dream of intentionally causing someone else to feel guilty, it points to personal issues of inadequacy.

guitar

To play a guitar (whether or not you actually can) is to express your emotional turmoil in a way that won't threaten or agitate others. Rather than trying to avoid controversy, reveal your true thoughts: They will come across gently and sincerely. *See also* **music.**

gun

If you are merely holding a gun, you feel threatened by something that isn't obvious. To actually shoot a gun indicates your need to establish or reclaim control of a contentious situation. *See also* **knife.**

guru

This image is more common than you might think and usually reflects an attempt to gain a better understanding of yourself. Pay attention to what the guru says, as this figure represents wisdom of the unconscious. *See also* **wise old man/wise old woman.**

gymnast

A gymnast signifies flexibility, strength, and discipline. If you are the gymnast, you possess a freedom of expression that many others lack.

gypsy

As a dream symbol, a gypsy can represent unbridled wanderlust that may take you down the wrong path. If you dream of having your fortune told by a gypsy, you will soon receive advice from an unexpected source. Think carefully before you heed that advice.

H

hail

Feeling bombarded by responsibilities, either at home or at work? Try to weather the storm with a clear head: It won't last long, but overreacting will just bring on more stress.

hair

This dream theme represents energy, strength, and sexuality. If you are cutting someone's hair, you are either trying to exert power or reduce someone's control over you. If your hair is being cut, your position in life (socially or at work) is being threatened. To lose your hair entirely points to insecurities about your appearance or anxiety over growing older. The sidebar below offers other interpretations. *See also* **bald.**

hallway

This is another representation of your journey through life.

Look at other symbols in the hall—for example, whether or not it is obstructed (and by what or whom), or if there are doors (opened or closed)— and consider these as opportunities or impediments in your life. *See also* **door, gate, passageway, roads.**

halo

This is most often a symbol of purity and goodness, but in more general terms, it can

---

Interpreting Your Tresses

Throughout time and across cultures, hair (or the lack thereof) has defined people—not only in terms of their perceived beauty but also as it relates to their personalities. Therefore, it's no surprise that hair is a universal and common dream symbol. Dreams related to one's hair often point to character traits. Here are a few:

Clean, healthy hair: vitality, pride, stability

Dirty, unkempt hair: authenticity, independence, indifference

Curly hair: authority, stubbornness, determination

Straight hair: thoughtfulness, discrimination, persistence

Long hair: reliability, intuition, fortitude

Short hair: authority, respectability, shyness

Hair loss: powerlessness, vulnerability, anxiety

Haircut: dissatisfaction, transformation, vulnerability

Dyed hair: curiosity, pretension, gullibility

Hairpiece/wig: vanity, secrecy, insecurity

also indicate that you expect perfection from yourself or others (depending on who is wearing it). *See also* **angel**.

hammer

A hammer indicates determination and persistence but not necessarily strength. If you are using a hammer, you would benefit from being more assertive in making important points. Alternately, it can be a sign that you need to rebuild or alter a relationship.

hammock

This can be a soothing dream image, a sign of a relaxed state of mind. However, it can also indicate that you need a break from your hectic, everyday routine.

hands

If they are your hands and they're empty, consider whether you are in a position to offer someone help, or if you are the one in need of assistance. Full hands can have opposing interpretations: You either are enjoying an abundant life or you feel overburdened. Hands that are larger or smaller than normal reflect the impact you have on those around you.

handshake

You will soon strike an agreement that proves profitable. Alternately, you will end a relationship that has caused you distress.

hanger

You are ready to step out on your own and express your individuality—you have been stuck in the same spot and with the same people for too long.

hanging

If you dream of hanging something on a wall, for example, you are trying to put issues or situations into perspective. To hang up a phone implies that you are ready to give up on something. Your own public hanging (execution) points to feelings of guilt or humiliation.

hangnail

To be bothered by a hangnail indicates that a seemingly harmless error or omission will lead to more problems if you don't tend to it soon.

happiness

Are you happy and content in your waking life? If not, your dream self may be trying to compensate. Otherwise, this dream feeling reflects a period of pleasant satisfaction. *See also* **love, sadness.**

harbor

Seeing or being in a harbor suggests that you need a place to recoup from turmoil. Also, consider the symbol metaphorically: Are you harboring negative thoughts?

hare

See **rabbit.**

harness

To dream that you are wearing a harness implies that you are holding back emotions; to place a harness on a person or an animal points to a need for control. *See also* **collar, yoke.**

harp

The instrument is often a symbol of a relentless problem or a nagging (harping) person. To hear harp music reflects a peaceful state of mind.

hat

A hat is a reflection of your role in life. Consider the type of hat, as well as its condition and fit. A worn-out cap or a fancy bonnet can represent your current level of satisfaction. A hat that is too big or too small shows whether you are doing more or less than what is expected of you.

hate

Feeling that you hate someone or something indicates real-life frustration and anger, but usually not actual hatred. Who or what evokes this feeling?

haunting

Are you obsessing over past mistakes? Guilt is making it hard for you to let go and move on. *See also* **demon, ghost.**

hawk

To dream of a hawk in flight indicates that you will be rewarded for your watchful eye and keen observations. *See also* **eagle.**

hay

If you are walking through a field of hay, expect a period of hard work. Stacks of hay represent the bounty you will soon enjoy.

haze

Hazy weather represents muddled thinking or confusing information. Alternately, it can point to harassment, given or received. *See also* **fog.**

head

First, consider the position of your head—that is, whether or not it is on straight. If you dream of seeing your head in profile, you are likely at a standstill in life. If seen from the front, you are heading in the right direction; if you see the back of your head, you will regret a recent decision.

hearing

See **deafness, ears.**

hearing aid

Wearing a hearing aid indicates that you are facing an incomprehensible situation. Listen closely to all sides before you make judgments.

> *So, if I dream I have you, I have you,*
> *For, all our joys are but fantastical.*
> —English poet John Donne

hearse

If you see or are riding in a hearse, expect an unplanned but temporary separation from someone close to you.

heart

Most often, this is a literal symbol of love. Metaphorically, it can indicate a need to get to the center of an issue or to put more effort into a task. To hear a heartbeat signifies self-reflection and acknowledgment.

heat

Are you feeling pressured to perform or to meet high standards? To heat up something is to stir emotions, either in yourself or in others.

heather

This flower, particularly white heather, symbolizes good fortune and health. *See also sidebar on page 115.*

heaven

To dream of heaven represents your desire for the absolute best in a relationship or situation. Consider whether your expectations are reasonable. Alternately, heaven can reflect a spiritual quest. *See also* **hell.**

heavy

This dream feeling often means that you are feeling overwhelmed or bogged down. It can also refer to someone or something that may be a burden to you.

height

In general, dreams that focus on height or heights refer to high standards or lofty ideas that may be separating you from others. If you are afraid of heights in a dream but not in your waking life, you lack confidence in your ability to reach the top. *See also* **ladder.**

heirloom

You will soon receive something special, though not necessarily from a family member. It could be material, monetary, or in the form of a heartfelt message.

helicopter

This symbol is a reminder to view the bigger picture before you draw conclusions or make commitments.

hell

This image often depicts a depressed state of mind or one of extreme anger. It can also refer to a worst case scenario or the absence of spirituality. *See also* **heaven.**

helmet

A helmet signifies safety and can be a warning to take precautions. To wear a helmet is a sign that you are not easily influenced by the words or opinions of others.

helplessness

This dream feeling indicates that you are at a crossroads and aren't sure which way to turn. It can also be a sign that a lack of knowledge or credentials is preventing you from advancing. Seek the advice of someone you respect, perhaps a mentor.

hen

Considered metaphorically, are you being relentlessly attacked by someone? This image can also symbolize distracted or scattered thoughts. Another interpretation is one of motherhood and nurturing.

herbs

To grow or use herbs means that you or someone close to you can expect healing and better health.

hermit

You are overcommitted and would benefit from taking some time to be alone. Alternately, address your fears of isolation or your inability to connect with others.

hero

The archetype represents salvation and the part of you that can handle crises. If you dream of being a hero, you will overcome trying times. If you are in search of a hero figure, help is on the way.

hibernation

You are likely in need of rest and rejuvenation, but also consider whether you have a tendency to withdraw when conditions aren't exactly to your liking.

hiccups

To have hiccups in a dream is an omen of small disruptions in your schedule. Ignore them and proceed with your plans.

hiding

To dream that you are hiding indicates that you are trying to keep a secret or are reluctant to reveal something about yourself. Hiding objects implies possessiveness or a fear of being exploited. To find something that has been hidden symbolizes an awakening.

high school

See **school.**

highway

How do you feel about your progress in life? Because faster speeds are required on this type of road, consider whether you

---

Hopeful Dreams

This dream prayer is from a clay tablet in the royal library of the Assyrian emperor Ashurbanipal, who ruled from 668–627 B.C.:

My gracious god, stand by my side...
My friendly god will listen to me:
God Mamu of my dreams,
My god, send me a favorable message.

are moving too slowly, keeping up, or pushing the (your) limit. *See also* **roads.**

hijack

If you dream of being hijacked, you may be forced to take an alternative route or approach to something. Don't panic, though: This may work out better than your original plan.

hill

This symbol points to your goals and successes. Examine your proximity to the hill. If you are at the bottom gazing up, do you feel overwhelmed or excited? If you are climbing the hill, do you do so with ease or difficulty? *See also* **climbing, mountain.**

hippopotamus

This image foretells a slow period followed by an increase in activity. You have the power to change an unproductive situation into one that will benefit many.

hitting

Hitting in anger reflects a fight against some aspect of yourself. Other interpretations include hitting a jackpot or, relative to flirtation, hitting on someone you find attractive.

hobby

Pursuing a hobby that you are unfamiliar with in your waking life implies that you need to explore your creative side or to think outside the box.

holding

This is a feeling with varied implications. Holding something can be a sign of support and protection or one of control and manipulation. Examine what or whom is being held and why.

hole

To dream of a hole in the ground warns against making commitments that will be difficult to get out of. To fall into a deep hole indicates that you are in over your head. Holes in objects represent faults or errors. *See also* **ditch.**

holidays

The interpretation depends on your personal experiences with the holidays: whether they are happy celebrations or solemn obligations. Despite their joyous portrayal, the symbolism of holidays frequently points to hurtful family issues.

home

This symbol represents any place, environment, or structure that makes you feel comfortable and secure. If it's not where you currently live, you will soon change residence.

honey

Honey reflects sweetness in demeanor and love in the home.

hook

To hook something in a dream is to make a good decision. A crochet hook or rug hook encourages creative pursuits.

hoop

You may need to take unusual steps to achieve your goals. A hoop can also represent wholeness or completion.

horn

The horn of an animal denotes sexual prowess. A musical horn heralds surprising news or a special event. If you are blowing a horn, you will enjoy success; however, make an effort to be humble about it.

horoscope

If you dream of checking your horoscope, you are relying too heavily on the direction or advice of someone else. A horoscope also means that you question your future or desire spiritual guidance.

horse

This animal signifies power and passion. If you are riding a horse confidently, you will exert your will and achieve control. Riding a wild horse reflects unbridled enthusiasm that may not always serve you well.

horseshoe

Traditionally, this symbolizes good fortune. If you are shoeing a horse, luck will come as a result of your efforts. To play a game of horseshoes is a sign that the odds are in your favor. Take a chance!

hospital

This image often reflects a desire to heal, either emotionally or physically. Sometimes, though, it has to do with a need to be nurtured or protected. What is your role in this dream? Are you a patient or a healthcare worker?

hotel

You are facing a transition: Consider the condition of the hotel—whether it's luxurious or dilapidated indicates the new direction your life will take.

hourglass

An hourglass signifies a sense of urgency. Be aware of how quickly time is passing. *See also* **clock, watch.**

house

A house symbolizes the self, and its appearance represents your self-image. There are several possible scenarios: Perhaps the exterior of the house is run-down but the inside is clean and tidy; maybe the house has curb appeal, but its interior is in shambles. These inconsistencies are reflections of personal conflicts.

housekeeper

If a person cleans for you, someone is toiling behind the scenes in your favor, likely in the workplace. If you are the housekeeper, you may be taking on someone else's responsibilities.

howl

The howl of any animal is a warning of unfavorable news.

hugging

If you receive a hug in a dream, expect a visit from someone you haven't seen in a while. If you are hugging someone, is it with affection or because you feel insecure or vulnerable?

humming

To hear humming is a sign of harmony in your life. It can also indicate the arrival of a joyful message.

hummingbird

This dream symbol can represent either perseverance or a fear of commitment.

hunger

To feel hunger denotes an intense desire for something lacking or absent. If you observe someone who is hungry, try to pay better attention to the needs of others.

hunting

Hunting can symbolize a spiritual search, but one that

provokes anxiety. A peaceful or mindful approach will prove more satisfying. If not spiritually related, hunting can mean a determined focus on a specific goal.

hurricane

To see or be caught in a hurricane indicates impending arguments, anger, and upheaval. If you maintain control of your emotions, the storm will be short-lived.

husband

Not necessarily a literal interpretation, a husband can refer to any male partner or mate, whether in business or in relationships. *See also* **family.**

hut

This symbol represents the simple things in life, the basic necessities. The dream may be emphasizing the importance of restraint. *See also* **cabin.**

hypnosis

Being hypnotized indicates that you neeed more control over your life. It can also represent a fear of humiliation or domination. *See also sidebar below.*

I

ice

As a dream symbol, ice represents rigid behavior. It can also indicate a lack of feeling and an aversion to change. If you are slipping on or stepping through ice, you are unsure about your path in life.

Daydream Believers

Among the many misconceptions about hypnosis is that this state of mind is equivalent to being asleep or unconscious. In fact, many people who undergo hypnosis report that they feel fully awake and actually more observant during the process. Hypnotism is often equated with "daydreaming": The mind is focused intently, sometimes to the point that it is difficult to be distracted. It is thought that this period of mental relaxation helps us process and work through complicated waking-life issues.

iceberg

This image represents limited consciousness. Be aware that there is more to you (or other people or situations) than meets the eye, and what exists under the surface has the potential to cause harm.

icicles

To see icicles suggests that your personal life is lingering or at a standstill, as if it's been frozen in time. If the icicles are dripping, the source of your problems will dissolve quickly.

igloo

You are seeking refuge from a harsh environment, whether it is your home or workplace. Think carefully before you take shelter elsewhere, as that may be equally inhospitable.

ignore

In your waking life, are you ignoring someone or something that needs your assistance? If you are the one being ignored, contemplate your feelings of being unworthy of attention. Then speak your mind and make sure you are heard! *See also* **ears.**

illness

Dreams in which you are ill should first serve as warnings that you may in fact have an undiagnosed physical ailment. A secondary interpretation is that the ailment is an emotional wound that won't heal until you address it. *See also* **disease, infection.**

immobility

Being immobile in a dream represents helplessness or fear. It is common to feel unable to move when trying to flee something that threatens you, but if you face and accept the situation, you will no longer feel trapped by it. Many people experience this feeling during REM sleep. *See also* **paralysis.**

imposter

To dream of someone who is an imposter is actually a reflection of you. Consider what the imposter is pretending to be. *See also* **disguise.**

impotence

Rarely is this type of dream associated with sexuality. Rather, it means that you feel powerless in a situation that you once had control over. *See also* **castration.**

imprisonment

This symbol of confinement and restriction means you are limiting your potential or denying yourself something. Another interpretation is that you feel you have little personal freedom in a relationship with a domineering partner. *See also* **captivity.**

inarticulation

You have been trying to make an important point but feel that no one understands you. The real problem is that your thoughts on the issues are mixed. Clarify them in your own mind before you express them to others.

incense

Incense symbolizes an emotional or spiritual search. To light it is to discover and acknowledge your inner strengths. To smell incense that is appealing indicates that the path you are on is right for you.

incest

Unless you have had a real-life incestuous experience, this is most often an exaggerated symbol of a negative relationship, but not necessarily of a sexual nature, nor with a family member.

income

A frequent interpretation points to financial worries, but the symbol can foretell rewards or benefits you will receive. Also consider the play on words: Expect an announcement that

---

Your Nose Knows

Many aromatherapists believe that scents not only facilitate a good night's sleep, but also improve dream recall and may induce lucid dreaming. Dream-enhancing essential oils include rose, patchouli, sandalwood, mugwort, anise, palo santo, helichrysum, and clary sage.

something is incoming. *See also* **money.**

independence

This dream feeling indicates your self-worth. If you are striving for independence, you are more self-reliant than you give yourself credit for. To lose your independence is a favorable reflection of trustworthiness and responsibility.

indifference

To feel indifferent to something or someone could reflect mild depression in your waking life. If someone shows indifference toward you, expect a new romance that is both enticing and challenging.

infant

The archetype represents innocence, purity, and potential. As a dream symbol, an infant reflects the beginning stages or baby steps in an endeavor that promises to be successful. *See also* **baby.**

infection

Although not usually an indication of poor health, an infection frequently represents negative influences. It can also mean that there is a "bug in the system," whether at work or on the home front. If not corrected or removed, the problem will spread and get worse. *See also* **disease, illness**.

infidelity

See **adultery.**

inheritance

Expect valuable advice that will provide you with profitable opportunities.

initiation

Being involved in an initiation indicates a desire to move beyond your current status at work or in society in general. If you are willing to go through the required ritual, you will achieve your goal.

injury

To experience an injury foretells dire consequences due to negligence or carelessness. Consider other symbols in the dream for clues on how you can prevent such a situation. *See also* **accident.**

ink

A jar of ink is a warning to read the fine print in a financial or legal transaction. Spilled ink indicates your concern over an issue that could cause you embarrassment.

innocence

To feel the innocence of youth highlights your ability to connect with your inner child. Alternately, you are burdened with responsibilities and want a more carefree life. To plead innocence suggests that you feel defensive or insecure around others. *See also* **youthfulness.**

insanity

Feeling that you are insane means that your judgment is skewed or that you are in the midst of a confusing situation and are unable to cope.

insects

Insects often represent life's little annoyances that aren't worth making a fuss over. On the other hand, they can highlight the importance of persistence and hard work, even if the effort isn't always acknowledged. *See also individual insects,* **itch.**

interview

To conduct an interview is a sign that you are questioning your own abilities (consider what you are asking the interviewee). To be interviewed means you are about to make a lifestyle change.

intrusion

Seeing an intruder portends a temporary period of disruption in your quest to accomplish something. Stay focused to minimize setbacks or damages.

inventory

Checking inventory is equivalent to taking stock of one's life or a current situation. Consider the state of the inventory: Is it complete, overabundant, or lacking?

invisibility

This dream symbol represents hidden aspects of your unconscious. If you are invisible, why do you feel overlooked or neglected, or what part of yourself are you refusing to see? The inability to see someone you care about means you should examine your relationship with that person more closely.

iron

If it is iron metal, this symbol warns to exercise willpower. To dream of ironing clothes is a sign that you will work out difficulties at your own pace.

island

An island can represent solitude or vulnerability. If you are on an island surrounded by calm waters, it is a good time to be alone. If surrounded by rough waters, it would be better to ask for help rather than tackle a problem unaided. *See also* **water.**

isolation

This dream feeling suggests an unbalanced sense of self. Avoid social activities if they cause you stress, but seek them out if you are feeling lonely or depressed.

itch

You have been dwelling on minor irritations that do not concern you. If you ignore them, they will resolve themselves. *See also* **insects.**

ivy

This symbol often represents a tangled, dependent relationship. It also suggests that you are clinging too tightly to an ideal or something from the past. If you don't let it go, it will hold you back. *See also* **vine.**

The Gates of Horn and Ivory

Experienced dream interpreters refer to the Gates of Horn and Ivory as dream gates from which two types of dreams emerge. The Gates of Ivory bring dreams that are "false," whereas the Gates of Horn bring "true" dreams. True dreams are considered to be profound or deeply meaningful to the dreamer, and "false" dreams can be either ordinary or confusing. Before they go to sleep, these interpreters often request a true dream from the Gates of Horn to help solve problems or answer questions. The earliest reference to the dream Gates of Horn and Ivory can be found in Homer's *Odyssey.*

J

jack

If you are using a mechanical jack during a dream, you will soon be relieved of burdens. To see someone using a jack implies that you would benefit from more independence.

jacket

See **coat.**

jack-in-the-box

This image symbolizes someone who is intrusive or insensitive, or who gets attention by shocking others with words or actions. Do you recognize the face of "Jack"?

jade

Jade is an omen of financial gain and prosperity. It also signifies personal growth.

jail

See **imprisonment.**

jam

To dream of making or eating jam signifies domestic contentment. Alternately, it can represent impediments in your life or a bothersome situation that you are having trouble extricating yourself from.

jar

You will soon face circumstances that require a great deal of physical or mental endurance. Conserve your energy now so you don't run out later.

jasmine

Jasmine is a good omen regarding relationships. To smell jasmine in a dream predicts a new romance. To pick jasmine portends newfound harmony with someone in your workplace.

jasper

This gemstone represents misunderstandings that are causing competition and envy. A peaceful resolution will not be reached until the facts of the matter are known to all.

javelin

As a dream image, a javelin symbolizes precision and tenacity. If you throw a javelin, you will refuse to give up on long-term goals despite minor setbacks.

jaws

If you see or are aware of your own jaws, you will summon the strength and determination to conquer a current problem. To dream that you are caught in the jaws of an animal implies the need for a creative solution to a problem.

jaywalking

Don't cut corners when it comes to performing important duties at work or at home. To do so will jeopardize your employment status or personal safety.

jealousy

See **envy.**

jellyfish

You are being threatened by something or someone but are afraid to stand up for yourself. Be more assertive, and the threat will slip away.

jewelry

This dream symbol represents your sense of self. If you are wearing a lot of jewelry, you would enjoy being in the spotlight but feel you don't deserve it. To receive jewelry is a sign that your self-esteem will improve, perhaps as the result of a new romance. Looking for lost jewelry signifies that a current relationship has stalled.

jig

See **dance.**

job

Whether or not it's related to your current employment, this type of dream often reflects doubt or anxieties about being able to provide for yourself or your loved ones. It can also indicate that you have taken on too many tasks and as a result are doing an inadequate job at all of them.

joke

To dream of telling a joke suggests that something in your waking life requires more serious consideration. The message behind or theme of the joke is important, as it will point to what (or who) needs your attention.

joker

As a wild card, a joker may indicate that unpredictability in a relationship could be more valuable than you thought. Conversely, it could place you in an embarrassing situation. *See also* **court jester.**

journey

A journey of any type symbolizes the direction

your life is taking, and the destination represents your goals. Pay attention to the people and objects you encounter on your dream journey: Do they impede or facilitate your progress? Also consider your emotions: Is this a trip you want to take, or should you embark on a different trip? *See also* **travel.**

judgment

If you dream of being judged by people in general, it indicates that you feel guilty or are too self-critical. If you dream of appearing before a judge in a courtroom, be prepared to defend words or actions that have caused others to question your character. *See also* **courtroom.**

jug

If the jug is full, your friends will soon be the source of much-needed support. If you are drinking from a jug, your physical health will improve.

juggling

Do you feel stressed because you have too much going on at once? You will accomplish more if you rearrange your schedule and delegate some duties to others. Alternately, if you are good at multitasking, this dream symbol underscores your ability to focus and prioritize.

jumping

To dream of jumping up or over something indicates your desire to get ahead in life. If you are jumping rope, the energy you are putting into a work project or personal relationship may seem pointless, but it will ultimately prove beneficial.

jungle

To avoid feeling overwhelmed by life's fast pace and demands, don't become entangled in someone else's problems.

junkyard

This image represents the memories you have accumulated throughout your life. Carefully consider the items in the junkyard and then get rid of anything you deem worthless. *See also* **garbage.**

jury

If you are serving on a jury, you will soon make a decision that will alter your life. Be sure to solicit input from people you trust before you take action.

K

kaleidoscope

To dream of a kaleidoscope signifies that you have a keen mind and can perceive aspects of a situation that most others would miss. To look into a kaleidoscope is a message to view all sides of situation or argument before you form an opinion.

kangaroo

A kangaroo symbolizes restless movement, whether from place to place or from one relationship to another. This dream image indicates that now is the right time settle down.

keepsake

See **heirloom.**

keg

What does the keg contain? A keg of beer suggests that you need to enjoy yourself more. A powder keg warns of a potentially explosive situation.

kennel

If you are in a kennel, your feelings of either security or isolation correspond to a situation in your waking life. To put an animal in a kennel indicates guilt or inattentiveness.

Dreaming the Day Away

Many of director Luis Buñuel's movies were inspired by his dreams and, in fact, seemed oddly dreamlike onscreen. The opening scene of his film *Un Chien Andalou* (*An Andalusian Dog*) was based on a combination of dreams: his own (a cloud slicing the moon in two) and artist Salvador Dali's (ants crawling out of a hand).

Regarding dreams in general, Buñuel once told an interviewer: "If someone were to tell me I had twenty years left and ask me how I want to spend them, I'd reply, 'Give me two hours a day of activity, and the other twenty-two in dreams.'"

kettle

A whistling kettle foretells pleasant news regarding a family member. Alternately, it can be an indication of familial strife. To pour water from a kettle points to a need for relaxation.

keys

As a dream symbol, keys represent control and access to opportunities. If you find a key or set of keys, you have what you will need to succeed with a plan or solve a problem. If you lose your keys, there is something in your life that's missing or is beyond your grasp entirely. If you give a key to someone, you will receive assistance from a friend or associate.

keyhole

To peer through a keyhole suggests that you have a distorted or limited view of someone and should avoid making judgments or assumptions about his or her private affairs.

kicking

If you are kicking someone in a dream, you're expressing frustration at your inability to drive home a message. To see someone kicking signifies that someone in your life lacks tact and discretion. Alternately, kicking a can or a ball suggests that you "kick up your heels" and have some fun.

kickstand

This is a symbol of support. A broken kickstand is an omen that someone you consider reliable will let you down.

kidnap

If you are the one kidnapped, you have either lost control of a situation or your goals have been compromised. If you are the kidnapper, you are trying to claim something you are not entitled to. *See also* **abduction.**

killing

There are varying interpretations of dreams in which you kill a person or an animal. Killing someone usually reflects anger or envy (though not necessarily toward anyone in particular), whereas killing an animal often points to issues of power and domination.

Killing can also represent suppressed emotions or personal traits that you wish to rid yourself of. *See also* **murder.**

kilt

Regardless of your heritage, this symbol serves to remind you of the importance of creating and celebrating family traditions.

king

The archetype represents lawfulness, leadership, authority, and justice.

kissing

For many people this is a sign of affection, warmth, and intimacy. To receive a kiss portends a new, positive relationship (though not necessarily romantic). If you are kissing someone familiar, you will soon reveal a secret to that person. However, to watch others kiss implies that you are prying into someone's personal life.

kitchen

A tidy, sterile kitchen highlights issues of control, inflexibility, or close-mindedness, whereas a kitchen filled with warmth and activity reveals a creative and nurturing personality. *See also* **baking, cooking.**

kite

A high-flying kite represents your ability to achieve whatever you want. Go after your dreams, but maintain a down-to-earth attitude. A kite that gets loose or tangled in a tree reflects your desire for more personal freedom. *See also* **airplane.**

kitten

This image symbolizes your playful personality but can also reflect a desire for offspring.

kneel

Depending on the context of the dream, kneeling represents either humiliation or respect. Kneeling in prayer suggests a need for spiritual reflection.

knees

As a dream image, your knees represent the level and quality of support you have in your life. Sore or scraped knees

> *Existence would be intolerable if we were never to dream.*
> —French writer Anatole France

point to vulnerability and can also reflect painful childhood memories.

knife

Various interpretations include betrayal (stabbed in the back), assertiveness (cut to the chase), or defensiveness. To cut with a knife implies severing ties or eliminating something from one's life. *See also* **cut**.

knight

This hero archetype means you will find relief from a distressing situation or conflict.

knit

Knitting indicates that long-lost family or friends will soon be brought together. Alternately, it can represent disapproval (knitted brow) or imply that someone is in need of your healing energies.

knocking

If you hear knocking in a dream, someone or something requires your attention. It can also mean that you will make new friends or receive news from a stranger.

Dream a Little (Bothersome) Dream

It is frequently thought that insomnia prevents people from fully exploring or benefiting from their dreams because they seldom experience the REM stage of sleep in which dreams occur. But according to a study published in the *Journal of Sleep Research*, participants with insomnia who woke frequently during the night did so just at the point of entering REM sleep. Consequently, they reported better dream recall than the participants who slept soundly through the night.

Not surprisingly, the insomniac patients recalled dreams that were largely negative (or at least troubling), and the themes of their dreams reflected the stressful waking-life issues or emotions that were preventing them from getting a good night's sleep in the first place.

knots

This symbol often represents a complicated situation or person. If you are tying knots, you are creating or contributing to something problematic. Knots also reflect your connection to family members—are the knots loose or difficult to untie?

laboratory

A laboratory is a place of experimentation and discovery. If you dream of working in a lab, you will achieve success through trial and error. In the process, you will learn a great deal about yourself.

labyrinth

See **maze.**

lace

If you see or handle lace, you should approach a sensitive issue delicately. Lace curtains warn that private matters will be revealed.

ladder

If you dream of climbing a ladder, you will achieve greater social prominence. If you are descending a ladder, you are insecure about your current position in life. *See also* **climbing.**

ladybug

A social function will require formal attire, but don't be afraid to show your individuality. A ladybug walking over green leaves is a sign of good luck.

lake

If the lake is calm, anticipate a period of rest and reflection. Rough water represents a tumultuous state of mind. *See also* **water.**

lamb

This dream symbol points to your gentle soul, but it can also be a sign of vulnerability. To eat lamb is to attempt to find spiritual peace.

lamp

A lamp signifies enlightenment. To turn on a lamp is to offer wisdom and hope during a time of despair. To turn off a lamp means it is best to keep someone in the dark about a potentially hurtful issue. *See also* **light.**

landscape

Characteristics of the landscape—e.g., gently rolling, rocky, or barren—reflect your unconscious. If you dream of landscaping, you are doing well in creating the life you want.

landslide

To observe a landslide from afar indicates your desire to release pent-up emotions. To be caught in a landslide warns that too many responsibilities could quickly overwhelm you. *See also* **avalanche.**

lantern

Holding a lantern suggests that someone is in need of your guidance. To put out a light in a lantern portends the dissolution of a partnership. *See also* **lamp, light.**

Dream Catchers

A dream catcher is a Native American craft that originated with the Ojibwa Nation and was used as a tool to capture the wisdom of nature. Its primary purpose was to protect people from nightmares or other negative dreams while enabling them to benefit from positive dreams. The dream catcher—typically a small wooden hoop crisscrossed with leather and decorated with beads and feathers—resembles a spider's web and is placed over a bed or near a window in the bedroom. According to legend, the dream catcher attracts all the dreams that fill the night air and then holds them in the webbing. The bad dreams become entangled and cannot escape, while the good dreams slip through the webbing, slide down the feathers, and gently find their way to the sleeping person's unconscious. As the first light of morning hits the dream catcher, the bad dreams that were captured throughout the night are destroyed.

lap

If you dream of sitting on someone's lap, you want to be cared for or listened to. If someone sits in your lap, you are taking on more than your fair share of a project.

lapis lazuli

This stone is a symbol of luxury and perfection. To wear it foretells a formal celebration.

lasso

If you dream of swinging a lasso with confidence, pleasant opportunities will come your way. The inability to swing a lasso denotes confusion or entrapment.

last

Interpretations of being in this position can mean you are trying to catch up with peers or coworkers. Alternately, it points to your ability to hang in there when others can't.

lateness

This common dream feeling represents unmet goals or missed opportunities. Don't expect more of yourself than you can realistically attain.

laughter

Laughing represents a desire for happiness, which eludes you in your waking life. If you hear laughter, avoid potentially humiliating situations.

laundry

Soiled laundry means you have been inattentive to or ignorant of someone's feelings. Clean laundry drying on a clothesline represents confidence and self-sufficiency.

lava

Flowing lava portends an explosive situation. Tend to a troubling matter before it erupts. *See also* **explosion.**

lavender

This dream image represents fond memories. Lavender can also predict enjoyable times with friends or family.

lawn

Consider the condition of the lawn and to whom it belongs. Greener grass doesn't always mean better circumstances.

lawyer

If you are practicing law, you are feeling defensive and argumentative. Taken literally, this dream may reflect anxieties about an actual legal matter. *See also* **argument, jury.**

laziness

To dream that you feel lazy could simply mean you are physically exhausted. Alternately, it could be a sign of reluctance or indecision with regard to a personal or business relationship.

leadership

If you are leading others, do you do so confidently or with malevolence? This dream image points to either helpful guidance or a need for control.

> Twenty years from now you will be more disappointed by the things that you didn't do than by the ones you did do. So throw off the bowlines. Sail away from the safe harbor. Catch the trade winds in your sails. Explore. Dream. Discover.
>
> —Mark Twain

leak

Detecting a leak suggests that you are wasting your efforts. Reevaluate your relationships before your emotional or financial reserves are drained. *See also* **faucet.**

leaping

See **jumping.**

leash

This symbol represents restrictions and limits. Which end of the leash are you on, and how much leeway is there?

leaves

To dream of green leaves wavering in the sunlight predicts abundance and prosperity. Falling leaves are signs of positive life changes, but dry, dead leaves symbolize crushed hopes.

lecture

Do you feel that you are being nagged, or are you nagging someone else? Listen to the opinions of others carefully, and express yourself with tact and respect.

ledge

Standing on a ledge means you are involved in a precarious

situation. Take a step back to get a better perspective. *See also* **cliff.**

leeches

This symbol warns of a freeloader or someone so needy that he or she is draining your energy. Be sure to set boundaries. *See also* **barnacles.**

legs

To dream that your legs are strong indicates that you will have to defend yourself against false accusations. Broken or weak legs represent a need for stability, structure, and balance.

lemons

If you are eating a lemon, a good relationship will turn sour. To dream of picking ripe lemons represents good health and vitality. *See also sidebar on page 101.*

leopard

Consider the proverbial reference to someone who is unable to change. Accepting people the way they are will make your life easier.

letter

To dream that you receive a letter suggests that someone is having difficulty communicating with you. To write a letter reflects your desire to know and express yourself better.

levitation

This feeling or image suggests that you will rise above a situation and become more objective about it. Alternately, you may feel depressed and need something to raise your spirits. *See also* **floating**.

library

A library symbolizes a search for answers or your ability to access information. To work in a library points to the need for better organization.

license

This image signifies permission and freedom. Proceed with what you have planned, and you will encounter minimal interference.

lies

To dream of being lied to can point to feelings of suspicion or mistrust. If you are telling a lie, something in your waking life is causing you shame or embarrassment.

lifeguard

To ensure your safety, heed the advice of others and accept offers of assistance.

light

Light represents your spiritual energy and creativity. If a light comes on, expect to benefit from inspiration and fresh ideas. Dim or burned-out lights indicate a lack of insight or self-awareness. *See also* **lamp.**

lighthouse

You will be guided through your darkest moments by someone who radiates hope.

lightning

The interpretation depends on the feelings this symbol evokes. If you are entranced by the sound or sight of lightning, expect a streak of luck and creativity. But if it elicits fear, destructive forces are trying to enter your life.

lily

To dream of a lily portends a period of rest and relaxation. Alternately, lilies symbolize illness, death, and mourning. *See also sidebar on page 115.*

limousine

If you are riding in a limousine, you will be recognized for your talent and achievements. To drive a limousine reflects frustration in the workplace.

lines

Lines symbolize boundaries or limitations. Are you drawing the line or crossing the line?

lion

As a dream symbol, a lion signifies strength and power. To see a lion in the distance indicates a desire for more respect or authority. A lion in close proximity represents your tendency to intimidate people. To hear a lion roar warns against making boastful claims. *See also sidebar on page 54.*

lisp

See **inarticulation.**

list

Making lists in a dream points to problems in your waking life

brought about by forgetfulness
or inattention to detail. Losing
a list may be a humorous way
of depicting listlessness. Time to
get energized!

litter

To litter signifies a lack of
respect or concern for yourself.
It can also imply that you are
trying to keep track of things
that are insignificant. *See also*
clutter.

living room

Occupying this particular part
of a house suggests that you are
comfortable being the center of
attention.

lizard

This symbol represents your
adaptability, dexterity, and
capacity to handle criticism.

lobster

Catching or eating lobster
means that someone with
a seemingly harsh exterior
will prove to be pleasant and
generous.

lock

A lock represents self-imposed
barriers. Only you hold the key
to happiness and fulfillment.

locker

If you cannot find your school
locker or have forgotten the
combination to the lock, you
are facing a threatening or
confusing situation and don't
know which way to turn.

locket

A locket is a symbol of affection
between lovers or loved ones.
An empty locket indicates
a need to reconnect with
someone who was once close to
your heart.

log cabin

See **cabin.**

lollipop

To be given a lollipop is to be
taken advantage of or mocked.
Someone underestimates your
abilities or perception. Consider
the meaning of the slang term
"sucker."

lose/losing

Losing an object reflects
unacknowledged grief about
the absence of something or
someone in your life.

lost

The common dream feeling of
being lost can imply that you
are having trouble reaching

a goal. To be unable to find your way to a place that was once familiar foretells a sudden change of residence or employment.

lottery

Playing the lottery means that a seemingly risky pursuit in business or romance will be worth the investment. *See also* **gambling.**

lotus

The archetype represents the higher or inner self, perfection, and purity. A lotus floating in water means that arcane knowledge will provide a spiritual awakening.

love

To feel love toward someone in a dream but not in your waking life means that you admire and respect that person. To express love can indicate that you are receiving an insufficient amount of it. *See also* **hate.**

low

Dreams of being in this position can reflect depression, guilt, or inferiority. They can suggest that you are trying to pass under the radar.

luggage

This dream represents emotional baggage. If you are carrying a piece of luggage, is it light enough to handle or so heavy that it slows you down? If you have the latter feeling, consider what or whom presents a burden in your life. To lose luggage indicates that you have forgotten to do something. *See also* **bag.**

lying down

To dream of being in a prone position is a sign of neutrality. This is a time to stay out of arguments and avoid taking any sides.

"I Don't Want to Wake Up!"

The "natural alarm clock" that enables some people to wake up more or less when they want to is caused by a burst of the stress hormone adrenocortico-tropin. Researchers say this reflects an uncon-scious anticipation of the stress of waking up.

M

madness

Are you actually angry or do you feel you are going mad? Differentiate between less-severe issues and matters too big to handle. *See also* **insanity.**

maggots

Interpretations range from thoughts of dying or death to the image of someone who takes advantage of your vulnerability. Maggots on your body represent someone who makes your skin crawl. *See also* **barnacles, leeches.**

magic

This dream symbol foretells unexpected changes. To perform magic is a sign you will undergo a positive transformation brought about by a strong belief in yourself. To watch someone perform magic means you want to change but can't summon what it takes to make it happen.

magician

The archetype represents someone who can offer knowledge and intuition. *See also* **wise old man/wise old woman.**

magnet

Using a magnet can reflect conflicting thoughts related to a romantic pursuit. There is someone you are simultaneously attracted to and repelled by, so examine those feelings before you make a commitment.

magnifying glass

This symbol reflects either scrutiny or distortion. To use one can signify a desire for clarity. Alternately, it warns against overanalyzing people or situations. *See also* **mirror.**

mail

Mail represents communication with your unconscious. If you are waiting to receive mail, look inward for the answers you seek. Sending mail suggests that there are more effective or efficient ways to make your point. *See also* **letter.**

makeup

Whether you are a man or a woman, to dream of applying makeup foretells a social event for which you will have to "put on a happy face." If you dream of wearing too much makeup, you are either trying too hard to impress someone or you're not revealing your true self. *See also* **disguise.**

male

The archetype represents the provider and the intellect as well as typically masculine qualities such as strength, aggression, and competitiveness.

manipulation

To experience this feeling points to issues of power, though they are not as obvious as they seem. If you are being manipulated, you have neglected responsibilities and blame others for the consequences. To manipulate others signifies a lack of control.

mannequin

You should try to be more expressive. You lack independence and often come off as cold, unfeeling, or rigid.

mansion

This dream image reflects your inner self. You have the desire and capacity to grow both emotionally and intellectually. These pursuits will prove profitable. *See also* **house.**

map

To see or study a map in your dream means that you will alter the course of your life. Don't worry if you can't make sense of the map: Someone will be there to guide you. *See also* **atlas, globe.**

maple tree

This symbolizes prosperity and growth through cooperation. Tap into the resources of others to bring about pocket change.

marble

Marble structures or statues symbolize a rigid or cold attitude. Alternately, they

> *In dreams, we all resemble this savage.*
> —Friedrich Nietzsche

reflect reliability and fortitude. Marbled images also represent diversity and cohesion. To dream of playing marbles recalls the simplicity of childhood.

marching

Do you feel concerned about being out of step with others? If marching in a parade, you take pride in your achievements; if marching in protest, your convictions will serve you well. *See also* **drumming, parade.**

marigolds

Contrary to their association with death, marigolds also signify health and prosperity. *See also sidebar on page 115.*

marionette

You will be unwittingly involved in a business situation with strings attached. Examine your options closely to avoid financial collapse. *See also* **dummy, puppet**.

market

Walking through a market indicates that you are facing a big decision. Don't choose the first option you are given, or the one from the loudest vendor. *See also* **shopping.**

marriage

The archetype represents a merging of masculine and feminine energies or qualities. *See also* **wedding.**

Mars

Dreams of the planet portend petty misunderstandings or arguments. To dream of the mythological god Mars predicts conflicts on a larger scale.

marsh

You are feeling bogged down. To slog through a marsh is a sign that you will eventually achieve your goals, but that progress will be slow. *See also* **quicksand.**

martyr

The archetype signifies sacrifice. The dream message: Don't compromise your ideals.

mask

See **disguise.**

massage

To dream of getting a massage is to reassure yourself that a period of stress will be short-lived. If you dream of being a masseuse, you are still working through the kinks of a problem.

master

Consider whether the image portrays authority and malevolence or skill and proficiency. Are you the master, or do you feel you are under the thumb of someone? *See also* **mistress.**

maze

Wandering through a maze highlights the importance of thoughtful navigation. Pay attention to the details of your journey, as they will determine where you end up.

meadow

Images of a meadow reflect tranquility and peace of mind.

measure

This dream image reflects your personal standards. If something or someone can't measure up, perhaps you have unrealistic expectations.

mechanic

Symbolically, a mechanic represents someone who offers help in an uninspired or perfunctory way (perhaps in your workplace). If you are patient, you will benefit from such assistance.

medal

Although you may think otherwise, your hard work has not gone unnoticed. To watch someone else receive a medal reflects your appreciation and respect for someone who has made an extraordinary effort.

medicine

This dream symbol reflects healing energy. To receive medicine recommends that you make the small changes necessary to improve your life. To dream of giving medicine means that someone is in need of your help or advice but is afraid to ask. *See also* **doctor.**

meeting

A meeting represents a negotiation or exchange of ideas. Noting the reason for the meeting, the facilitator, and the attendees will help you address the real-life issue that prompted this dream.

melting

The general interpretation is transformation. Melting ice can represent the dissolution of a relationship; alternately, it can suggest that you become less rigid and go with the flow. *See also* **ice, iceberg, icicles.**

memorial

Attending a memorial service means you will be asked to assist someone in physical or emotional pain. If you are the one being memorialized, evaluate how well you take care of yourself. *See also* **funeral.**

menstruation

Most often, such dreams reflect anxiety over becoming a parent. Less obviously, they raise the issue of whether you are moving smoothly through life and are on schedule with regard to specific goals.

menu

To dream of reading a menu foretells opportunities for fulfillment: Choose carefully among them.

Clairvoyant Dreams

A clairvoyant dream is one in which you obtain information about the location or physical properties of a distant object or of events occurring at a distance while you are sleeping. If you want to develop clairvoyant dreaming skills, you could try the following exercises.

May I Have the Envelope, Please?

Have a friend or relative select several pictures from magazines and seal each in a separate envelope. Choose one envelope, then attempt to incubate a dream with the request to your dream self that you will dream about the picture sealed inside. Place the envelope on your nightstand or under your pillow—wherever you like. In the morning, record the dream, open the envelope, and compare the picture with your dream. Make a list of your hits (and misses) in your dream journal.

mercury

If you dream of the planet or the element (e.g., the mercury in a thermometer), expect an elevated financial or social status. If the dream involves the mythological god, expect a heated argument.

mermaid/merman

Such images reflect the feminine or masculine aspects of your unconscious that will bring you tranquility in a sea of confusion.

merry-go-round

See **carnival, circles.**

mesmerized

To be mesmerized in a dream is a sign that you are strongly influenced by or attracted to something or someone—to the point that you are neglecting what really needs your attention. *See also* **hypnosis.**

mess

This image reflects disorder in your waking life. Consider whether the phrases "mess around" or "mess up" pertain to you. *See also* **clutter, garbage.**

message

Your unconscious is trying to relay important information to you: Look for personal symbolism and significance in the message. See also **letter.**

metal

There are differing interpretations: Your character is strong or you should soften

Art Imitates Life

Early in the morning of June 28, 1914, Hungarian bishop Monsignor de Lanyi awakened from a startling dream in which he received a letter that read "I herewith inform you that today my wife and I will fall victims to an assassination. We commend ourselves to your pious prayers." He wrote down his dream and also drew an image of how he envisioned these mysterious deaths. That afternoon, the bishop received word that two close friends, Archduke Franz Ferdinand and his wife, had just been assassinated. The bishop's post-dream drawing bore an eerie resemblance to photos of the scene that appeared in newspapers.

your approach to people. Also consider the homonyn "meddle."

meteor

Forthcoming troubled times can be minimized if the underlying causes are detected early enough. Alternately, a meteor foretells a streak of creativity that will get you noticed.

mice

See **mouse.**

microscope

This symbol of focused intent or scrutiny has differing meanings. If you are looking through a microscope, you may be making minor problems seem bigger than they are. Don't get bogged down in details. On the other hand, your sharp perception could help clarify a situation for everyone involved.

mildew

Mildew signifies the slow deterioration of a long-standing relationship. *See also* **mold.**

milk

This is most often a sign of nurturing and nourishment. To dream of drinking milk is a sign of emotional contentment.

But if you are pouring milk or milking a cow, someone is taking advantage of your kindness.

mime

Watching a street mime means you have problems communicating with people in general. If you dream of being a mime, you feel that you are misunderstood or aren't being taken seriously. *See also* **mute.**

mimic

To mimic someone in a dream indicates that you admire or covet the qualities or abilities of that person. If you are the one being mimicked, speak cautiously, as someone may repeat your words.

mine

A mine represents the deepest recesses of your unconscious, the parts of your mind that are waiting to be tapped. To work in a mine reflects a quest for greater self-awareness that ultimately brings enlightenment and possibly wealth. Also consider the word as it relates to possession: Is something you feel you own being threatened? *See also* **ore.**

mirror

In dreams, mirrors reflect the way you see yourself, and the image is often distorted because of unrealistic expectations or idealizations. Do you see yourself as younger or older, heavier or thinner, introverted or extroverted? Your dream self sends such images to help you discover, accept, and embrace the "real" you.

missing

To miss an appointment warns against overcommiting your time or emotions: Your efforts won't be acknowledged, so it is time to prioritize and delegate. To miss something because you simply forgot reflects overall apathy or carelessness. An object gone missing reflects confusing or unacknowledged losses in your waking life.

mist

The image of mist reflects a lack of clarity or a mysterious environment. Try to discern images that are obscured, as they represent what you have lost sight of. *See also* **fog.**

mistake

This is both a warning and a reassurance: The mistake you dream of making can be avoided, but only if you evaluate other symbols in the scenario. Pay attention to people or objects that seem particularly odd or out of place.

mistletoe

Despite its traditional association with holidays and potential romance, mistletoe is classified as a semiparasitic plant. Beware of an attractive person who will prove to be clingy and needy.

mistress

Whether you are a man or a woman, this image represents a distorted sense of self combined with a need for (or desire to be) controlled. *See also* **master.**

A dreamer is one who can only find his way by moonlight, and his punishment is that he sees the dawn before the rest of the world.

—Oscar Wilde

moat

A moat emphasizes measures to protect or defend. It can also represent one who prefers to be cut off or distant from others, one who guards his or her privacy.

molasses

Things are progressing too slowly, so make an effort to push a project or relationship along. At the same time, be wary of sticky situations, and get out of them while you can.

mold

A mold can represent a vessel to be filled (often your inner self) or an opportunity to be creative. What or whom are you trying to mold? On the other hand, mold is also a fungus: a source or result of neglect and decay. *See also* **mildew.**

money

Literally, dreams of money point to financial concerns. Finding money on the street reflects stress over a lack of resources but assures that you have what you need to survive. Losing money is a sign that something important is coming your way.

monkey

Is the monkey in a zoo or in the wild? After a period of great stress, you are feeling uninhibited and carefree. Take advantage of this state of mind and be frivolous, even mischievous.

monster

The archetype represents unconscious anxiety, which often reflects what you fear most in yourself. *See also* **demon.**

moon

The moon reflects the cyclic phases of life. Individual interpretations depend on its phase. A new moon suggests success with impending projects; a full moon indicates dramatic affairs of the heart; and a harvest moon foretells financial rewards. *See also* **planets.**

moonstone

Mystical forces and spiritual experiences are associated with this symbol.

mop

A clean mop is a sign that an enjoyable activity (such as a hobby) could become profitable. A stiff or dirty mop highlights neglected responsibilities. To use a mop affirms your attempt to clean up your act. *See also* **broom.**

morgue

This image can reflect the end of a dying relationship, or it can warn that cold attitudes will ultimately leave you lonely.

mosquito

If you are bitten by a mosquito, you will host visitors who get under your skin. Set boundaries with those who have unreasonable demands. *See also* **insects.**

moss

Green, healthy moss predicts social advancement as the result of your solid family history. Dry or dying moss foretells the loss of a long-standing friendship.

mother

The archetype represents a feminine authority figure, a caretaker, fertility, and birth. Dreams of your own mother symbolize the bond you have (had) with her, which in turn influence the quality of your relationships throughout life. *See also* **family.**

mountain

A mountain symbolizes your professional standards. If you are climbing a mountain, you will receive recognition in the workplace. To reach the top of a mountain predicts that you will achieve a position in which you oversee many people. If you are descending, you will take the fall for the errors of others. *See also* **climbing.**

mourning

Whether or not you have suffered an important loss, this dream feeling reflects unacknowledged grief, regrets, or persistent malaise. More immediate is its relevance to "morning": There may be something you dread or fear doing upon awaking. *See also* **depression, grief.**

mouse

You will soon have to summon the strength and courage necessary to tackle a gnawing problem.

mouth

An open mouth displaying teeth warns of a false friend; if no teeth are showing, you will receive shocking news. A closed mouth can point to either loyalty (zipped lips) or secrecy. *See also* **dentist, teeth.**

mouthwash

To use mouthwash in a dream reflects guilt over bad mouthing someone or spreading hurtful gossip.

moving

Moving symbolizes the threat of change or the possibility of a new beginning. At what pace and in which direction are you moving? The image can also foretell a separation or relocation. *See also* **crossroads.**

mud

This image can reflect muddled or slow thinking that is making you feel stuck. It may also represent guilt or a need to come clean. Consider such idioms as "mud-slinging" and "your name is mud." *See also* **dirt, quicksand.**

mummy

You could have a fear of growing older and want to preserve your youthful appearance or attitude. Alternately, you are vulnerable and want to be swaddled or protected.

murder

This is most often an exaggerated symbol that indicates the death or end of negative issues, situations, or relationships. But to commit murder is also an expression of deep-seated rage, whether it's toward yourself or someone else. *See also* **killing.**

> *Those who dream by day are cognizant of many things which escape those who dream only by night.*
>
> —Edgar Allan Poe, "Eleanora"

museum

Old friends and cherished memories are important now. If wandering through a museum, you are examining the choices you have made in life and how they will affect your future.

music

If the music is soothing and pleasant, it heralds peace of mind and encourages creative expression. Discordant or loud music indicates an unbalanced or conflicted sense of self. *See also sidebar below and individual musical instruments.*

Music in Dreams

For centuries, there have been anecdotal reports about famous musicians who have created important works based on sounds or images they received through dreams. But until 2006, there was little scientific evidence to support the possibility. That's when researchers at the University of Florence conducted a study that involved 65 people: 35 were professional musicians, and 30 had received little or no musical training.

For 30 days, the subjects recorded their dreams in journals. After analyzing these journals and interviewing the subjects, lead researcher Valeria Uga claimed that "Musicians dream of music more than twice as much as nonmusicians [and] musical dream frequency is related to the age of commencement of musical instruction, but not to the daily load of musical activity. Nearly half of all recalled music was nonstandard, suggesting that original music can be created in dreams." The specifics of the findings are as follows:

The 35 professional musicians reported 244 musical dreams, more than half of which were similar or identical to pieces they already knew well. Another 41 dreams involved familiar tunes with unusual variations, and in 68 dreams, the dream music was unfamiliar to the dreamers.

musk

Depending on your reaction to the scent, musk can foretell a passionate and exciting love affair or point to a heavy or lingering problem.

mute

To be mute is to be withdrawn or secretive. Talking to a mute person represents an inability to communicate effectively. A "mute" button indicates that you refuse to listen to what someone is trying to tell you. *See also* **inarticulation, mime.**

N

nagging

Nagging represents persistent and annoying problems. If you keep ignoring or avoiding them, they will never go away.

nails

You will be required to fix a situation or hold things together and will succeed through hard work, tenacity, and accuracy.

names

Names are one way that your dream self conveys information to you. If they don't refer to someone you actually know, individual names are often a play on words. For example, "Lucy" is derived from the Latin for "light" and foretells enlightenment or illuminated ideas. Consider puns related to names: "Lucy" suggests that you loosen up in your daily life, whereas "Carrie" represents burdens or responsibilities. To be referred to by a nickname or the wrong name points to identity issues.

nap

This is often a sign that you are growing weary of a relationship or situation. A temporary break will prove invigorating.

napkin

A folded napkin foretells enjoyable social activities. A crumpled napkin conveys a satisfaction regarding your home and family.

narrow

Navigating narrow spaces implies that you are unwilling to accept the ideas or behavior of others. This lack of approval puts limits on your own life. *See also* **hallway, tunnel.**

nature

Nature represents elements of yourself that are changing and evolving. To seek out or explore a natural environment reflects a quest for a new way of life, one with less materialism and greater independence. *See also* **earth, woods.**

nausea

The feeling of nausea in a dream is a sign that worries or anxieties are taking a toll on you. It can also indicate that you find someone or something distasteful or repellent. Alternately, it simply means that you are coming down with an illness.

neck

Dreams that feature your neck reflect the relationship between your mind and body. An overly long neck represents a disconnect, whereas a short neck means that your emotions often interfere with rational thought. Also consider idioms such as "pain in the neck," "stiff-necked," and "up to your neck."

neck brace

A neck brace indicates that you will receive moral support from family or friends. To wear a neck brace is a warning against action or words that will make it difficult for you to hold your head up in public.

necklace

This symbol is an omen for a strong new relationship. However, if you dream of a lost or broken necklace, anticipate domestic conflicts. *See also* **jewelry.**

necktie

Being unable to tie a necktie (yours or another's) implies that a work project will take longer to finish than you expected. A tie that is too tight means that you feel out of place socially or professionally. *See also* **knots.**

need

What do you feel is lacking in your life? Be sure to differentiate between what you simply want and what you really need.

Also consider the homonym "knead," in reference to working the kinks out of an issue.

needle

A needle indicates that something is bothering (needling) you or that a relationship requires mending. If you dream of losing a needle or have trouble threading a needle, you are too bogged down in the details of a problem to reach a resolution. If you are stuck with a needle, issues in your waking life that are causing you pain are only temporary. *See also* **pin.**

neighbor

Dreaming of someone who lives nearby represents a real-life relationship that is about to change (for better or worse). For clarification, examine your attitude toward the neighbor (and his/hers toward you): Is it contentious, friendly, or distant?

> *For my part I know nothing with any certainty, but the sight of the stars makes me dream.*
> —Vincent van Gogh

nest

A nest represents a home and family. If the nest contains eggs, anticipate financial problems that are offset by abundant joy; an empty nest foretells sadness or loneliness that will soon be replaced by a sense of achievement and freedom. The idiom "nest egg" emphasizes the importance of foresight and planning.

net

Differing interpretations include feelings of possession or entrapment. Are you casting a net or tangled in one?

newspaper

Reading a newspaper reflects an intellectual search—but you will put forth minimal effort and reach insignificant or irrelevant conclusions. Look beyond the headlines for more satisfying information.

new year

To dream of an impending year indicates a deep desire for positive changes or new beginnings. However, images of a New Year's Eve celebration or party negate the sincerity of such hopes. Focus on your goals, and pursue them with quiet thoughtfulness. *See also* **birthday.**

nibble

To dream that you are nibbling on food indicates trepidation or doubt about a relationship or an endeavor. Gather all the facts before you dig in deeper. *See also* **eating.**

nicknames

See **names.**

nightingale

This bird foretells an awakening. If you hear the song of a nightingale, expect a fleeting romance.

nightmare

To dream of having a nightmare and to actually have one are distinct experiences that reveal the level of consciousness with which you deal with everyday stress. Enabling yourself to recognize and come out of a nightmare is the goal and result of lucid dreaming. *See also sidebar on page 194.*

nighttime

Dreams that occur in a dark nighttime atmosphere can have several meanings. To many people they facilitate rest and recuperation, and the themes are nonthreatening. But to some people who work at night and sleep (and dream) during the day, these images emphasize stress, boredom, or confused thinking. Another common response to the darkness of night is a fear of the unknown. *See also* **darkness.**

An "Amazing" Nightmare

John Newton, who composed the hymn "Amazing Grace," was the captain of a slave ship when he dreamed that he saw "all of Europe consumed in a great raging fire." According to Newton, this nightmare brought about a "spiritual transformation" that prompted him to become an ardent antislavery activist.

noise

Noisy dreams reflect the fact that you always have a lot to say but no one seems to listen. Find a more subtle way to make your point and disregard the adage "the squeaky wheel always gets the grease." It's not working in your case.

nomination

To nominate someone in a dream is to avoid responsibilities. To be nominated implies that you will soon take on more than you bargained for. *See also* **election, voting.**

noon

This time of day symbolizes your creative and intellectual peak. Take advantage of this message and arrange forthcoming plans or projects to coincide with the hour. Noon can also represent the midpoint in life.

noose

To see a dangling noose means an important deadline is approaching. To be in a noose implies that you are unable to extricate yourself from a troubling situation. Stop swinging back and forth and choose a side.

north

Dreams that reference this direction indicate that you have your sights set on positive goals and are working hard to achieve them. To dream of seeing the North Star suggests that you should follow your intuition.

nose

This common dream symbol reflects intuition. If you dream of your own nose, you should trust yourself in decisions regarding business or romance. If your nose is proportionately oversized in your dream, stop meddling in someone's life. Dreams of having a nosebleed indicate that you need to pour out your heart to someone.

novel

Something unpredictable or unusual is about to enter your life. To write a novel is to develop character; a sign that you are growing as a person.

nudity

Dreams involving nudity reflect your self-esteem. If you are comfortable being nude, you are secure about exposing your feelings and have nothing to hide. Embarrassment about nudity implies vulnerability, guilt, or shame, whereas being oblivious to it reveals a lack of self-awareness. Nudity can also reflect honesty, freedom, and nonconformity. *See also* **clothing.**

nugget

To receive a nugget of gold predicts a profitable opportunity. You may be offered a bit of information that will have a big impact.

numbers

Many people count things to fall asleep, and those things have meanings that are personal to the dreamer—as do individual numbers. They can represent money, family members, commitments, deadlines, etc. On the other hand, they can reflect lost identity or the fact that you feel like just another number. *See also sidebar on page 175.*

numbness

Feeling numb often reflects avoidance or repression. Alternately, it can point to commitment problems or overall feelings of detachment. If a particular body part feels numb, consider whether there is an undisclosed health issue.

nun

This symbol can reflect obedience, self-sacrifice, or dedication; a different interpretation points to repetitive behavior (a habit) that is causing you guilt or regret. To dream of a nun who is praying is a sign to count your blessings.

nurse

A nurse can reflect the desire for a mother figure, someone

Dreams Count!

Whether you are counting sheep days before a deadline, or neglected household chores, numbers are a frequent dream image. But they don't always appear as actual digits. Instead, they can present themselves in the form of people, objects, money, repetitive actions, or stages of personal growth. Although the interpretation of numbers as dream symbols is particular to the dreamer and his or her life experiences, here are the general meanings of the basic numbers:

Zero: timelessness, eternity, completion, emptiness

One: beginnings, ego, leadership, loneliness

Two: duality, opposites, unity, opposition

Three: trilogy, bravery, fulfillment, separation

Four: earth, strength, consciousness, insecurity

Five: awakening, courage, transformation, resentment

Six: balance, harmony, creativity, ostracism

Seven: illumination, abundance, mysticism, restlessness

Eight: rebirth, development, infinity, indecision

Nine: purity, achievement, wisdom, imperfection

Ten: experience, cooperation, lawfulness, depression

When examining the significance of numbers, it is also important to consider their symbolism in everyday life. For example, three represents a triangle or triad (past, present, and future; mind, body, soul; earth, wind, and fire, etc.). There are seven days in a week and seven easily identifiable colors in a rainbow. For many people, six (particularly 666) implies evil, and the number thirteen has long been associated with bad luck. If you are so inclined, take the analysis a step further by applying mathematical formulas to interpret larger numbers.

who will tend to your needs or offer unconditional love. To dream you are a nurse suggests that you should focus less on others and more on yourself. To dream of being cared for by a nurse can reflect unresolved childhood issues of physical or emotional neglect. *See also* **doctor.**

nuts

A nut foretells great potential in future endeavors. To eat nuts is to mull over new ideas. To buy or be given nuts is a sign to make preparations or take preventative action. Also consider the word in reference to being emotionally unbalanced. To dream of only the shell of a nut denotes that you need more details to make an informed decision about an issue. *See also* **acorn, seeds, trees.**

oak

This type of wood symbolizes strength and endurance. To see an oak tree in a dream indicates that you have a strong character and a solid family life. *See also* **trees.**

oar

If you dream about rowing a boat with two oars, you will achieve balance in what has been a precarious situation. Using only one oar predicts that you will go in circles or repeat the same mistakes, getting nowhere in the process.

oasis

This symbol predicts success and profit when you least expect it. It can also suggest that you take a restful break from your busy schedule. *See also* **desert.**

oath

To take an oath in a dream recommends that you follow through on recent commitments to avoid damaging personal or professional relationships. It can also be a sign that you are ready to make a commitment. *See also* **initiation.**

oats

This symbol is an omen of newfound friendship that will prove long-lasting. If you dream of harvesting or eating oats, take more time to socialize and enjoy yourself.

obedience

To be obedient in a dream indicates that you should be more respectful of others. However, blind obedience to unreasonable rules reflects low self-esteem or a lack of good judgment.

obelisk

An obelisk is often interpreted as a phallic symbol but also denotes anything of significance. If people are present around the obelisk, someone will soon send you an important message.

obituary

This is not necessarily related to death but instead can herald the end of an era. To read your own obituary suggests that you should acknowledge and take pride in your achievements.

See also **death, funeral, memorial.**

obligation

To dream of fulfilling an obligation is a reminder that someone is depending on you. To feel a sense of obligation means that you too often take on the problems of other people.

obscenities

Using obscenities indicates your dream self's way of compensating for your inability or unwillingness to express your anger. Although you don't have to start swearing at people, you should make an effort to unburden yourself of such feelings. *See also* **anger.**

observatory

This symbol reflects a need to explore the unknown or what

America is a land of big dreamers and big hopes. It is this hope that has sustained us through revolution and civil war, depression and world war, a struggle for civil and social rights and the brink of nuclear crisis. And it is because our dreamers dreamed that we have emerged from each challenge more united, more prosperous, and more admired than before.

—U.S. President Barak Obama

seems beyond your grasp. If looking at the stars while in an observatory, you will soon reach a higher level of self-awareness. *See also* **laboratory.**

obsession

To feel obsessed with something or someone reflects unrelenting guilt or regret. It also indicates that you admire, covet, or envy certain qualities in another person.

obstacles

Encountering obstacles in a dream represents real-life physical or emotional barriers. Consider the obstacle itself for clues on how to overcome it. For example, if you come upon an obstacle in the road, consider taking an easier path in life. To run an obstacle course means you need to improve your health in order to achieve a certain goal. Keep in mind that the obstacles we face are often created in our own minds.

occupation

See **job, office.**

ocean

An ocean represents the unconscious, and the movement of the water (calm,

swirling, turbulent) reflects your state of mind. If wading in an ocean, you are afraid to explore your deepest emotions. Gazing out across an ocean foretells that your expansive knowledge will help others broaden their horizons (perhaps teaching is in your future). *See also* **tide, water.**

octagon

Because an octagon is the shape of a stop sign, this dream symbol is a warning to halt something that's already in progress or a reminder to stop and think before you act. For further clarification, examine symbols in the vicinity of the octagon.

octopus

Encountering an octopus implies that you will overcome a seemingly daunting challenge handily. Alternately, it could reflect the fact that you are trying to juggle too many tasks at once. An octopus that squirts ink warns of clouded thinking or an obscured view. *See also* **spider.**

odor

This represents the memories associated with a particular scent, and your reaction to it (whether it was pleasant or offensive) reflects your true feelings about those memories.

office

Dreams that involve the office in which you work reflect real-life stresses that aren't necessarily related to your job. If you dream of holding a particular office, you will eventually achieve the goals you are striving for. *See also* **job.**

oil

Oil represents an attempt to keep things running smoothly, even when they start to falter. An oil spill signifies contamination—in other words, problems that have far-reaching implications. Dreams of striking oil emphasize that happiness and fulfillment don't come easily. You have to put forth effort. *See also* **gambling.**

ointment

To apply ointment or a salve means that your emotional wounds need to be tended to in order to heal. The word *ointment* is derived from the Latin *unguere*, which means "to anoint." To be anointed in a dream foretells a ritual acceptance or a spiritual revelation. *See also* **bandage, baptism.**

old

The interpretation of this image varies. Old objects in a dream can represent either cherished memories or outdated ideas. An old person suggests that you seek out someone who has gained wisdom through experience. Alternately, an old person predicts a decline in physical or mental health or a fear of aging. *See also* **wise old man/wise old woman.**

> *I prefer to be a dreamer among the humblest, with visions to be realized, than lord among those without dreams and desires.*
>
> —Kahlil Gibran

Mutual Dreaming

As you record, explore, and express your dream content with other people, you may discover that some themes are eerily similar—or seemingly identical. This concept is referred to as mutual dreaming, in which two or more people share the same dream (or elements thereof). Mutual dreams can occur spontaneously, or you can program or incubate them (that is, you wish them to be), and they are most common between two people who know each other well. In the most extreme examples of mutual dreaming, two dreamers see or meet each other in their dreams and proceed to communicate.

Common Ground

A classic example of mutual dreaming was reported by Hugh Calloway, who wrote under the pen name of Oliver Fox, in the early 1900s. One evening, Calloway and his two friends Elkington and Slade were discussing dreams. They decided to try an experiment where they would all meet in their dreams that night. They chose a place called Southampton Common as their location.

That night, Calloway dreamt that he went to Southampton Common, and there he met Elkington, but Slade was missing. In the dream, he and Elkington greeted one another, and both commented that Slade was not there.

The next day, Calloway asked Elkington what he had dreamed the previous night. Elkington reported that he had met Calloway at Southampton Common, and that they both remarked upon the absence of their friend, Slade.

When they contacted Slade to find out what he had dreamed, Slade reported that he did not remember any dreams for that night at all.

Not all mutual dreams will be this precise. Remember, everyone experiences and interprets their dreams differently. There may be only some symbolism or events in a dream that match with someone else's. If you have a friend or family member who is keen to try mutual dreaming experiments, you might want to set up some target dates and places. Give it a try and see what happens!

olives

Eating olives or cooking with olive oil predicts good health and longevity. An olive tree or olive branch symbolizes forgiveness and peace. Mythological references contend that olive trees facilitate beneficial dreams.

Olympics

Dreams in which you participate in an Olympic sport reflect your desire or need for improved fitness but also warn against trying to achieve too much too quickly.

onions

An issue or problem that seems obvious or easy to solve will require more scrutiny: You will have to peel away the layers to reveal the cause. If you dream of cooking with onions, think before you speak to avoid offending someone. To smell onions signifies deception. *See also sidebar on page 101.*

onyx

This gemstone suggests that you are living beyond your means. Use restraint to ease your financial problems.

opal

Opal jewelry warns that someone outwardly dazzling is emotionally vulnerable.

open/opening

Depending on the context of the dream, something that is open can represent opportunities and revelations. On the other hand, the image means you should open your eyes to a growing problem or be more open in expressing your feelings. To attend the opening of a show or a business heralds newfound prosperity.

opera

To attend an opera foretells a situation that will cause emotions to run high. Keep a level head, and don't get distracted by the drama. If you appear in an opera, a passionate but fleeting romance may be in your future. *See also* **theater.**

operation

If you undergo an operation, you are trying to unburden yourself of negative influences. These can be people, habits, or your own self-defeating thoughts. To perform an operation is to examine something closely or to get to the heart (or guts) of the matter.

opponent

To face an opponent is to challenge yourself or question your own judgment. This image can also reflect a struggle with your conscience. You are opposing something you have done or said that you aren't particularly proud of. *See also* **argument.**

opposite

Dream images that appear opposite to what is considered normal reflect conflicted or contradictory emotions. They will sort themselves out if you follow your intuition. Opposites can also reflect that you seek in others the qualities that you feel you lack. Consider whether this serves you well.

orange

The fruit represents your positive disposition, but the color can symbolize either warmth or deception. *See sidebar on page 85.*

orchard

If walking through an orchard, expect your personal life to grow and flourish. The image can also reflect fertility or ripe opportunities.

orchestra

Do you feel you are in tune or in synch with others? Thoughtful listening makes for harmonious relationships. Alternately, this dream symbol recommends that you be more independent (march to your own drummer).

orchids

To grow orchids indicates that a once-devoted relationship is growing fragile and needs more attention. *See also sidebar on page 115.*

ore

Ore symbolizes inner wisdom and resourcefulness. To mine ore means that inspiration or a hunch will come from an unusual source.

> *All night I dreamed I was surrounded by the bodies of those who had been murdered … now I know it was the souls of the trees crying out to me.*
>
> —Hasidic Proverb

organ

If you dream of a specific organ of the body, such as your lungs, heart, or liver, a medical check-up may reveal an illness. If you are playing an organ, hold on to traditional values but rethink old-fashioned ideas.

ornaments

Beware of admiring someone for his or her looks alone. To receive an ornament as a gift reflects a growing friendship.

orphan

If you dream that you are an orphan, you are concerned with being abandoned or rejected. To dream of adopting a child from an orphanage reflects guilt about neglecting someone close to you.

ostrich

Take this symbol as a warning to face and deal with problematic issues. Burying your head in the sand won't make them go away.

outbreak

To dream of an outbreak—anything from acne to a contagious disease—means that a troubling situation will get out of control if not handled quickly and properly.

outcast

Often, dreams that involve social ostracism are contrary. If you are the outcast, congratulate yourself for staying true to your beliefs rather than going along with the crowd.

outdoors

See **nature.**

outspokenness

An outspoken individual symbolizes free expression. To be outspoken in a dream is an omen that your opinions will encourage a positive change.

oven

A plan or project in its early stages will develop into something that alters your life for the better. This dream symbol also represents the womb and may reflect thoughts of or issues with your mother or with motherhood. *See also* **baking, mother, stove.**

overcast

See **fog, mist.**

owl

Pay close attention to the owl in your dream, as it can represent either guidance and wisdom or mystery and death. If the owl gazes at you, expect to receive important advice. If the owl's head is turned away from you, anticipate a loss of something or someone.

oxen

This dream symbol reflects the strength of your character, will, and work ethic. It can also serve as a warning against taking on too much responsibility.

oxygen

To dream of oxygen often foretells freedom from worries or troubling situations. If there is a lack of oxygen, however, consider if something in your waking life is depleting your energy.

oyster

Traditionally thought to be an aphrodisiac, oysters can reflect your need or desire for a fulfilling sexual relationship. Alternately, an oyster can suggest that you are closing yourself off from people, preventing them from seeing the pearl that lies within. *See also* **clams, lobster.**

P

pacifier

This dream symbol reflects either your need to care for someone or your desire to be cared for. To search for a lost pacifier suggests that you are feeling emotionally empty.

pacing

Pacing back and forth means you are feeling anxious or confused over a recent decision. Accept things as they are and move forward. *See also* **walking.**

package

An unopened package can be an omen of a surprise, whether good or bad. To open a package is to explore one's hidden talents or abilities. *See also* **box, letter.**

packing

To dream of packing something, whether it's a suitcase or moving boxes, indicates that you want to change your life. The process of packing recommends that you put away painful memories, or it may symbolize a need for freedom and independence.

page

If reading a page of text, you are facing a situation that requires close examination. For clues, try to decipher what is written on the page. To see a blank page reflects either an opportunity or a lack of awareness. If you dream of turning several pages, expect significant changes in a personal relationship. *See also* **reading.**

pail

A pail that is full can imply abundance, but if you are carrying a full pail with difficulty, consider whether you have more in life than you really need. If the pail is empty, expect to be relieved of stress or burdens.

pain

This dream feeling doesn't always indicate physical ailments; rather, it may reflect emotional damage. Pain can also symbolize someone who is getting on your nerves. *See also* **injury.**

painkillers

Taking painkillers (aspirin or anything stronger) suggests a need to diminish something unwanted or unfavorable. To take a great quantity of painkillers is a sign that you are trying to avoid an unpleasant situation altogether; however, that will just make things worse. *See also* **addiction, pills.**

paint

The scent of fresh paint foretells a restorative period, whereas images of peeling paint warn of a difficult or repetitive task.

painting

Although usually a reflection of your creativity, this dream action can have other implications. If you are painting an image, carefully consider the details. Does it relate to something in your waking life that you are trying to generate, change, or cover up?

palace

A palace is an omen of both financial gain and leisure. Expect a change in lifestyle for the better. *See also* **castle, mansion.**

palette

To dream of a palette full of paint predicts creative productivity. A bare palette indicates a lack of fulfillment or imagination.

pallbearer

This symbol assures that old burdens will be laid to rest. To be a pallbearer foretells that you will be asked to help shoulder a significant burden. *See also* **burial, funeral.**

palm trees

Tropical symbolism often points to the need for relaxing or romantic getaways.

pan

If the image is of a cooking vessel, anticipate a heated social or family gathering. If you are panning for gold, you will seek something that is difficult to achieve. If you dream of being panned, consider whether you are overly sensitive or defensive.

pancakes

Eating or making pancakes represents boredom with professional or family obligations.

panic

This is usually a literal symbol of anxiety, stress, or confusion in your waking life. Can you pinpoint what might be causing these feelings?

pansy

You are fortunate to appreciate and enjoy simple pleasures, but beware that someone may take advantage of your easy-going nature. *See also sidebar on page 115.*

panther

To dream of a panther reflects your intelligent and agile mind, as well as your instinct. To be chased by a panther foretells a confrontation with a formidable opponent.

> *Dreams come true. Without that possibility, nature would not incite us to have them.*
> —John Updike

pantry

A full pantry often reveals that you are secure with where you are in life, but it can also mean that too many choices are making you indecisive. An empty pantry, or one that is poorly stocked, reflects financial concerns.

pants

See **clothing.**

paper

Is it a clean, single sheet of paper or are they meaningless scraps? This dream symbol can indicate either a need for organization or a desire to reinvent yourself. To dream of papyrus paper suggests that you listen to and learn from those you consider wise and experienced.

paper clip

Take this image as a reminder to make sure your personal papers are in order.

parachute

To descend by means of a parachute foretells security amid dangerous or tumultuous circumstances. An unused parachute warns that you

need a contingency plan for a current project.

parade

Watching a parade implies that you feel insignificant and that life is passing you by. If you are marching in a parade, consider whether you are comfortable going with the flow or if you should strike out on your own.

paradise

To dream of a place you consider paradise indicates that something may be too good to be true in your waking life. Examine every detail of that something and check for faults.

paralysis

This common dream feeling can have many meanings. Physiologically, it simply reflects the paralysis you experience during REM sleep (e.g., feeling unable to walk or scream). Alternately, paralysis represents fears that are holding you back.

paranoia

This feeling, which is often exaggerated in dreams, indicates that you are too concerned with how others perceive you. Chances are that they aren't paying that much attention to you.

parasites

A parasite represents someone who feeds off of another's

Prodromal Dreams

The ancient Greeks referred to a particular type of dream as *prodromal,* from the Greek words *pro* (which means "before") and *dromos* ("running"). They believed that prodromal dreams could predict anything from mild ailments to life-threatening diseases before any symptoms appeared. Hippocrates, often cited as the "father of modern medicine," encouraged his patients to incubate prodromal dreams. Aristotle, who was born shortly after Hippocrates died, helped promote the idea that prodromal dreams were an important diagnostic tool—and, if used during the course of treatment, often facilitated healing. In his book *Prophecy in Dream,* the Greco-Roman physician Galen (who often used his own dreams to guide him through surgeries) described a patient who had a recurring a prodromal dream. The man, who was healthy and in fine physical condition, frequently dreamed that his left leg had turned to stone. After many such dreams, the man inexplicably developed paralysis in that same leg, and the condition persisted until the man died.

Skip to the mid-1900s: Psychiatrist Vasily Kasatkin, working at the Leningrad Neurosurgical Institute, began a 40-year study that involved 1,200 people who recalled and recorded the details of more than 10,000 dreams. The result of Dr. Kasatkin's research was that illnesses could be detected through dreams that are especially poignant or disturbing. In Dr. Kasatkin's words: "Dreams are sentries that watch over our health."

success. Avoid this kind of individual. *See also* **barnacle, leeches.**

parcel

See **package.**

parchment

An important and valuable document may soon be placed in your care. This dream symbol may also point to outdated attitudes.

parents

Dreams involving your parents often reflect deep-seeded feelings about them or even their relationship. Sometimes, however, these dreams refer to your responsibility for another, perhaps as a guide or guardian. *See also* **father, family, mother.**

park

Examine the feelings this image evokes. For some people, a park represents leisure and respite; for others, it can suggest loneliness or isolation, or it can represent a stalemate. What type of park is it— a playground or a public walkway?

parking

To park a car predicts a pause or standstill in a relationship or a work project. If you dream of parking cars as a job, you aspire to achieve an elevated lifestyle and are encouraged to take the wheel and make it happen.

parrot

A parrot perched on your shoulder represents an overbearing, persistently vocal person. If you are that type of person, don't mock others or repeat idle gossip.

parsley

To dream of growing or eating parsley suggests a need for physical or spiritual purification.

party

You will soon have something to celebrate, and all eyes will be on you. Examine your participation in the party: Are you the host, a wallflower, or the one wearing a lamp shade? *See also* **celebration.**

passageway

This dream symbol predicts a discovery. If you come upon a hidden passageway, expect new opportunities that will reveal something about yourself.

passenger

Consider whether you are in a position to be taken for a ride. Alternately, the symbol can warn against being critical of someone in the driver's seat. *See also* **car, driving.**

passport

To possess a passport suggests that you explore different avenues in life. This is a good time for personal development and growth. *See also* **travel.**

password

To have access to a password indicates that you will be awarded privileges that are denied to others. Keep the matter to yourself to avoid jealousy or conflicts.

past

Dreams often revolve around our personal pasts, but are you dwelling too much on situations that cannot be changed? To dream of the past in general is a warning to not let history repeat itself. Also think about the homonym "passed." Don't pass a good opportunity by.

pasture

It is time to turn out negative habits or worn-out ideas.

path

This image represents your direction in life. Is the path straight and free of obstacles? Are there twists and turns ahead? Are you tempted to wander off the path? *See also* **highway, roads.**

patterns

If you dream of unfamiliar, intricate patterns, you have a lot on your mind and are having difficulty keeping things organized. If you envision a simple pattern, your everyday routine needs some pizazz.

pawn

If you are selling a personal possession to a pawnbroker, you are not giving yourself enough credit for your achievements. Dreams of the chess piece warn against being duped.

Alternately, don't pawn off your responsibilities on others.

paws

If an animal extends a paw to you, a new acquaintance will grow into a close friendship. Also consider if the homonym "pause" has any significance.

payment

Making a payment reflects anxiety or guilt over neglecting your financial or personal obligations. It can also warn against overindulgence. *See also* **money.**

peach

To pick a ripe peach foretells a sensual but short-lived romance. To eat a peach means that you will soon enjoy the best life has to offer.

peacock

This symbol emphasizes that there is a fine line between confidence and vanity. On which side of the line do you stand?

peanuts

Are you being paid (monetarily or in terms of attention) what you are worth, or are you working for peanuts?

pearl

A pearl represents high intellect. To be given a pearl necklace indicates that a friend will offer you wise advice.

peas

Peas imply that ideas considered insignificant have more value than you think. Give someone's suggestions another chance.

pedestal

Consider whether the person you idolize is worthy of your admiration and respect. On the other hand, there may be someone you would like to knock off his or her lofty perch.

peel

To peel something is to search for hidden meanings or qualities. Be warned that you could discover imperfections. *See also* **onions.**

> *Only the dreamer shall understand realities, though in truth his dreaming must be not out of proportion to his waking.*
> —Chinese Proverb

Pegasus

Wild horses symbolize freedom, and the mythological winged horse Pegasus foretells a life-changing transformation.

pendulum

A pendulum in motion suggests that personal or professional circumstances will change unexpectedly. A resting pendulum implies indecision or a stalemate.

penguins

Penguins can't fly, and they all seem to look alike. The message from your dream self is to rise above the crowd and make yourself stand out.

pen name

Using a pen name or an alias indicates a desire for privacy. Alternately, you are trying to conceal your true self out of fear of judgment.

penny

To count pennies in a dream points to financial concerns, but if you find a shiny penny, expect a boost in your bank account. Pennies also represent small problems that could accumulate quickly. *See also* **coins, money.**

penthouse

This symbol reflects a desire to live the high life, but be aware that the image is superficial. You actually want to have a higher opinion of yourself.

pepper

Cooking something with hot peppers means it is time to spice up your life. Using plain black pepper symbolizes minor irritations.

peppermint

If you are eating peppermints, expect a boost in energy and motivation. This would be a good time to tackle household jobs or to get a jump on that looming project at work.

percolator

This dream symbol represents ideas that are bubbling just

below the surface. If you are patient, important goals will come to fruition.

performance

If you dream of watching a performance (e.g., a play or recital) someone close to you is putting on a front. Hurtful truths will be revealed when the performance ends. If you are putting on a performance, your character or portrayal is likely contrary to the real you. *See also* **acting.**

perfume

To smell perfume in a dream is an omen of good luck. To put on perfume indicates a need for attention. To spray someone with perfume is a sign of possessiveness (think of the way an animal marks its territory). *See also* **incense.**

peridot

This gem portends emotional healing through forgiveness.

periscope

Your intuition will enable you to see beyond the surface of a murky issue. Use your insight to help those who seem stuck. *See also* **telescope.**

permanence

Dreams in which something seems permanent can reflect either security with or anxiety over change, For further clues, consider what in the dreams has permanence.

permit

Being given a permit (or to be granted permission) is a sign to move forward with plans or express ideas. Alternately, it reflects self-doubt or indecision. *See also* **license.**

perspiration

To perspire in a dream foretells a period of difficult but profitable work. To see a person perspire indicates that someone close to you is working hard to hide his or her true feelings.

persuasion

To persuade someone is to talk yourself into accepting something you have long rejected. It's time to listen to that inner voice.

> *I never paint dreams or nightmares. I paint my own reality.*
> —Frida Kahlo

petals

Love and romance will soon consume your thoughts. Enjoy the feelings but keep a clear head and be realistic in your expectations. *See also sidebar on page 115.*

pets

Dreams that involve your own pet(s) in general point to your need to nurture or to be nurtured. Pets you had in childhood symbolize the freedom and loyalty you felt at that time, and to search for a missing pet indicates a longing for security.

pharaoh

This dream symbol means you will achieve a position of authority and great wealth.

Night Terrors

Night terrors are a common sleep problem among children between the ages of two and six, but they can occur well into adulthood. Studies have shown that approximately 15 percent of younger children have occasional or frequent night terrors. The causes can include inadequate sleep the previous few nights, inconsistent bedtimes, or an unusually active or hectic daytime schedule.

Parents commonly describe night terrors this way: The child appears extremely panicked, and his or her eyes are wide open. What follows are screams of terror, accompanied by rapid breathing and an elevated heart rate. The child will usually appear confused and can't be comforted or calmed. The duration of a night terror can range from 5 to 45 minutes.

A child should not be awakened from a night terror, as that can just exacerbate the fear. Instead, stay with the child to make sure he or she is safe; most children fall back asleep as soon as the incident is over. Unlike a nightmare, which children often recall vividly, night terrors are forgotten immediately.

It can also indicate a desire to investigate your ancestral roots. *See also* **pyramid, ruins.**

pheasant

See **quail.**

phone numbers

It is common to dream that you can't remember your phone number or home address. This theme points to a need or desire for independence.

photograph

Obviously, the objects or people in the photo can offer further clues, but dreams in which you look at photographs serve to evoke memories or images that you have put out of your mind. Consider reconnecting with distant friends or family members.

photographer

To dream that you are taking photographs can mean that you prefer to see things from your own point of view. It can also point to a desire to capture or own something that is otherwise elusive.

piano

To play a piano skillfully reflects your overall creativity and an appreciation for the benefit of hard work. To hear pleasant piano music highlights the harmony in your life, but a piano played poorly warns to get in tune with friends or coworkers. *See also* **music.**

pickles

If pickling (preserving) foods, this dream image indicates a desire to adopt a simpler lifestyle. Alternately, it points to insecurities about your ability to provide for (feed) yourself or your family. Another interpretation is taken from the metaphor "in a pickle," relating to feelings of entrapment or embarrassment. *See also* **jam.**

pickpocket

To be the victim of a pickpocket suggests that you are being deceived or taken advantage of. If you are the one picking pockets, whatever you are pursuing requires more effort than you are putting into it.

picnic

Preparing or attending a picnic reflects a disdain for formality but highlights your casual attitude toward life and simple enjoyment of family and friends.

pie

Dreams of serving pie reflect insecurities about equality or fairness—is everyone getting an equal amount of your attention? To bake pies suggests that you are trying to please someone who doesn't appreciate it. *See also* **baking.**

pier

Gazing across a body of water from a pier points to introspection and a desire to go beyond what is currently expected of you. To jump off a pier is a sign that you will exceed those limitations.

pig

Consider your own opinion of pigs. To some people, these animals represent lazy, slovenly, or overindulgent behavior, but to others they are symbols of self-security and sensuality. *See also sidebar on page 54.*

pigeon

To dream of a pigeon in flight portends messages from afar. Exercise judgment as to their veracity. To feed pigeons reflects your compassionate nature.

pilgrim

This dream symbol typically corresponds with the bounty of Thanksgiving, but it can also represent a pilgrimage or a quest to find a lifestyle that puts less emphasis on materialism. *See also* **Quaker.**

pillars

In general, concrete pillars symbolize strength and support. As a dream image, they reflect the stability of your family life or your social or professional status. What is the condition of

---

Say the odds are a million to one that when person has a dream of an airplane crash, there is an airplane crash the next day. With 6 billion people having an average of 250 dream themes each per night, there should be about 1.5 million people a day who have dreams that seem clairvoyant.

—Robert Todd Carroll, author of
The Skeptic's Dictionary

the pillars? Are they new and sturdy or old and crumbling?

pillows

This is a symbol of comfort. Do you have enough pillows, and do they provide adequate support? Dreams of sleeping without a pillow can point to insecurities about where or with whom you are sleeping.

pills

To dream of taking pills points to an attempt to relieve yourself of someone who is annoying (being a pill). However, if you do find relief, it will be short-lived, so consider a more permanent solution to the problem. *See also* **painkillers.**

pilot

You will be asked to guide someone through a difficult time. Your steadfast reliability has encouraged that request.

pimples

See **outbreak**.

pin

To dream of a sewing pin reflects your creativity and desire to design a life that is suited to you. Alternately, to feel pricked by a pin warns against being too thin-skinned with regard to the opinions or remarks of others.

pineapple

Eating pineapple foretells a relaxing, much-needed trip. To peel and cut a pineapple points to a laborious household project that will provide much satisfaction.

pine tree

Walking peacefully among pine trees means you will have a long, healthy life. To gather pinecones predicts fertility. A lone pine indicates that you will soon weather a storm. *See also* **trees.**

pink

This color traditionally connotes femininity and affection. *See also sidebar on page 85.*

> *Since that deluge of newspaper articles I have been so flooded with questions, invitations, suggestions, that I keep dreaming I am roasting in Hell, and the mailman is the devil eternally yelling at me, showering me with more bundles of letters at my head because I have not answered the old ones.*
>
> —Albert Einstein

pioneer

To dream that you are a pioneer is a sign that you should forge ahead with a plan that may seem unrealistic to others. Your ingenuity will bring success and recognition.

pipes

Pipes can represent the connections you have with coworkers and the ease with which communication flows. Pay attention to signs of leaks or blockages. Drainage pipes indicate that someone or something unwanted or no longer useful will soon be flushed away. *See also* **plumber.**

piranhas

This dream symbol represents a fear of being confronted by a group—whether family, friends, or authority figures. Consider recent behaviors or comments that would warrant such a situation, and try to redeem yourself as quickly as possible.

pirate

If you dream that you are a pirate, you are violating the personal space or emotions of someone. Another interpretation is that you don't deserve whatever you are trying to take credit for. Alternately, this symbol can refer to your adventurous spirit and desire to play by your own rules.

pistol

See **duel, gun.**

pit

Digging a pit indicates that you are ready to dispose of negative feelings, behaviors, or relationships. If you dream of being in a pit (metaphorically, your life is in the pits), consider whether you are trapped there or are trying to climb out. *See also* **burial, ditch.**

pitcher

To dream of being a baseball pitcher means that it is a good time to present ideas that you have been holding on to. You feel more in control now and can make your point more accurately. To pour water, milk, or some other liquid from a pitcher foretells a refreshing flow of emotions.

pitchfork

This is typically a symbol of dark forces or influences, but it can also predict a difficult and seemingly pointless task.

pizza

You are facing a difficult decision with a lot of options and feel divided over which choice to make.

plague

Overwhelming or troubling thoughts could get out of hand if not dealt with properly. This can also be a literal dream that reflects concerns about your health or that of people close to you. *See also* **outbreak.**

plaid

Wearing plaid predicts social activities that will raise your spirits. *See also* **patterns.**

planets

To dream of traveling to or living on other planets points to lofty goals and your ability to attain them. As the saying goes, the sky is the limit!

plank

Walking the plank often reflects feelings of guilt, punishment, and vulnerability. Do you feel doomed because of something you have done? Images of planks positioned as ramps represent unstable emotions.

plants

Plant growth reflects personal development. To care for withering plants suggests that you attend to what is ailing within you so you can heal. Watering or pruning healthy plants means you are emotionally attentive to those close to you—they may now be able to thrive on their own.

plaque

Consider the contrary meanings of the word: a plaque can be a symbol of tribute and honor; it also signifies something unsightly or unhealthy that threatens your vitality. Examine the context of the dream to determine whether this is a positive or negative symbol.

plaster

Working with plaster in a dream often reflects a real-life attempt to reinforce or strengthen a weak situation or relationship. In a different view, plaster can point to a hardened heart or an attempt to impose your opinions on others.

plastic

To dream of plastic objects reflects fears or guilt concerning artifice. Do you suspect that someone isn't who you thought they were, or are you hiding your true self from someone? This dream symbol can also point to rigid attitudes or a lack of emotion. *See also* **rubber.**

plate

This dream symbol typically points to personal or professional responsibilities. A full plate can elicit feelings of being either satisfied or overwhelmed. An empty plate indicates that you are not working to your potential.

platform

See **stage.**

play

To dream that you are playing reflects your tendency to put on a happy face even when you are feeling low. Alternately, it can symbolize creativity—you are toying with a hobby that will prove profitable.

playground

You are reflecting on favorable childhood memories. It can also suggest that you get in touch with your inner child and enjoy life more.

plow

Plowing through what you deem to be obstacles has the potential to alienate people in your path. Patience and consideration are better approaches.

plug

Putting a plug into an electrical socket means you need to connect with your inner power. Also consider the use of the word as it relates to promoting something (that something is likely you). To plug a leak represents a temporary but ultimately unsuccessful attempt to fix a problem.

plum

Picking or eating a plum predicts that you will make a wise choice about an important matter. To dream of rotting plums indicates that you have let a good opportunity slip by. *See also sidebar on page 101*, **grapes.**

plumber

If you dream of being a plumber, expect twists and turns in a project or plan, but know that everything will work out fine in the end. To clear clogged plumbing indicates your need to release anger or frustration. Leaky plumbing warns against spreading rumors. *See also* **leak, pipes.**

pockets

Obviously bulging pockets reflect an over inflated ego and a need for attention. If the pockets are empty or turned inside out, expect financial troubles.

poetry

To write or recite poetry to someone is a sign of reverence and dedication. If you are reading poetry, you should try to solve a troubling situation with a more creative, less obvious approach.

pointing

Dreams in which you point at someone or something

If we want to realize our dreams, we have to stay awake.
—Swami Tejomayananda

serve to remind you of what is important and should not be overlooked. Consider what or whom you are pointing to. To be pointed at can represent either admiration or accusation.

poison

Poison as symbolized by a skull and crossbones is a sign to avoid people or situations that don't feel right to you. To take poison in a dream foretells regret over an old or recent action or comment.

poison ivy

Poison ivy is a warning to watch your approach when dealing with irritating personal or professional relationships. A misstep will only exacerbate the situation.

poker

See **cards, gambling.**

police

This image encourages you to make better decisions. Messages from your unconscious are warning you to watch yourself.

polishing

Polishing something in a dream indicates that you are honing skills or talents that you have neglected. It can also refer to putting the finishing touches on a project or presentation.

politician

This symbol warns that someone may be telling you only what you want to hear. You are unaware of underlying,

Precognition or Coincidence

Prophetic dreaming (and precognition, in general) has been documented and debated since biblical times. Aristotle questioned its validity and called such dreams "mere coincidences," and psychologist Sigmund Freud referred to the phenomenon as "nonsensical." Because precognitive dreams frequently involve the harm or death of a loved one, if you actually know someone who is gravely ill or engages in life-risking behaviors or activities (anything from an addiction to high-wire walking), these images can be coincidental. But if you have such a dream only once and just prior to an accident or a death, it is thought by many to be truly precognitive.

negative aspects of the story.

polka dots

You need more variety in life; a change of scenery or a new hobby would brighten an otherwise bland routine.

pollution

This dream image signifies an unfavorable atmosphere, either at home or in the workplace. Do what needs to be done to clear the air. *See also* **air.**

pomegranate

To dream of eating this fruit means that despite your sweet soul, you appear tough or impenetrable. Let more people see the real you.

pond

A pond means that introspection will bring you peace of mind. Ripples on a pond predict minor but temporary problems in an otherwise smooth relationship. *See also* **lake, water.**

pool

A pool of water symbolizes hope and promise. It also suggests the potential benefit of pooling your resources. To dream of playing pool suggests that you are aiming for and achieving goals.

poor

See **poverty, wealth.**

popcorn

Dreams in which you make popcorn foretell busy activities that will end in a celebration.

poplar tree

Although you see yourself as a people-pleaser, not everyone appreciates your efforts. *See also* **trees.**

poppies

Remembrance of past hardships will put current difficulties into perspective. Things are not as bad as they seem. *See also sidebar on page 115.*

popularity

To feel that you are popular in a dream can indicate confidence or a need for attention. To perceive another as popular represents admiration.

porch

This symbol can reflect your generous and welcoming spirit and your ability to connect with those around you. Alternately, it can warn against disclosing personal information to casual acquaintances.

porcupine

To dream of a porcupine predicts a situation in which you will need to protect your integrity or that of someone close to you.

porpoise

See **dolphin.**

port

To dock a boat in a port means that after much searching, you will find the answers necessary to improve a relationship that seems doomed.

porthole

Gazing out of a porthole suggests that you are not seeing the whole picture. You should broaden your perspective to gain better insight. *See also* **telescope.**

pose

To strike a pose for a photo-grapher or an artist is a sign of confidence. It can also indicate that you are at a point in life well worth remembering. However, it warns against insincerity or deception.

postcard

A postcard represents limited information. To send a postcard suggests that a message you are trying to convey is confusing or incomplete.

post office

If you dream of working at or waiting in line at a post office, expect important business negotiations to go slowly. However, they will be fruitful if you are patient.

posture

Your posture in a dream reveals your mood or state of mind. Are you slouching (lethargic, depressed)? Straight-backed (strict, unbending)? Relaxed (graceful, flexible)?

potato

This symbolizes your basic needs in life. To cook or eat potatoes suggests that you are satisfied with what you have. To cultivate potatoes implies that you are digging for something more.

potholes

It has been a rough ride lately, but you have developed a keen awareness that will help smooth things out. *See also* **roads.**

potpourri

To dream of making potpourri means you need more variety in your life. Don't be afraid to mix things up, but keep in mind the importance of balance. *See also* **patterns, quilt.**

pots

See **pan.**

pottery

If you dream of being a potter, consider whether you are creating something new or trying to mold or manipulate what you deem imperfect. Broken pottery foretells problems that will be difficult to mend.

poverty

This image is often attributed to concerns over money, but it can also represent physical weakness or emotional emptiness. To experience poverty in a dream indicates that you can't muster what it takes to be at peace with yourself. To see conditions of poverty warns against dwelling on what could go wrong. The overall message is to appreciate what you have. *See also* **money, wealth.**

power

If you dream you have no power or that your power has been diminished, consider your interpretation of the word. To you, does "power" represent control or manipulation, or does it bring to mind subservience? Dreams that place you in a position of power mean that the focus will fall on your ability to influence (but not control) others.

prank

Playing a prank in a dream means you are not taking something or someone seriously enough. The cost to you will be alienation or embarrassment.

> *Your old men shall dream dreams, your young men shall see visions.*
> —Joel 2:28

praying

Though not necessarily related to religion, this is frequently a literal symbol that points to a spiritual search or a desperate cry for help.

preacher

This particular religious image (distinguished from, say, a rabbi, priest, minister, etc.) serves to remind you that actions speak louder than words; one-sided conversations are fruitless, and forcing your ideas on people can cause resentment.

pregnancy

If you are not actually pregnant, this dream theme often predicts that a developing project or endeavor will enhance your life. It is common for women who are pregnant to have odd or anxious dreams of pregnancy or delivery. *See also* **baby**, **birth.**

premature labor

Whether or not you are pregnant, this implies that you are working harder than is necessary. It can also symbolize that recent frightening news was merely a false alarm.

prescription

Though not necessarily health-related, a dream in which you are prescribed medication recommends that you seek advice from someone you hold in high regard. You will benefit from his or her experience and wisdom.

present

To interpret this dream word or image, consider the different uses and meanings of the word (it may not imply a gift). Are you concerned about a forthcoming presentation? Are you expected to be present somewhere? Do you feel unable to live in the present?

preserves

Making preserves represents both forethought and an appreciation for simpler times. You will soon enjoy the fruits of your labor. *See also* **jam.**

pressure

To feel physical pressure in a dream usually represents emotional burdens or obligations. Also consider the immediate implication of a physical ailment. If you dream that someone is pressuring you into something, remove yourself from that source of heat before making a decision.

price

Examining the price tag on an item reflects concerns over the worth of something or someone in your life. Consider the value of the object and whether the price you are paying is too high. *See also* **shopping.**

pride

This dream feeling indicates satisfaction with your approach or reaction to a difficult situation. It can also represent a content family life.

priest

This archetype usually conjures issues of spirituality, but it can also represent guilt or rigid ideals. *See also* **preacher, rabbi.**

prince/princess

To dream of meeting a prince or princess suggests that your life will soon be influenced (though not necessarily in a positive way) by an important man or woman. If you dream that you are a prince or princess, you have the power to control your destiny. *See also* **royalty.**

principal

This symbol reflects anxiety or guilt because you haven't met a certain standard. The interpretation of the homonym "principle" is similar.

prism

Looking through a prism warns against someone with a seemingly multifaceted personality. There is an underlying lack of dimension.

prison/prisoner

See also **imprisonment.**

privacy

Desiring or seeking privacy indicates that you are tired of being manipulated or coerced. You are ready to start making

> *Dream no small dreams. They have no power to stir the souls of men.*
> —Victor Hugo

your own decisions, and your life will improve as a result. Alternately, dreams of having private time can indicate regret or a fear of being exposed,

prize

To win a prize in a contest suggests that you work harder for what you want or need, because it won't just be handed to you. *See also* **lottery.**

probation

Dreams in which you are put on probation are often omens of a new phase in life. It is up to you whether this phase will be positive or negative.

procession

See **parade.**

prodigy

Don't be afraid to show off your intellect or talent. You you have a lot more to offer than people realize. However, brace yourself for potentially harsh scrutiny or judgment.

program

To program a recording device is a reminder to plan ahead. To program an alarm clock is a hint to be more alert. If you program a computer, you desire more control or authority, but to achieve that, pay closer attention to the tasks at hand (get with the program). *See also* **computer.**

project

It is common to dream of job-related projects, and these

The Dream Accident

Famed racecar driver A. J. Foyt credits a dream for his winning the 1967 Indianapolis 500—and claims it also saved his life. In his dream, Foyt was racing the last lap when a crash happened ahead of him, requiring him to brake suddenly and sharply. In the actual race the next day, he was taking the last lap and suddenly recalled his "dream accident" and adjusted his speed. As he rounded the corner, he encountered a crash just the way it had happened in his dream. If he hadn't slowed down, he would have been part of the crash. Fortunately, he maneuvered through it and went on to win the race.

images often are driven by stress or anxiety over deadlines or the quality of your work. But this type of dream can also serve to reinforce and encourage your efforts. Also, consider the word as a verb: Are you trying to project your insecurities on others?

promises

If you make and then break a promise, you are taking on too much responsibility at home or work (or both). If someone breaks a promise to you, beware of anything that appears too good to be true.

promotion

To dream that you receive a promotion indicates that your hard work is appreciated, even if it isn't rewarded. *See also* **job.**

propeller

The image of a propeller in motion means that you will soon be inspired to move forward in life after being stalled. Set your sights high! *See also* **engine.**

property

To dream that you own or buy property implies that someone is encroaching on your space. You are trying to claim what you feel belongs to you. To sell off property is to release burdensome feelings.

proposal/propose

A marriage proposal foretells an important commitment, which may not have to do with romance. Regardless, an important decision must be made or considered. If you are writing or submitting a proposal, be warned that a superior at work is taking credit for your efforts.

prosthesis

Dreams in which you wear a prosthetic device mean it is time to look at other options or for help on a home- or work-related project.

prune

The journey toward prosperity or success will proceed much faster once certain obstacles have been cleared (pruned) away. To dream of eating prunes foretells the elimination of emotional obstructions.

pry

To pry something open warns against insinuating yourself into the affairs of another. It can also suggest that you are ready to examine repressed or hidden emotions.

psychic

See **wise old man/wise old woman.**

puddle

Remember to take care of the small things in life before they accumulate into one big problem. Similarly, don't be afraid to bypass (or step over) people who are impeding your progress.

pulley

If you dream of operating a pulley, you have tedious tasks ahead. Rest assured, though: with little effort, a lot of work can be accomplished smoothly and efficiently. A broken pulley suggests that you single out members of the team who aren't pulling their weight.

pumpkin

Typically a symbol of the harvest season, a pumpkin emphasizes the importance of patience. To carve a pumpkin is to show pride for a job well done.

punch

If you dream of delivering a physical punch, you should be more assertive in order to be heard. To get punched predicts the arrival of surprising information. If preparing or serving punch at a celebration, consider whether working behind the scene serves your best interest.

punishment

You are punishing yourself with with negative thoughts that may include guilt, regret, doubt, etc. To mete out punishment indicates that you feel vengeful toward someone. Before you act on those feelings, carefully consider the repercussions.

puppet

To dream that you are a puppet means you should stop relying on others to get you where you want to be in life. If you are a puppeteer, you will be asked to help or pull strings for someone. Alternately, this suggests that you have a tendency to manipulate people into doing things they wouldn't normally do.

purple

This color symbolizes luxury, royalty, lawfulness, and order. It reflects your confidence and the respect you command from others. *See also sidebar on page 85.*

purr

To hear a cat purr is a sign of personal contentment. If a cat purrs while you are holding or petting it, expect to receive something you have long desired.

purse

This dream symbol usually represents ideas, identity, or the self. Examine the contents of the purse for further clues, and note whether it is full, messy, empty, etc. *See also* **wallet.**

putty

Working with putty signifies your efforts to fill gaps in your personal or professional life. Alternately, putty can imply that you are too malleable and should be less easily influenced by others. *See also* **clay, plaster, rubber.**

puzzle

If putting a puzzle together or working a puzzle, you will soon be dealing with a perplexing situation. It will come in bits and pieces, but eventually you will clear up the confusion.

pyramid

To dream of seeing or exploring a pyramid foretells access to mystery and arcane or lost knowledge. Look to those who are older and wiser to help you interpret this information. *See also* **ruins.**

pyrite

Also known as fool's gold, pyrite is an omen that what at first appears to be a good opportunity may turn out to be less than expected.

> Nothing can be so stupid, so impossible, or so unnatural that it cannot happen in a dream.
>
> —Cicero

Q

quagmire

You are on unsteady ground and risk getting in over your head. Take a step back, and don't get distracted by (or mired in) extraneous details. *See also* **quicksand.**

quail

Because this bird is so closely associated with hunting and hiding, as a dream symbol it reflects vulnerability and a fear of exposure.

Quaker

To dream that you live or dress like a Quaker reflects your desire for a simple and spiritual life. Alternately, whatever is making you "quake" in your waking life isn't as threatening as it seems.

qualms

You are second-guessing yourself about a recent decision but should trust your initial reaction. To behave without a qualm indicates insensitivity to the feelings of others.

quarantine

To dream that you are put into quarantine suggests that you withdraw from a potentially explosive situation that has little to do with you. Your input is being disregarded.

quarrel

See **argument, duel, quibble.**

quarry

A quarry symbolizes a source of wisdom or knowledge, and this image points out that those qualities lie within you and simply need to be mined. Alternately, this image reflects an emotional void or lack of self-awareness. *See also* **mine.**

quartet

To participate in a musical quartet signifies domestic harmony. It could also refer to the number four, which represents stability and strength.

quartz

Clear quartz symbolizes your keen perception and good judgment. Colored or smoky quartz suggests confusion and stubbornness in thoughts or behavior.

quasar

A quasar represents great stores of energy. Tap into yours, and your future promises to be bright. *See also* **meteor.**

quavering

A quavering voice is a sign of suppressed sadness or an indication of deceit. Does the person speaking sound depressed or nervous?

queen

The archetype represents equality, emotions, harmony, and intuitive guidance. A queen can also represent a female authority figure or a desire to achieve a higher social status. *See also* **royalty.**

quench

To dream of quenching your thirst is to seek satisfaction. To quench a fire is to deny passion toward someone or to deny yourself an opportunity for enjoyment. *See also* **drinking, thirst.**

quest

Embarking on a quest foretells a spiritual journey that will provide the meaning and purpose you have been searching for.

question

To question someone or something in a dream points to self-doubt. To be asked questions means you should be more forthcoming with your opinions.

quibble

Quibbling, in the context of a dream, represents minor, irritating distractions rather that arguments. Choose your battles wisely, and don't get caught up in petty issues.

quiche

Quiche is a symbol of nurturance and femininity. Baking or eating quiche

---

Bes to the Rescue

In ancient Egypt, the cheerful dwarf-god Bes was believed to protect households from nightmares and ominous dreams. The god's image was often carved into headboards of beds, and some people kept small statues of the god close to where they slept.

indicates that your feminine and masculine sides are well balanced.

quicksand

Beware of becoming stuck in a problematic situation that will prove difficult to get out of. If you are currently in such a situation, a calm demeanor will serve you better than an aggressive attitude. *See also* **quagmire.**

quicksilver

This dream image refers to a slippery or silver-tongued individual who should not be trusted. Quicksilver is also another name for Mercury, a planet that represents fire and passion.

quiet

A dream atmosphere that is noticeably quiet represents the calm before the storm. Prepare yourself for a period of trouble or unrest. If the quiet is disrupted mid-dream, consider adding some adventure to your life. *See also* **noise.**

quills

A quilled feather predicts that sharp-tongued comments will not fall lightly. If you dream of writing with a quill pen, beware that the words on the page could be read the wrong way.

quilt

Sewing a quilt is an omen of security and balance. You have an opportunity to bring together a group of people (family, friends, coworkers) that has been disconnected or discordant. If you encourage a cooperative effort among those involved, relationships will be mended and harmony will return. *See also* **knit, sewing.**

quitting

There are varying interpretations of this image. Giving up on something or someone can reflect a lack of confidence, desire, or motivation, especially if you quit a creative pursuit, a relationship, or a job. The dream can also point to fears of abandonment or a need to quit a bad habit. The overall message is: Don't give up on yourself or your dreams.

quiver

If you are holding a quiver full of arrows, you are on target with regard to reaching your goals. An empty quiver suggests a need to define your target more clearly. To feel the sensation of quivering implies nervousness. *See also* **arrow, target.**

quiz

The common dream image of taking a quiz suggests that you are anxious because your potential has been assessed inadequately or too quickly. The onus is on you to prove what you are capable of.

quote

To hear or repeat a quote reflects insecurity about expressing your thoughts or opinions. Try to identify and interpret the quotation for further clarification.

R

rabbi

Whether or not you are Jewish, this dream symbol reflects a desire for spiritual growth, but you are wary of being preached to. *See also* **preacher, priest.**

rabbit

A rabbit traditionally symbolizes luck, fertility, abundance, and productivity. Alternately, to dream of a rabbit that's hopping means you are taking shortcuts or have a fear of commitment. *See also* **frogs, jumping.**

rabies

You fear being attacked by someone who is particularly vicious. Do what you can to

Humanity needs practical men, who get the most out of their work, and, without forgetting the general good, safeguard their own interests. But humanity also needs dreamers, for whom the disinterested development of an enterprise is so captivating that it becomes impossible for them to devote their care to their own material profit. A well-organized society should assure to such workers the efficient means of accomplishing their task, in a life freed from material care and freely consecrated to research.

—Marie Curie

avoid such a confrontation, because the consequences will be serious and long-lasting.

raccoon

This dream symbol warns of covert behavior of any kind. It can also mean that you are masking your feelings. *See also* **disguise.**

race

If it's not a literal dream about a forthcoming competition, participating in a race suggests that you are more concerned about your destination than the journey toward it. It also represents a racing mind. Don't get ahead of yourself.

rack

As an instrument of torture, a rack represents guilt or regret. Do you fear humiliation or that someone will try to make an example of you? To see someone else on a rack warns against making indiscriminate judgments.

racket

Consider the possible meanings: A racket could warn against associating with people who appear unseemly or threatening. If the dream involves a tennis (or racquetball) racket, are you using it in a pleasant pursuit or as a means to defend yourself?

radar

Your personal radar (intuition) will serve you well. Pay attention to potentially dangerous or negative situations in your waking life. Try to discern the objects or people you detect on your dream radar, as they will provide clarification.

radiation

You radiate light and positive energy. To undergo radiation treatment or to be exposed to radiation reflects concerns of being scrutinized or exposed. Don't disregard the possibility of an actual physical ailment.

radio

Listen carefully, because you are hearing your inner voice. Disregard opinions (static) that

> *Friends cherish each other's hopes, they are kind to each other's dreams.*
> —Henry David Thoreau

don't sound right. A warning delivered via radio portends bad news that will take a while to reach you.

radish

To plant, harvest, or eat radishes emphasizes harsh or bitter relationships.

raffle

See **gambling, lottery.**

raft

Although usually associated with rescue, a raft can reflect self-imposed isolation or a lack of direction. You may feel lonely or that you are merely drifting through life. Alternately, floating on a raft indicates that you are working your way out of a sea of trouble. *See also* **boats.**

rage

This emotion is usually exaggerated in dreams and reflects frustration with yourself. What or whom has provoked this feeling has more significance than you think. *See also* **anger, hate.**

rags

Clean rags are an omen that you are ready to make better choices in your personal life. Dirty rags point to self-neglect.

raid

Being involved in a raid (e.g., if your home is raided) can indicate vulnerability or the feeling that you have something to hide. To conduct a raid indicates fear that important information is being kept from you.

railroad

An imminent journey will go smoothly. To stop at a railroad crossing indicates a minor but temporary setback that will require patience. On the other hand, this symbol reminds you to guard yourself: Don't be railroaded into doing something you are unsure of.

rain

Walking in the rain implies that persistent problems or worries will be washed away. To see or hear rain falling recommends that you release some of that pent-up emotion. *See also* **shower.**

rainbow

A rainbow reflects harmony, balance, and completion. It

represents a reprieve: You have expended considerable effort and learned difficult lessons.

raincoat

Disregard anything or anyone who tries to dampen your spirit.

rain forest

This dream image represents conflict: You have a lot to offer but feel that you are being used up.

raisins

Although you think a ripe opportunity has passed you by, better options remain. *See also* **grapes.**

rake

You will be asked to perform a repetitive and unsatisfying task at work or home (or in your community). Also consider the noun if it relates to someone who tries to get your attention with excessive behavior.

ram

This dream image warns against being overly assertive regarding a matter that requires a more subtle approach.

ramp

To dream of going up or down a ramp represents the easiest way into or out of a predicament.

ransack

This symbolizes pent-up anger and frustration. To walk into a ransacked room warns that someone close to you is losing control over his or her emotions. Beware of an outburst! *See also* **anger.**

ransom

To dream of being held for ransom indicates an over-inflated sense of self. Take time to contemplate your worth.

rash

Minor irritations are distracting you. Address them while they're relatively small. *See also* **insects, poison ivy.**

raspberries

If picking raspberries, expect blatant or inappropriate defiance from an unexpected source. If you are eating raspberries, you have the strength of character to deal with the situation.

rats

Your interpretation depends on how you feel about rats. For some people, they invoke fear and repulsion; for others, they represent experimentation, fertility, and the potential for discovery. Additionally, rats can signify a harried, chaotic situation at work or at home. *See also* **mouse.**

rattlesnake

See **serpent, snake.**

raven

A raven is widely considered a symbol of negativity, depression, or dark experiences.

razor

Is the blade sharp or dull? A sharp blade can represent a keen mind or cutting wit, but it could also point to someone with a sharp tongue. *See also* **cut, scissors.**

react

Are you reaching for something beyond your grasp? Consider the specific object and how it relates to your goals and desires.

reading

The text itself could hint at or be a direct message. This dream action is also associated with a search for knowledge or understanding, or a desire to broaden one's horizons.

rebirth

Dreams in which you feel that you have been reborn portend a spiritual or emotional awakening that could give you a fresh start in life.

rebound

If an object rebounds in a dream, it is a sign that you will quickly get your energy and drive back after a minor setback. It can also point to improvements in your health or financial situation.

receipt

This image symbolizes proof of payment. If you are looking at

Continued on page 222

Like Snowflakes, No Two Dream Interpretations Are Alike

Because your dreams are unique to you, the personal associations you have with their symbols and images help you interpret the messages. So if two people were to have the same dream, they would certainly interpret it in different ways. This is particularly true if one person has more experience with dream interpretation. Let's say Tom and Tanya have the same dream. Tom has been recording and interpreting his dreams for years and is familiar with how his dream self speaks to him. Tanya is just becoming acquainted with her dream self and isn't quite sure of all the messages it sends.

Their Dream Description: I am walking in the woods, carrying heavy file folders from work. I hear a dog barking, but I can't see it. I'm excited by the sound of the barking and curious to see if I know the dog. I drop the folders on the ground and climb a tree. From this vantage point, I can see the dog in the dis-tance, standing with its front paws on a large tree. It seems to be barking at something high in the branches.

Tom's Interpretation

When Tom went to bed that night, he was exhausted—not only from a stressful day at work but from poring over manuscripts he had taken home that evening. He's been doing a lot of work at home lately. As he fell asleep, he was curious about what his dreams that night might reveal.

Upon waking, Tom examined how he felt: Surprisingly, he was refreshed and invigorated. He then examined the various images and symbols: woods, work files, a dog, and trees. These immediately brought to mind happy childhood memories of summer vacations at his grandparents' cottage. He had spent many hours exploring the nearby woods with his dogs, looking for the best climbing trees. When he found one and navigated his way as far up as he could, his dogs would wait patiently for his safe return to solid ground. Tom has always appreciated the woods and equates it with his life-long love for animals and the relaxed, carefree days of his youth.

Upon further examination, Tom realized that the file folders represented his workload, and that by carrying them in the woods (or his "home"—a stress-free environment where he relaxes with his faithful dogs), he was invading his private or "comfortable" space with something that should be kept separate. In other words, he was allowing his work to dominate his time at home.

Tom took the advice from his dream and planned a rustic vacation with his dogs—no work allowed!

Tanya's Interpretation

Tanya had also had a stressful day at work and had been taking work home in an effort to pull together a proposal for an important but demanding client. It had not been going well. She went to bed tired and anxious—despite her nightly yoga routine, which usually leaves her relaxed and calm.

Tanya awakened perplexed by her dream. She had always lived in a city environment, and though she jogs through a nearby park almost every morning, she had never even considered climbing a tree, and she has never owned a dog. But Tanya knows that her dream is work-related because of the image of file folders. After she looked up the other symbols in her dream dictionary and mulled over the general meanings of *woods, trees,* and *dog,* she suddenly burst out laughing as she realized that her dream self had sent a playful message: While in the woods (which represents her workplace), Tanya "can't see the forest for the trees." But by climbing the tree, she gained a better perspective and can "see the bigger picture." She knew then that she should drop the idea she had been proposing to her client, recognizing that she had been "barking up the wrong tree." That day, she started working on a new approach.

Tom's and Tanya's interpretations, though quite different, are equally valid. Both offered them productive advice, which they acted on to their benefit.

receipt, *continued from page 219*

a receipt, you will be recognized for your contributions. To look for lost receipts reflects concerns over monetary matters.

reception

To dream of attending a wedding reception predicts success with business or social partnerships. A reception given to honor you foretells an unexpected windfall.

recipe

This dream symbol suggests that everything you need to proceed with a plan or project is available. However, old, tattered, or unreadable recipes reflect sadness over lost loved ones or long-held traditions.

record

The interpretations of this symbol depend on the context of the dream. If you are listening to records, consider the feelings the music evokes—relaxation, enthusiasm, or perhaps reflection? Whichever it is, you need more of it in your life. To dream of recording or keeping a record of something is a reminder from your dream self of an important event. *See also* **calendar, schedule.**

recycling

This can indicate your resourcefulness and ability to make practical use of things thought worthless or damaged. Something thought to be of no value will turn out to be very useful under different circumstances. Alternately, it can imply that you should let go of objects or relationships that no longer serve a purpose. *See also* **garbage, junkyard.**

red

The color red often represents energy, physical strength, and fiery emotions, but it can also be a way of telling you not to proceed with something. *See also sidebar on page 85.*

redwood

To dream that you are among redwood trees symbolizes your endurance, patience, and high ideals. *See also* **trees.**

reef

Are you caught on the reef or exploring it? This dream symbol can reflect your desire or need for freedom or your curiosity and sense of adventure.

referee

If you are the referee, you have the ability and responsibility to resolve an unsettled situation in your waking life. To simply see a referee in a dream suggests that you have conflicting thoughts about something and could benefit from the advice of another.

reflection

If you dream of seeing yourself in a mirror, consider whether it is a true reflection or one that's distorted. What you see is likely the way you want others to perceive you. *See also* **mirror.**

refrigerator

A full refrigerator portends social celebrations, but an empty one can reflect a lack of feeling or emotional warmth toward someone who needs your attention.

rehearsal

To dream that you are rehearsing for a performance suggests that you are unsure how to react to something in your waking life. Make sure your mind is set before you proceed—it could save you from considerable embarrassment.

reincarnation

If you are reincarnated in a dream, what new form have you taken? If it's a person, consider whether he or she has qualities you admire or dislike. They may reflect the ways in which you would like to change yourself. If you take the form of an animal, is its demeanor passive or aggressive?

Recurring Dreams

Dreams that play the same events over and over are referred to as recurring dreams (think of the Bill Murray movie *Groundhog Day*). It often feels as if you are talking with someone who isn't paying attention, but that someone is actually you. Another example: Have you ever been chased in a dream and can't seem to get away? When you are running from someone or something unknown to you, you are running from yourself. However, denying emotions or situations won't get you anywhere, and it's best to turn around and face them.

rejection

This common dream feeling most often directly reflects fears or insecurities about being rejected in your waking life. Examine who is rejecting you for a clearer interpretation.

relatives

Dreams that involve relatives aren't necessarily about the family members themselves but may instead represent objects that relate to something or each other. Connections and patterns are also indicated by dreams that involve relatives. When specific family members are present, your perception of (or reaction to) them in the dream often closely reflects your real-life feelings toward them (although some people have never recognized these feelings). *See also individual family members,* **family.**

religion

Dreams about religion, whether your own faith or another, are often associated with a desire to be more spiritual. Alternately, though, they can represent the rejection or acceptance of conformity and compliance.

remote control

This dream image seems silly but is suprisingly common. If you're using a remote control, you likely have all you need at your fingertips. Alternately, it suggests that you have a controlling nature or want to be the sole decision-maker in the household. To operate a remote-controlled object (car, plane, etc.) implies that you can easily manage situations without much help from others.

renovate

Dreams in which you are renovating something imply that you are examining your life and recognize a need for change. It may be difficult, but your efforts will ultimately make your life better.

rent

To dream of paying rent is a reminder that you owe someone a favor. If your rent is overdue, greater attention to your

> *The world is full of kings and queens who blind your eyes and steal your dreams.*
> —Anonymous

finances will alleviate a lot of stress in your life.

repetition

It is common to dream about doing something repeatedly but accomplishing nothing, and this often reflects the tedium and routine of everyday life. The message is: You are stuck. Add some variety to your routine.

report

To write a report in a dream indicates a need to organize your thoughts regarding a confusing situation. If it is apparent what you are writing, clues can be gleaned from the words themselves. To dream of reporting or relaying information to someone reflects a need to be better heard.

reptile

See **lizard, snake.**

repulsion

This is a contrary feeling that suggests you reexamine the merit of a current action or idea. Alternately, the feeling can reflect low self-worth or offense at the behavior of another.

reputation

Dreams in which your reputation is called into question often reflect guilt or anxiety regarding something in your waking life. It can represent false accusations, whether made by you or against you. *See also* **gossip.**

rescue

If you dream of being rescued, you likely feel stuck in an unpleasant relationship or situation in your waking life and don't know how to get out of it. If you rescue someone, expect that someone will ask for help or a favor. *See also* **lifeguard.**

reservation

Dreams about making reservations can imply that you are uneasy about forgetting or being left out of a social situation. Alternately, it can mean that you are concerned about a recent decision or are having second thoughts about it.

reservoir

This symbolizes your personal storehouse of energy. If the reservoir is full, you have the stamina to finish a project or reach a goal. If empty, you should explore what is missing from your life.

resignation

To resign from a job, public office, or any other position indicates that you feel ineffective or inadequate and desire to change your life for the better. You may feel resigned to your fate, but it doesn't have to be that way—you have many options.

restaurant

A restaurant can be a symbol of emotional nourishment. Consider whether you're dining alone or with a group and if the situation makes you feel tense or relaxed. To gaze through a window of a full restaurant suggests a need for more social interaction.

restraint

See **paralysis.**

resuscitation

To dream of resuscitating someone suggests that you need to breathe life into a tired relationship or situation. To be resuscitated foretells personal revitalization that will bring many benefits.

retire

Dreams in which you retire from a job indicate that something has run its course and is no longer useful. Another meaning is that you have been working too hard and need some time away.

retreat

Whether you dream of retreating from a situation or that you are attending a retreat, you clearly have a lack of drive or energy that needs to be addressed.

reunion

This common dream theme suggests that you will soon make important connections, either with alienated relatives or long-lost friends (or vice versa).

revenge

To seek revenge in a dream is often an exaggerated symbol that simply reflects the frustrations you feel about minor problems in your waking life. It would be wise to take responsibility for your actions and not blame others.

revolution

This dream symbol often reflects emotional conflicts. If you participate in a revolution, expect major changes in a troubled personal relationship. If you oppose the revolution, your problems will persist and grow.

revolving door

To enter a revolving door may indicate feelings that you are getting nowhere in life despite your efforts to move forward. Alternately, it can represent your tendency to go with the flow or a dependence on others to lighten your load.

reward

If someone offers you a reward, your work and abilities will be praised by others. *See also* **money.**

rhinestones

This is typically a symbol of imitation or deception. To receive rhinestones as a gift suggests false friendships. Someone is not who you think they are.

rhinoceros

If in the wild, a rhinoceros is a symbol of fertility. A rhinoceros in a zoo reflects frustration, anger, and a feeling of being powerless.

rhubarb

Unexpected but welcome visitors may soon arrive bearing abundant gifts.

rhythm

See **drumming.**

ribbon

A tied ribbon symbolizes promises that will be kept. An untied ribbon implies that plans or projects will have to

> You see things, and you say, "Why?" But I dream things that never were, and I say, "Why not?"
>
> —George Bernard Shaw

be finalized sooner than you thought.

rice

You may soon hear of a hasty wedding, possibly an elopement. To eat rice in a dream may be an indication that you would feel better by watching what you eat. *See also* **food.**

rich

See **affluence, wealth.**

riddle

If trying to solve a riddle, you will soon be enlightened about a perplexing situation. To tell a riddle implies that you are keeping important information from someone.

riding

If you are riding a horse, bicycle, etc., skillfully, it foretells success using inborn talents. If you are riding with difficulty, expect to face obstacles in

---

A Psychic President

As you pay closer attention to your dreams and maintain a record of them, you may discover that some seem to predict events. Many people refer to such dreams as "psychic," "prophetic," or "precognitive" (and to similar thoughts in their waking lives as "premonitions"). Abraham Lincoln often spoke of his psychic dreams. Here is one:

In 1865, President Lincoln claimed he'd had a dream in which he heard muffled noises that sounded as if people were weeping. In his dream, he got out of bed and went to search for the source of the sounds. When he entered the East Room of the White House, he saw scores of mourners gathered around a coffin on a raised platform, which was guarded by soldiers. The face of the body in the casket was covered. Lincoln asked one of the guards, "Who has died here?" The guard answered, "Why, sir, it's the president. He was killed by an assassin." Two weeks later, President Lincoln was assassinated by John Wilkes Booth. After his death, Lincoln's coffin lay on a platform in the East Room, guarded by soldiers.

the workplace that you will ultimately learn from.

rifle

See **duel, gun.**

ring

Any kind of ring represents completion, union, and inclusiveness. To dream of wearing a ring foretells a harmonious relationship. To give a ring as a gift indicates your desire to better connect with someone, though not necessarily in a romantic way. *See also* **circles.**

rink

Skating in a rink predicts effortless success in business. If watching a sport played in a rink, stiff competition will encourage you to overcome self-imposed limitations.

riot

To see or hear of a riot foretells strife in the workplace. To participate in a riot suggests that you need to express pent-up feelings. *See also* **raid.**

rising

To feel that you are rising off the ground represents your lighthearted nature and willingness to take the higher road in matters of dispute. You have a better perspective. *See also* **floating, levitation.**

risk

See **gambling, lottery.**

ritual

A ritual points to your commitment to and appreciation of time-honored traditions. If you exhibit ritualistic behavior in a dream, you should strive to give up negative habits.

rival

Dreaming of a rival means you will soon experience a confrontation. To outperform a rival predicts difficult tasks that will ultimately bring benefits.

river

This dream image represents your life energy. If swimming in the river, are you going with the flow or fighting the current? Are you in over your head or afraid to get your feet wet?

roaches

See **insects, itch.**

roads

Dreams that feature roads usually refer to one's destiny

or path in life. Consider the condition of the road (e.g., smooth pavement or dirt, straight or winding, wide or narrow) as these features often indicate the ease with which you will reach your goals. Roadblocks represent obstacles that require patience.

road signs

Road signs in a dream are fairly literal indications of how you should proceed in life, whether it's with a relationship, a business project, or a family situation.

roast

To roast meat or other types of food predicts that you will have to question the integrity of a friend's word. Someone is talking behind your back.

robbery

To be involved in a robbery (whether you are the perpetrator or the victim) suggests that the credit you deserve is being given to someone else.

robin

If you dream of this bird, expect a renewed interest in life and perhaps a fresh start.

robot

You likely feel that some activity has become routine and boring and that you are just going through the motions. It can also point to a lack of emotion toward someone.

rocket

To dream of traversing space in a rocket implies that you would like to find an easier way out of a current situation. Alternately, it points to your drive and ambition—you operate on full throttle.

rocking chair

Most typically a symbol of ease and relaxation, dreams involving a rocking chair often indicate a need for emotional comfort. It can also be a symbol of retirement.

rocks

This symbol, particularly if you're climbing among several, often reflects your stability, strength, and endurance. The image can also point to rigid attitudes and emotions.

rodeo

To ride a bronco in a rodeo reflects your desire to control a situation that is quickly getting out of hand. To watch a rodeo implies that you enjoy the unpredictability of life.

roller coaster

This common dream symbol often corresponds to insecurities you have in your waking life, likely related to questions about your future, or what lurks around the bend. Alternately, riding and enjoying a roller coaster symbolizes your adventurous spirit and ability to roll with the punches.

rolling pin

Using a rolling pin reflects an attempt to smooth out the rough edges of a personal (romantic or family) relationship and turn it into something positive.

romance

This is one of the most common dream feelings, yet it isn't often a literal one. To have romantic feelings toward someone (known in your waking life or not) can reflect a variety of feelings (e.g., respect, envy, anxiety). It can also represent a need for affection or closer personal relationships.

roof

To dream about being under the shelter of a roof signifies the safety and security you feel in your waking life. If you are perched on top of a roof, consider whether you feel empowered (on top of the world) or vulnerable. To repair a leaking roof implies that you should attend to persistent family issues.

room

This particular dream symbol represents areas of your life that need attention. If the room is familiar, what feelings does it evoke? If unfamiliar, do you feel lost in the room (implying intimidation) or comfortable (implying a willingness to explore)? Explore objects in the room for further symbolism.

> *Dreams are the touchstones of our characters.*
> —Henry David Thoreau

rooster

A rooster is an omen for monetary gains made through persistent pursuit. To hear a rooster crowing warns that boasting of your achievements may evoke jealousy or resentment in others.

roots

To dream of the roots of plants or trees signifies that you are examining the genesis of a current situation and its development over time. On the other hand, it can point to an appreciation for your heritage or deep-rooted traditions. To yank roots (or weeds) from the ground indicates a desire to move beyond your current situation.

rope

This is a dream symbol that can represent either attachment or restrictions—or both. Examine how the rope is used, who is using it, and whether the rope is strong or threadbare.

rosary

Even among people who are not familiar with this religious symbol, a rosary indicates wish fulfillment or introspection.

It can also signify a need for security and nurturing.

rose

The meaning behind this powerful dream symbol depends on your interpretation of the flower. For many, roses can represent fond attention or love, while for others they evoke images of absence or death. Also consider the color of the roses; there are interpretations as to the meanings of each, but how you feel about them is what really matters. *See also sidebar on page 115.*

rosemary

This herb relates to lost loved ones or sadness over the passing of time.

rot

To see something rot in a dream is a fairly literal symbol of wasted emotions and efforts. Consider whether the object, situation, or person depicted as rotting (or rotten) is worth your time and consideration.

roulette

See **gambling.**

rowboat

See **boats.**

rowing

This dream symbol corresponds to the effort you put forth in your personal and professional life. *See also* **boats.**

royalty

To dream of someone considered royalty suggests that you may soon be treated with respect and reverence, whether or not you are worthy of it. This dream image can also signify your desire for authority or a better lifestyle.

rubber

This dream image can have contrary meanings. To feel rubbery in a dream may symbolize your emotional flexibility and refusal to be influenced by people's harsh words. On the other hand, it can imply that you comply too easily to the whims of others.

ruby

A ruby is a symbol of good luck and vibrancy, particularly in romantic situations.

ruffles

To dream that you are dressed in ruffled clothing implies that frivolous details may be distracting you from more important matters.

rug

See **floor.**

ruins

If you dream of visiting architectural ruins, you are fulfilling a need to connect with your ancestral past. If you are walking among ruins, you are searching for some sort of meaning in your waking life. Alternately, this symbol can represent a negative emotional attitude of futility.

ruler

As a measuring tool, a ruler can represent the gauge by

All dreams spin out from the same web.
—Hopi Proverb

which you judge others, or it can imply a concern that you aren't meeting someone's expectations. Dreams of a ruler in reference to an authority figure can be interpreted in the same way.

running

This common dream theme is often the result of the perceived paralysis you feel during REM sleep—i.e., that you are trying to run toward or away from something but aren't getting anywhere. But it also points to waking-life desires to escape from or be involved in something and an inability to realize those desires.

rushing

This dream feeling indicates anxiety over meeting deadlines or everyday expectations. It is often accompanied by a sense that you are achieving little in the process.

rust

To dream of scrubbing the rust off of something indicates that you are trying to let go of outdated ideas or behaviors. To

---

Digging Through Dream Messages

In 1893, renowned German–American archaeologist H. V. Hilprecht was having trouble classifying two inscripted agate fragments excavated from a Babylonian temple because he had only sketches to work from. He theorized that they were rings that had been worn on the fingers of a Babylonian priest, but he was never quite satisfied with his translation.

Soon after that, Hilprecht reported a dream in which he was visited by an ancient priest who told him the fragments had in fact been part of a votive cylinder that was cut to make earrings for a Babylonian king. When Hilprecht was finally able to see and examine the fragments, he knew that the dream priest had been correct. The inscription read: "To the god Ninib, son of Bel, his lord, has Kurigalzu, pontifex of Bel, presented this."

dream that rust is forming on something reflects behaviors or actions that no longer serve a purpose.

sabotage

Dreams of sabotage reflect paranoia and self-doubt. Make the decision that feels right to you, because the input of others could prove disastrous. *See also* **suicide.**

sack

If you dream of an empty sack, you lack confidence, but affirmations from others won't fill it—that's your task. A full sack represents emotional and financial security. *See also* **bag.**

sacrifice

Sacrifice points to emotional strain. You are investing a lot in a personal relationship, but the other person is not. Sacrifice can also be an exaggerated symbol suggesting that compromises will restore harmony.

saddle

A saddle predicts that you will acquire a position of leadership—you have shown that you can take the reins. If you are sitting in a saddle, you will soon encounter a situation that requires you to guide someone who seems lost. *See also* **leadership.**

sadness

As a dream symbol, sadness can point to dissatisfaction or loneliness. In your waking life, you are likely carrying a heavy emotional weight. *See also* **depression.**

safari

This represents your adventurous spirit. You are treading through unfamiliar territory in a job or a relationship. The best map to consult in this situation? Your instincts.

safe

To dream of a safe symbolizes a desire or need for stability. If the safe is closed or locked, circumstances are within your control. If it is open, you fear that everyone will see what's inside (of you).

safety

If you are concerned for your safety in a dream, you are dissatisfied with or unsure of your direction in life, and it is causing intense anxiety. If you are worried for someone else's safety, pay better attention to people close to you—their cries for help are going unnoticed.

safety net

A safety net represents preparedness in a crisis. To hold a safety net for someone means you are equipped to handle conflict. To fall into a safety net means you can rely on the support of others. *See also* **trapeze.**

saffron

Saffron is a symbol of loyalty. If you dream of eating food made with saffron, someone has spoken of you as a particularly good friend.

sage

If you dream of sage, wisdom and clarity with regard to an important decision are close at hand. Look within yourself.

sailing

Sailing represents a need for change. In your professional or personal life, why not try to navigate new waters? Consider the size of the sailboat for clues about the degree of change required. *See also* **boats, ocean, water.**

sailor

Dreams that involve this figure indicate that someone will enter your life for a short time and leave a lasting impression—it's not clear whether that's good or bad. A sailor in a dream can also represent a desire for independence and freedom.

saint

To envision someone you perceive to be a saint represents a cry for help. Don't hesitate to reach out for assistance. This can also be a request for attention from your spiritual side. *See also* **angel, praying.**

salary

It is likely that you are preoccupied not only with

financial matters but also with being acknowledged as an individual. Perhaps you feel undervalued—emotionally or otherwise. *See also* **job, peanuts.**

sale

This symbolizes the give-and-take nature of your closest relationships. Pay attention to what kinds of transactions take place in the dream. Are you buying or selling? *See also* **shopping.**

salt

To dream of salt means that you or someone close to you will be recognized and honored for their wisdom. It can also represent a down-to-earth attitude. *See also* **food, pepper.**

sanctuary

This dream symbol indicates a need for retreat or escape from a particularly trying situation. Alternately, it can reflect your tendency to escape conflict and avoid confrontation.

sand

Sand represents shifting emotions or the passing of time. Perhaps you are not on solid ground in a friendship or a relationship with a family member, and it is leaving you anxious. A dream of sand dunes suggests that your perspective on a wavering issue will shift or that your opinion is inconsistent or unreliable. *See also* **beach, hourglass.**

sandals

Wearing simple sandals reflects your desire to escape responsibility. You may be feeling tied down and need more freedom. *See also* **feet.**

sandcastle

To see a sandcastle foretells of carefree days. To build a sandcastle implies that you are spending too much time daydreaming or fantasizing to the point that important personal issues are being ignored.

> *What if nothing exists and we're all in somebody's dream? Or what's worse, what if only that fat guy in the third row exists?*
> —Woody Allen

sandpaper

Using sandpaper indicates that you are bothered by someone with an abrasive personality. Used sandpaper predicts that minor annoyances will go away.

sandwich

To see or eat a sandwich foretells that you will be caught in the middle of a compromising situation. To make a sandwich warns against getting involved in a matter that does not concern you.

Santa Claus

Regardless of your religious or spiritual beliefs, a dream of a Santa Claus figure reflects your desire to make everything right. Do the best you can, and don't make unrealistic promises.

sapphire

This gemstone means that an interesting opportunity will come to you out of the blue.

sarcasm

Sarcastic comments in a dream reflect defensiveness or insecurity. Consider what was said, who was involved, and the topic of conversation.

satan

See **devil.**

satellite

A satellite in the night sky predicts a reunion with a long-lost friend. Or it may mean that through newly gained recognition, you will attract influential contacts or opportunities.

sauna

You have been sweating over an issue and are finally about to reveal it. *See also* **heat.**

saw

A handsaw implies hard work with little recognition or reward. A chain saw indicates that old ties are being severed and new relationships are forming. Also consider the past tense of "see."

saxophone

If you are playing a saxophone in a dream, rest assured that current conflicts will soon smooth themselves out. To hear saxophone music indicates a need for relaxation and contemplation. *See also* **music.**

scab

*See **bandage, injury, wound**.*

scale

Stepping onto a scale reflects an imbalance in your life that is causing distress. Alternately, it points to your ability to negotiate and tip issues to your advantage.

scandal

You are worried that those closest to you will learn something that will change your relationship with them. Release whatever you are holding on to; people will be more forgiving than you imagine.

scar

If the scar is on your body, painful memories are fading or hurt feelings are on the mend. To see someone with a scar is a warning to approach that person carefully in word and deed. *See also **injury**.*

scarecrow

This seemingly strange image means that someone is trying to mislead you or keep you from knowing the truth. Don't take their word at face value. *See also **birds**.*

scarf

If you are wearing a scarf around your neck, you have a desire to reveal something about yourself but are hesitant to do so. To wear a scarf on your head indicates your ability to keep your emotions under control. *See also **neck**.*

schedule

Consulting a schedule reveals that you are feeling stressed or disorganized and can't find a way to make things easier. To compile things into a schedule reflects your ability to keep things on track. *See also **calendar**.*

school

This common dream symbol often represents how smart you think you are. If you dream of waking up late for school

Those Crazy School Dreams

Most people have unusual (sometimes disturbing) dreams about their days in elementary school, junior high, high school, or college, and many of these dreams are recurring (that is, you have them frequently and throughout your life). Here are some common themes:

★ It is your first day of a new school year (but you are not in a new school), and you don't have a copy of your class schedule. You have a vague idea of the room(s) you are supposed to go to, but you can't find any of them.

★ You don't know in which hallway your locker is located, or you can't remember the combination to your lock. Even if you think you know the combination, your lock won't open, and everything you need is in the locker.

★ You are late for a class and the door of the room is closed. When you finally muster the courage to walk in, you find that the room is empty.

★ It is the day of an important exam, but when you sit at your desk, you suddenly realize you have never attended the class and have no knowledge of the subject. When the exam is put before you, you can't even decipher the language.

Students aren't the only ones who have haunting dreams about school. Teachers recall them just as frequently, but their perspective is, of course, different. Here is a common one:

★ In preparation for a new school year, you have spent days organizing and decorating your classroom. However, when you enter the room on the first day, the walls are bare and the only people seated at the desks are a few scowling parents and the school principal.

The general explanation for these dreams is simple: You are under a lot of stress or feel particularly scrutinized in your waking life. The good news is that you have likely survived the pressures of school well, and you can expect to do the same as you face your current challenges.

or missing classes, you are insecure about the knowledge you have gained through life. If you are lost in a school, you are not relying on lessons you have already learned. People who didn't finish school or those who didn't have an opportunity to attend college often dream of sitting at child-size desks or being taught their ABC's. *See also sidebar on page 240,* **university.**

school bus

A school bus represents opportunities for personal growth. Are you riding in the back or the front of the bus, or have you missed the bus once again? *See also* **bus.**

scientist

If you dream of being a scientist, you may be too rigid in thought and would be wise to acknowledge your creativity and intuition. Alternately, this image emphasizes that someone is depending on your advice.

scissors

The image symbolizes cutting away the ties that bind. If you are using scissors, you are ridding your life of unnecessary burdens. Unused scissors

in a dream indicate that it's time to decide what should be eliminated. *See also* **cut.**

scold

To be scolded in a dream is a warning to be cautious when dealing with an authority figure. Don't step on someone's toes or go over that person's head. To scold someone in a dream reflects a need for control.

score

Keeping score on a scorecard is to contemplate what is fair in life. Scoring a goal in a sports event means you will win someone's favor. Also consider the use of the word as a sexual metaphor. *See also* **sports.**

scorpion

Avoid putting on an intimidating front or using sharp words in an attempt to intimidate people. They know you're not as tough as you seem. *See also* **lobster.**

scrapbook

Looking through a scrapbook in a dream suggests that once forgotten memories will be brought to your attention, and you will consider them with a different perspective. You have grown as a person and will be able to see the bigger picture. *See also* **photograph.**

scream

To wake yourself with a scream or to dream of screaming is a plea from your dream self to pay attention to something that seems too disturbing to deal with. To hear a distant scream is to become aware that someone is unable to communicate his or her frustration.

screw/screwdriver

A screw symbolizes discernment. You have the ability to sort through information and focus on what's important. If you dream of using a screwdriver, you will soon have the opportunity to make important business connections—make sure your approach is straightforward.

sculpting

Sculpting is a way to emphasize that you are responsible for your own destiny. If you are viewing a sculpture, you have not yet fully realized that you have choices and can mold your future in any way. *See also* **clay, pottery.**

sea

This common dream symbol represents your current emotional state. Is the water clear, murky, calm, or turbulent? Are you sailing smoothly, or are you lost? Also consider the homonym "see." Are you ignoring something that's apparent to others? *See also* **ocean, water.**

seahorse

The image of a seahorse implies that you have unique abilities that lurk just below the surface. Don't be afraid to express your individuality.

seal

You have a playful, adventurous spirit: Nurture that gift, but realize that there are serious situations in life that need your attention (this is particularly true if the seal is barking).

searching

This is a common and often literal symbol: What in your

waking life is lacking or unfulfilled? Alternately, you need something to complete a project or bring harmony to a situation. Keep looking.

searchlight

Seeing or using a searchlight points to your ability to guide people through rough times. Close friends or colleagues may soon ask for your assistance. *See also* **light, lighthouse.**

seashells

If you are collecting seashells in a dream, expect to hear from a far-away friend or relative— someone you have missed dearly. *See also* **beach, ocean.**

seasons

To dream of changing seasons reveals concerns with aging or personal growth. You may be worried that time is passing

too quickly and you are not accomplishing all you set out to do. Alternately, you are ready to make significant changes in your life. *See also individual seasons.*

seatbelt

If you are wearing a seatbelt, your restraint and patience in a personal conflict will benefit you. An unbuckled seatbelt indicates indifference regarding that conflict's outcome. A vehicle without seatbelts predicts a precarious situation that requires slow caution. *See also* **car.**

seaweed

There are many ideas floating around in your mind. They are tangled, conflicting, or confusing. Sort through them before they pull you under. *See also* **ivy, vine.**

secrets

In dreams, secrecy can indicate shyness or low self-esteem. Are you concerned with what people think of you? Keeping secrets suggests that you are withholding information out of shame or guilt, or perhaps you think you have sole access to something. Chances are that a lot of other people are aware of what you are hiding.

sedation

A dream in which you feel sedated implies that you are overwhelmed by expectations. On the other hand, it can point to boredom and a need for more excitement in life. *See also* **painkillers, pills.**

seduction

To be seduced means you are susceptible to being distracted from certain goals. If you seduce someone, you desire immediate satisfaction, which will ultimately prove unsatisfying.

seeds

Seeds represent ideas that could develop into successful endeavors. If you are planting seeds, you have hope and faith in your future. Be attentive to ensure that things continue to grow and flourish. *See also* **plants, trees.**

seesaw

To ride on a seesaw indicates that your mood will drastically fluctuate for a time: up one day, down the next. Only you can restore balance.

selling

See **buying, shopping.**

separation

Being separated from something or someone means there is a rift between your emotions and intuition. What you feel like doing in a personal relationship or business venture does not align with what you are required to do.

sequoia

See **redwood, trees.**

serpent

A serpent is a common dream image that has several meanings. If you are trying to incubate a dream for healing, a serpent is a good omen because it traditionally symbolizes a caduceus (snakes entwined around a staff), which represents the professional field of medicine. Serpents also depict enlightenment, as representatives of *kundalini*

(energy traveling up the spine). If depicted in a Christian context, a serpent warns of temptation. A serpent may also have sexual connotations. *See also* **snake.**

servant

To employ a servant means you like to dominate social interactions. Let others express themselves and listen to what they are saying. If you dream of being a servant, you are someone who gets lost in the shuffle; be sure to speak up for yourself. *See also* **housekeeper.**

service

In a dream, providing a service for someone (regardless of the task) indicates that you are feeling unappreciated or undercompensated. Make sure you are appropriately compensated (financially or emotionally) for your time and effort.

sewing

Use your know-how to stitch up a relationship or situation that seems to be falling apart. *See also* **knit.**

This Is No Fish Tail!

Harvard professor Jean Louis Agassiz was compiling a list of fossil fish when he came across a strange, incomplete specimen. After spending frustrating weeks trying to identify and classify it, he had the same dream on consecutive nights. In the dream, he could see the mysterious fish clearly, down to the most minute physical detail. But upon waking on those two mornings, he was unable to recall the dream image. At some point the following night, with pen and paper at his side, he awoke with a feeling of excitement. He then proceeded, and in total darkness, to draw a sketch of his dream fish. The next day when he returned to his lab and compared his sketch to the unidentified specimen, Agassiz discovered that the dream had provided him with the details he needed to make a sound classification.

sex

Sex is a universal dream image that reflects the basic human desire or need for intimacy and connection. However, as a dream symbol, it is often overanalyzed or misinterpreted. As with any other dream image (whether it's recurring or just occasional), the person or people involved are less important than the feelings the dream evokes. Those elements may give you insight into what you are suppressing in your waking life.

shade

To dream of relaxing in the shade reflects the heated demands of work or household duties. To dream of raising or lowering window shades often reflects whether you are an introvert or extrovert. *See also* **blindness, curtain.**

shadow

This symbol usually represents negative aspects of your

> *We are not hypocrites in our sleep.*
> —William Hazlitt, "On Dreams"

personality. A shadow can also reflect intimate thoughts. To dream that you are being shadowed points to guilt or paranoia. *See also* **light.**

shaking

To physically shake in a dream means you are apprehensive about a recent or pending decision. To dream of shaking something reflects your desire to change a bothersome situation.

shame

This common dream feeling indicates that you have been carrying regret or shame for past mistakes. To prevent its recurrence, go easy on yourself. *See also* **embarrassment, guilt.**

shampoo

Dreams in which you use shampoo on yourself or someone else suggest that you adopt a new approach to a troubling situation. Clear your head and preconceived notions and look at it with a fresh perspective. *See also* **hair.**

shamrock

If you see a shamrock in your dream, you should be more aggressive in pursuing your goals rather than relying on chance or lucky breaks. *See also* **clover.**

sharks

This dream symbol commonly represents intimidation, aggression, and greed, but for greater personal meaning, consider the feelings it evokes: power, fear, or vulnerability? *See also sidebar on page 54.*

shaving

To dream that you are shaving portends a turning point in your way of thinking or behaving—you are about to exert more control. Alternately, it may reflect a lack of personal growth because you are unwilling to accept change.

shed

This symbol implies that you should discard outdated attitudes that no longer serve a purpose. It can also represent aspects of your personality that should be brought to light.

sheep

The presence of sheep in a dream illustrates the way you behave in a group. Are you an assertive leader, or do you act sheepishly around others?

Consider if you tend to go along with the crowd but would rather break free and do things on your own. *See also* **cattle, parade.**

shelf

A cluttered or full shelf represents issues that have been put off but need to be dealt with before they become too burdensome. An empty shelf represents a lack of motivation—find something that excites you and pursue it.

shell

See **seashells.**

shelter

This dream symbol represents protection—whether you have that need or you feel someone needs your protection. If you are in the shelter, consider whom, if anyone, is with you.

shield

Wielding a shield reflects newfound confidence that will enable you to stand up to criticism or judgment that has previously caused you to cower. Alternately, hiding behind a shield indicates that you are being held back because of insecurities.

shine

See **polishing.**

ship

To see a ship on the horizon means that exciting news is coming your way. To dream of being a passenger on a ship indicates that you are seeking a new direction in life. Before you make any drastic changes, consider the weather and water conditions. *See also* **boats, sailing, water.**

shirt

Putting on or wearing a shirt indicates that you guard your emotions where affairs of the heart are concerned. Being shirtless can indicate either bravado or personal sacrifice. *See also* **clothing, disguise.**

shock

See **electricity.**

shoes

People often dream about wearing (or not wearing) shoes—either image represents your personal progress. What is the condition of the shoes? If they are old and worn, you are in a comfortable place in life. If they are new or unfamiliar, you should consider taking things in a different direction. If you are wearing another person's shoes, be conscious of making hasty judgments of character. Mismatched shoes or shoes worn on the wrong feet represent indecisiveness or confusion over an important issue. Wearing no shoes when they are required implies a disregard for authority that will ultimately serve you poorly. *See also* **barefoot, footprints.**

shooting star

This dream symbol represents hope and often suggests that personal wishes will soon be fulfilled. *See also* **star.**

shopping

Shopping in a dream implies that you are searching for something to make your life complete. This often relates to matters of the heart but can also point to professional or financial goals. To shop without making a purchase represents a stalemate. *See also* **spending.**

shoreline

If you are at sea, the shoreline represents safety or familiarity—there is someone or something in your life you can always rely on. If you are on the shore looking out to sea, you may feel restless but are too unstable to do anything about it due to commitments or responsibilities. *See also* **ocean.**

shorts

To dream of wearing shorts foretells a brief period of calm relaxation. Alternatively, consider how you feel wearing the shorts—are you comfortable or exposed?—and whether they are appropriate for the occasion.

shot

See **gun.**

shoulders

The observations you make about someone's shoulders reflect your opinion of that person's strength, reliability, and support. To dream of your own shoulders implies anxiety over your responsibility for the well-being of those close to you.

shovel

To use a shovel indicates that you are caught in a problematic situation and are trying to get out of it. It can also point to self-exploration. *See also* **burial, digging.**

shower

Taking a shower means you are carrying guilt, worry, or some other emotional burden. Consider showering yourself with kindness—you will likely feel considerable relief. *See also* **bath.**

> We are such stuff
> As dreams are made on,
> And our little life,
> Is rounded with a sleep.
> —William Shakespeare,
> *The Tempest*

shrine

A shrine implies that you see someone else as being in authority or in a superior position to you. This is a distorted image. *See also* **pedestal.**

shrinking

If you dream of shrinking in size, you feel intimidated or overlooked in some aspect of your waking life. To see other people shrinking indicates that you have lost or are losing respect for them. To try to put on clothes that have shrunk suggests that your overinflated ego is causing others to withdraw from you. *See also* **growth.**

shyness

Feelings of low self-esteem can sometimes manifest as shyness in dreams. Alternately, feeling shy reflects embarrassment or guilt.

siblings

Depending on your relationship with your siblings, there can be many interpretations to their appearance in your dreams. They often symbolize competition or unresolved issues, but you also may miss

their physical or emotional presence. Perhaps you aren't as close as you once were or vice versa. *See also individual family members,* **family.**

sickness

Not usually a literal symbol, sickness in a dream often implies that there is something unhealthy or even harmful about a personal relationship. *See also* **illness.**

sidewalk

The interpretation is similar to that of a path, but a sidewalk has the added significance of childhood memories and dreams you had as a child. Notice whether the cement is new or cracked. *See also* **path, roads.**

signature

To sign your name on a document suggests that you have made an important commitment. If the handwriting is small, too large, or illegible, you should rethink that commitment. Most often, though, to put your signature on anything is an affirmation of your self-worth. *See also* **writing.**

signs

See **road signs.**

silence

The interpretation of this dream sensation (a dream in which there is no sound) depends on your state of mind. Do you find it calming, or does it evoke feelings of loss or loneliness? Consider the implications of silence as it relates to a lack of emotion. *See also* **noise, quiet.**

silo

This dream image represents a storehouse of knowledge. It indicates that you are a deep thinker with important ideas that you have yet to put to use.

silver

This particular metal represents enlightenment and intuition. Also consider its association with Olympic medals: There's nothing wrong with second best! Take another look at something or someone you previously dismissed. You may have overlooked true potential.

singing

To sing in a dream represents the desire to express oneself artistically. To hear joyful singing is a sign that troubled times are over. To hear mournful singing could be an omen of an unfortunate turn of events. *See also* **music.**

sinking

Sinking can have two entirely different meanings. It can represent the fact that you are beginning to understand and accept new ideas and attitudes, or it can reflect that you are feeling pulled down by the weight of a personal or professional burden. *See also* **quagmire, quicksand.**

siren

This sound is a warning from your subconscious to stop ignoring a growing problem before it is too late. *See also* **alarm.**

> *Why does the eye see a thing more clearly in dreams than the imagination when awake?*
> —Leonardo da Vinci

sister

The archetype of a sister (even if she isn't your actual sister) represents feminine strength and support, someone you can rely on. *See also individual family members,* **family.**

sitting

If you are sitting when everyone else is standing, you are steadfast in your opinions and have little patience with conformity. It may also suggest that you have too much going on and should consider sitting the next one out. *See also* **standing.**

skating

To dream that you are skating—whether in a roller rink or on ice—reflects the balance you have between your social, personal, and professional lives.

Notice whether you are skating with ease, awkwardly, or just round and round in circles. Do the terms "skating on thin ice" or "skating through life" have meaning to you?

skeleton

This common dream image implies that secrets (whether yours or those of someone else) will be revealed. It can also represent a person who shows little positive emotion (no "heart and soul") and is losing the respect and esteem of others. *See also* **bones, fossil.**

skin

Your skin often symbolizes your ability to cope with criticism and controversy (as in thick-skinned). Blemished skin can point to health issues that you are not aware of—which may

Talking in Your Sleep

German linguist Johann Martin Schleyer (1831–1912), who spoke more than 50 languages, had long been searching for a way to express their common features. His attempts were frustratingly unsuccessful until one night (in 1879) when he dreamed that the forms, letters, and processes appeared "in an orderly array." He then went on to create a new language for the purpose of "international communication." Schleyer called this newly constructed language Volapük.

have nothing to do with your skin itself—but are about to come to the surface.

skis

To dream of skis or skiing indicates that you will reclaim control of a situation over which you have recently relinquished power. Alternately, the image can reflect that a personal relationship or business venture is going downhill fast.

skull

This image can be foreboding, but it can also imply that you are developing unique ideas that will get you noticed. On the other hand, be wary of someone who tries to fill your head with meaningless ideas. *See also* **skeleton.**

skunk

This is a contrary dream image. To see or smell a skunk is an omen to follow your intuition. It will lead you in the right direction and steer you away from negative influences.

sky

The sky generally symbolizes aspirations and ambition. A clear sky indicates that your

potential is limitless, but don't be discouraged by a dark, overcast sky. The sun is shining just above it, so aim your thoughts high.

skydiving

You have a lofty position in life (socially, professionally, or both), but someone close to you wishes you were more down to earth. Another interpretation is that your idealized view of freedom and adventure will set you up for a disappointing fall. *See also* **kite.**

sleep

This ironic dream symbol has differing explanations. If you occasionally imagine yourself in peaceful slumber, it is likely to your advantage: You are in a comfortable place in life that offers room for retrospection and relaxation. The negative implications of this state of mind are that you are shutting down or repressing feelings that should be expressed.

slow motion

It is common to dream that you are moving or speaking in an unusually slow manner that prevents you from accomplishing something or expressing yourself. For example, you are trying to run from a perceived threat but can't seem to get away or

you are calling out for help with unintelligible words. The interpretation is that you are hesitant about or fearful of something in your waking life. Take this feeling as a warning to slow down or to give more thought before you act. *See also* **immobility, paralysis.**

smell
See **odor.**

smile

To smile or see others smiling is often viewed as a positive symbol of contentment, but consider it in the context of accompanying symbols: Who is smiling, and what is your relationship to that person? If

---

A Weird Night's Sleep

In 1965, while the Beatles were filming *Help!* in London, Paul McCartney dreamed of hearing a melody played by a string ensemble. This is his recollection of the dream:

"I woke up with a lovely tune in my head.... There was an upright piano next to me, to the right of the bed by the window. I got out of bed, sat at the piano, found G, found F sharp minor 7th—and that leads you through then to B to E minor, and finally back to E. It all leads forward logically. I liked the melody a lot but because I'd dreamed it I couldn't believe I'd written it. I thought, 'No, I've never written like this before.'" McCartney's dream became known to the world as the song "Yesterday."

you are smiling at someone, is it sincere or fake (perhaps out of envy)? Smiles frequently hide feelings that contradict the supposed emotion. *See also* **face.**

smog

See **air, pollution.**

smoke

A smoky dream environment reflects the absence of clarity regarding an important waking-life situation. Alternately, it can represent an alluring romantic encounter that will quickly prove to be stifling. To dream that you are surrounded by or overcome by smoke is a warning that your safety or that of loved ones will soon be jeopardized. *See also* **fire, fog.**

smuggle

Smuggling in a dream indicates deception. The smuggler feels he or she cannot be truthful with others, usually due to a vain or defensive attitude.

snail

You are dissatisfied with the pace at which your life (specifically, a relationship or work project) is moving. Have patience: Things will soon pick up and you will reach your goal. *See also* **turtle.**

snake

A snake can represent creative energy, enlightenment, and spiritual growth. If the snake is shedding its skin, this is an omen of positive beginnings and improved health. A snake that slithers past you warns of encountering an untrustworthy person (as in the expression "snake in the grass"). *See also* **caduceus, serpent.**

sneeze

A sneeze is your body's way of fending off something disagreeable. In a dream, a sneeze reminds you to rid yourself of negativity. Pay attention to what or who makes you sneeze.

snore

To hear someone snoring (it may actually be you, which is an important observation) is a sign of restlessness and boredom. Alternately, it could mean that you are too easily distracted by issues that are causing you to lose sleep.

snow

This is a symbol with differing interpretations. Falling snow symbolizes a desire for purity, wholesomeness, and serenity. Alternately, it suggests that you harbor cold feelings toward someone. If you dream of melting snow, your relationship with that person will grow warmer. *See also* **ice, icicles.**

soap

To dream of using soap points to a need for emotional or psychological cleansing. *See also* **clean.**

solitaire

Playing the card game solitaire indicates that you are entering a period in life in which you should rely on your intuition. Don't bother consulting others for their opinions or advice, which may put you at risk. *See also* **cards, gambling.**

solo

If you are flying, singing, or engaging in any other activity by yourself, consider whether you do so with confidence or apprehension. The answer will reveal the success of an impending venture.

son

The archetype represents any masculine figure—usually someone close to you. Also consider the homonym "sun" in terms of warmth or closeness of a relationship. *See also individual family members,* **family.**

soup

Soup has a strong tradition as a source of simple nourishment and healing. It can also emphasize that diversity (a combination of different ingredients) produces something agreeable to almost everyone. *See also* **stew.**

south

In terms of directions, south often signifies warmth or comfort. In general or universal terms, it highlights the importance of being open-

> *What an air of probability sometimes runs through a dream!*
> —Jane Austen, *Emma*

minded to other cultures. It can also reflect guilt with regard to sexual feelings. *See also* **directions, north.**

space

To dream that you are floating or traveling in outer space symbolizes a desire to discover unrecognized creative abilities or push beyond your usual boundaries. Also consider whether you need more freedom, or space, in a relationship. *See also* **flying.**

spark

See **electricity.**

sparrow

This bird foretells fervent activity that will bring little reward. Use your energy in a more productive way.

speech

To give a speech in a dream means that in your waking life

you have someone's undivided attention. Make the most of this opportunity!

speeding

Speeding (whether in physical activity or while operating, say, a car) can signify impatience; you are taking a hasty or careless approach to something. If you slow down and practice mindfulness, you will achieve better results. Alternately, look at the symbol positively: You have the energy and drive to succeed! *See also* **race.**

spelling

To dream that you are unable to spell a familiar word implies that you are overwhelmed and can't think straight. To spell a word that doesn't exist (or spelling a word illogically) means you are trying to make better sense of your life.

spending

Spending money in a dream reflects how you expend your energy in real life. Are you using up your resources or are you conserving them? You will need them in the future. *See also* **money, shopping.**

spider

This is a dream symbol that may seem frightening; in fact, it most often represents your resourcefulness and creativity. But to kill a spider is an omen of a downturn in finances. To dream that you are caught in a spider's web warns that a personal relationship is becoming too complicated. *See also* **cobweb.**

spine

The spine symbolizes support, which in turn reflects responsibility and courage. To dream of your own spine means you are ready and able to stand up to a difficult situation. *See also* **back, legs, posture.**

spinning

Spinning (twirling) around in circles can point to the carefree days of childhood, when the resulting dizziness seemed fun. Alternately, if you experience this dream feeling as an adult, consider it a warning against repetitive efforts that are getting you nowhere or making you confused or overwhelmed. To spin yarn implies that you can take care of yourself and those who depend on you, regardless of the circumstances.

spit

Spitting in a dream (particularly if that isn't a regular habit) implies that a recent issue has left a bitter taste in your mouth. It can also mean that you have been speaking negatively of someone and feel guilty about it. *See also* **mouthwash.**

splash

To be splashed with water can be a wake-up call with regard to inappropriate behavior or words. A dive into water that creates a splash predicts that you will impress others with your accomplishments or talents.

sponge

A wet sponge signifies that it is time to stop cleaning up the emotional messes of others. On the other hand, a dry sponge symbolizes your desire to soak up new information and make a creative expression. *See also* **absorption.**

spoon

See **utensils.**

sports

Dreams about sports (basketball, baseball, fencing, football, gymnastics, volleyball, etc.) reflect your feelings about competition. Whether or not you play a sport in real-life, consider if you are playing for fun or exercise. Do you care about the final score? Competition can be motivating—use this to your advantage as you tackle issues in your waking life.

spruce tree

This dream symbol emphasizes a need for organization. Time to clear out unwanted clutter. To cut down a spruce tree foretells a festive celebration. *See also* **trees.**

square

As a dream symbol, a square figure represents stability and sensibility. If you see square shapes, you are at a balanced place in life, but perhaps you should be more expressive or creative. *See also* **circles.**

squash

To dream of cooking or eating squash indicates that you will stop a project or cancel plans for selfish reasons. Consider the feelings of others before you make any final decisions.

squeeze

Being squeezed or squeezing someone means you desperately need to release emotional tension. Alternately, consider whether this represents the fact that you have too many pressures in your life. *See also* **hugging.**

squirrel

This dream symbol can point to forethought and thriftiness. It may take considerable time and effort, but you should gather and protect your resources in the event of an unanticipated obligation. Another interpretation is one of deception or stealing.

stable

A stable is emblematic of emotional stability. If you feel penned in, do you desire or need freedom, or does this situation make you feel secure?

stage

This is often a literal indication of where you are in life. Do you feel comfortable with all eyes on you? Perhaps you could do your best behind the scenes. *See also* **acting, performance.**

stains

Dreams in which you see stains on objects such as furniture or clothing compel you to point out problems with family members that seem obvious only to you. On a positive note, these problems will prove to be minor and temporary if everyone attends to them quickly. Stains can also reflect shame over a tarnished image.

stairs

Climbing stairs portends a rise in social or professional status, particularly if you do so without the assistance of a handrail. Descending stairs suggests a lack of confidence. To gaze up a staircase represents opportunities: Don't be daunted—just take one step at a time. *See also* **climbing.**

stalk

Interpret this image as it pertains to your life circumstances. The word "stalk" has contradictory meanings. As a noun, it represents something upright or supportive (a healthy stalk of wheat, a crisp stalk of celery). But as a verb, "to stalk" denotes the stealthy, intuitive pursuit of something. That interpretation has acquired the negative connotation of obsession or harassment.

stamp

To dream of a rubber stamp can mean you are worried about receiving approval; more likely, you fear being considered the same as everyone else. In the same way, postage stamps point to insecurities about being passed over because you are perceived as dated.

stampede

Being part of a stampede warns against acting without thinking. To watch a stampede pass you by compliments your individuality and sense of caution.

standing

To dream that you are standing when others are seated reflects your desire for recognition and attention, especially among your peers. It also suggests that you speak up for yourself or take a stand on an important issue. *See also* **sitting.**

star

This sign of good luck predicts that you will achieve what you want in life. It can also indicate guidance, enlightenment, and insight as you forge ahead on a meaningful project or spiritual journey. *See also* **shooting star.**

starfish

This symbol reflects the fact that you adapt quickly to new situations. It is also a sign of regeneration and growth, especially if the starfish is missing an arm. *See also* **growth.**

staring

Staring indicates that you are reconsidering your opinion on something or someone. To feel that you are being stared at in a dream implies a lack of scrutiny on your part.

starvation

Feeling that you are starving in a dream often signifies a need for affection (familial or romantic love, or platonic closeness). Alternately, you may be starving for attention. Don't disregard that you may not be eating enough. *See also* **hunger.**

static

To hear static in a dream represents unclear or confusing communication. It can also represent unwanted advice.

statue

A statue of yourself portends that you will receive overdue recognition—personally or professionally. Alternately, that statue can represent an emotionless, unfeeling person. Consider who the statue depicts. *See also* **mannequin, sculpting.**

stealing

If you dream of stealing something, consider the object and why you can't acquire it by legitimate means. If something has been stolen from you, consider what worth that thing holds in your life. *See also* **thief.**

steam

This most often reflects a point of view that is distorted by heated or passionate emotions. *See also* **sauna.**

stew

If you are preparing stew, you are full of ideas that could enhance your life, but you can't distinguish between what's worthy or useless. The problem is you could end up with a confusing mess. Making a stew can also mean that people rely on your creativity for their basic needs. *See also* **soup.**

stilts

Walking on stilts represents a desire to stand out, to not be ordinary. But even if you are walking with ease, some people notice your confidence, while others see the deception.

sting

The dream feeling of being stung by an insect predicts temporary emotional pain. Also consider the implications of the word "sting" as it relates to being caught doing something untoward. Are you harboring guilt over something?

stones

See **rocks.**

stores

To dream of stores in a row represent options: You have all the resources you need at your fingertips. A single store implies that you may have to make some creative substitutions to acquire what you want. *See also* **shopping.**

stork

Usually associated with an announcement of pregnancy or birth, a stork in dreams is

> *O god, I could be bounded in a nutshell and count myself king of infinite space, were it not that I have bad dreams.*
>
> —William Shakespeare, *Hamlet*

a general omen of something new—whether a job, relationship, or financial opportunity.

storm

To dream of a storm signifies emotional rage or dissatisfaction. Is the storm approaching or passing, or are you caught in the middle of it? To facilitate calm feelings after the storm, keep in mind that it is temporary. *See also* **hail, hurricane.**

stove

Dreams in which you stand before a stove represent the need to formulate creative ideas. Consider whether you are actively cooking or have left something simmering on the back burner. You could profit from revisiting old ideas that have been put aside. *See also* **cooking, oven.**

stranded

If you are left stranded in a dream, you feel insecure about a waking-life relationship. To be stranded in an unfamiliar place reflects vulnerability and helplessness. *See also* **abandonment.**

stranger

When most people encounter this image in their dreams, they are fearful or confused about the reason for that person's presence. But this is a good opportunity to ask the dream stranger about his/her/its presence.

strangulation

Strangulation reflects the severance of a vital life force. To dream of being strangled indicates that you are cut off from something important to you. Alternately, someone may require too much of your energy. *See also* **choking, suffocation.**

strawberry

Picking or preserving wild strawberries foretells improved financial matters. Eating ripe strawberries predicts happiness in a romantic relationship.

strength

This is a compensatory dream that reflects waking-life weaknesses. *See also* **power.**

strike

Because of the many uses of the word, there are a variety of interpretations. If you participate in a labor strike, you need to be acknowledged, but only if you aren't perceived as being different. If you take a strike in a ball game, you are anxious about missing opportunities. If you strike out, a missed chance has brought you shame or embarrassment. (Also consider whether you feel the need to strike out at someone.)

string

This dream symbol brings to light business situations that carry hidden stipulations or strings. It's also a general warning of difficult attachments or dependence.

stripes

Stripes indicate that someone is reluctant to change a habit or routine and, as a result, has become stuck in a rut. *See also* **patterns.**

struggle

If you dream of any kind of struggle, you are wrestling with inner conflict and indecision. *See also* **argument, duel.**

studio

If you dream of a studio (as in an art studio), you may be neglecting your creative side. You will feel more balanced when you take time for hobbies or artistic work.

stumble

A stumble indicates that you may soon encounter difficulties in your path, but don't be intimidated by these obstacles.

stunts

To dream that you are a stunt person reflects a desire to reach beyond what you feel you are physically (or intellectually) capable of doing. It can also indicate you are someone who does all the dirty work while others take credit.

stutter

See **inarticulation.**

submarine

To dream of being in a submarine is to probe your inner psyche, the subconscious. To observe a submarine reflects a need for deeper thought—superficiality isn't working anymore. *See also* **periscope, porthole.**

subscription

Are you subscribing to someone else's opinions or beliefs, or do you need to embrace and feel pride in your own beliefs? What was being subscribed to in the dream? The answer will offer insight into what you believe.

subtraction

Subtraction indicates that something or someone has to be removed from your life in order for the equation to make sense. Are there any people or ideas that have bad influences on you? Parting from them might prove to be beneficial. *See also* **addition.**

suffocation

Suffocation can symbolize a lack of feeling or an inability to express yourself, but it most often indicates that you are feeling emotionally or creatively smothered. It can also signify actual health problems. *See also* **choking, strangulation.**

sugar

Sugar translates to sweetness, which as a dream symbol indicates that you overindulge or are too accommodating to those you care about. You have the right intentions, but it's time to set boundaries. *See also* **baking, cooking.**

suicide

Suicide is not often a literal symbol, but it has different interpretations. It can indicate that you are ready to give up on something or that you refuse to take responsibility for a situation that could imperil others. It can also indicate that your actions or inactions may prove final—incapable of being reversed or undone. *See also* **sabotage.**

suit

It is important to consider the fit and style of the suit. If you are used to or comfortable wearing a suit, this dream image confirms that business matters will prove prosperous. If not, think about a career that suits you better. *See also* **clothing.**

summer

The interpretation of this image depends on your reaction to the season. For some people,

summer is a time of relaxation; for others, it demands more activity and heated emotions. *See also individual seasons.*

sun

The sun is most often a symbol of warmth, nurturing, and rejuvenation. Particularly if you have been emotionally hurt, a sun-filled dream will comfort you.

sunflower

A sunflower predicts that a lost but devoted friend will reenter your life. *See also sidebar on page 115.*

superhero

A superhero image (whether it's of you or someone else) warns of expectations that are unrealistic.

superstition

This is another contrary dream: Superstitious behavior such as walking under a ladder or breaking a mirror foretells good fortune—provided you judge wisely.

surfing

If in a dream you are surfing with confidence, expect to do the same in an impending real-life situation. If you are just learning to surf or are surfing with difficulty, you will need more time than anticipated to get the job done. Practice makes perfect.

surgery

Surgery is a healing symbol. To undergo surgery is a sign that you are working on self-improvement. To witness surgery indicates that you are neglecting your physical or emotional health but are aware that it needs attention. *See also* **operation.**

> *All that we see or seem
> Is but a dream within a
> dream.*
>
> —Edgar Allan Poe,
> "A Dream Within a Dream"

surplus

See **inventory.**

surprise

To be surprised in a dream indicates happiness brought on by increased self-awareness. Strengths or talents you didn't know you had are making themselves obvious. A fear of being surprised points to repression or denial.

surrender

Typically, surrendering is an omen of positive changes in your life. By accepting things as they are and relinquishing control, you are opening yourself up to new opportunities.

suspenders

Wearing suspenders warns that your support system could let you down at any time or that an important project will be put on hold.

swamp

You are inundated with responsibilities and feel that you can no longer cope. You will have to wade through this period for a while, but help will come eventually. *See also* **marsh.**

swan

You like to surround yourself with beautiful people and objects, but be sure to look beyond the surface. A swan can also symbolize an impending transformation.

swearing

Swearing in a dream (especially if you don't swear a lot in real life) is an expression of normal, everyday frustrations that you usually hold in.

sweeping

Are you cleaning up your emotional debris or sweeping it under the carpet? *See also* **broom, clean.**

swimming

Swimming represents your flow of energy and how immersed you are in (or how well you know) yourself. If you are swimming with your head out of the water, you fear the unknown—the parts of you that lurk below the surface. To swim underwater represents curiosity and exploration: You may be surprised by what you discover. An inability to swim indicates denial; swimming smoothly (especially in rough water) signifies confidence. *See also* **drowning, water.**

swinging

Swinging on a swing set often reflects a happy and carefree childhood and can mimic a motion that you once found soothing. On the other hand, swinging may indicate that things just move back and forth, making no discernible progress. This dream image also has sexual undertones: You are weary of repetition and desire a different perspective.

sword

A sword warns to evaluate a problematic situation before you act on it. To brandish a sword signifies that the issue will come to an end, but in the process, you may lose the respect of people you care most about.

T

table

A table represents your connection with friends and family. If it's a dining table, are the people seated enjoying themselves? Also consider the use of the word in reference to postponing something. You may not have another chance. *See also* **dining room.**

tablecloth

You are protecting family secrets: Whether they are old or recent depends on the condition of the tablecloth.

table tennis

You are spending time in a relationship or disagreement that is going nowhere. Drop it and walk away. *See also* **tennis.**

taboo

Depending on the context and culture, something taboo is usually considered unacceptable or forbidden. As a dream symbol, engaging in something taboo can be a positive sign of independence or a rejection of what is considered normal.

tail

A tail can represent the end of something, and the movement of the tail reflects the feelings about that ending—is it raised, wagging, or motionless? Also consider the homonym "tale" in relation to this image: Are you sincere in your expressions, or are you saying what you think someone wants to hear?

talking

Who is speaking and what is being said? If you can't discern the words or they seem jumbled, pay attention to your communication skills. This is a time to ask your dream self for clarity. If the words are clear, pay attention to important clues or messages. *See also* **voices.**

tall

Anything that appears tall, such as a building or a tree, indicates something temporarily out of reach. Stay focused, and the image (goal) will seem less daunting. To grow tall in a dream is to gain self-confidence or feel proud of what you have achieved. Anything unusually tall warns that something is being blown out of proportion.

tambourine

You will hear unfounded rumors; save your energy and ignore them. To shake a tambourine predicts that you will profit through the departure of another, usually within the workplace. *See also* **music.**

tango

As the saying goes, it takes two to tango, so don't place all the blame on just one person. Listen to both sides of the story.

tantrum

Throwing a tantrum warns against displaying childish impatience or behavior in a personal relationship. The dream image can also encourage the expression of long-held frustrations.

tapestry

A tapestry symbolizes the events or progression of life on your terms. What is the condition of the tapestry— worn and frayed or vibrant and colorful? *See also* **patterns.**

tapeworm

Something or someone is sapping your energy or enthusiasm. *See also* **leeches, parasites.**

tapping

You will have to dance around an impending deception: To avoid this potentially embarrassing predicament, do what's right in the first place. Another interpretation related to the sound of tapping warns that someone's long-worn impatience is ready to give out.

target

If you feel your goals are well directed, go forward with your plans. If you are determined to hit your mark immediately, reevaluate your expectation. *See also* **arrow.**

tartan

Tartan is symbolic of family pride, alliances, and loyalty. The dream image is a reminder to cherish familial ties. *See also* **plaid.**

taste

Tasting something unfamiliar or even odd means you are ready for something new and exciting. Be ready for an unusual opportunity.

tattoo

A seemingly permanent situation can be changed, but it will take physically or emotionally painful work and ingenuity.

taxi

Do you feel you are being taken for a ride? Perhaps you are better off determining your own direction and finding the most efficient route.

tea

Sipping tea predicts pleasant moments with old friends or family members. To pour tea is a sign that someone will lend wise advice.

teacher

To dream of an actual teacher from your past (or one who is imagined) is a message that you are never too old to learn. What feelings does this dream teacher evoke? Do you feel intimidated, rebellious, disconnected, or inspired? If you explore those emotions, you may find your true calling. If you dream of teaching a class but have never done so, expect to be sought out for advice from someone long removed from your life. *See also* **school.**

tear
See **cut.**

tears
To shed tears is a sign of relief from stress, which will be followed by joy. *See also* **crying, sadness.**

teeth
Teeth are associated with your communication skills. Bared or outsized teeth warn to back away from a contentious situation. Do the teeth appear healthy, decayed, or false? See also **mouth, smile.**

telephone
Do you fear or become anxious at the sound of a ringing phone,

or do you leap at the chance to answer it? Your answer represents your ability to communicate with others.

telescope
Something obscured or misunderstood is being brought into focus—though it may be from your own perspective. To look through a telescope represents a search for knowledge of a deeper meaning in life. To look through the wrong end of a telescope is to minimize the significance of something or to keep it at a distance. *See also* **microscope, periscope.**

television
You are putting too much effort and energy into the affairs or fantasy lives of others. Take a step back and be more introspective.

Playing "Telephone" at Night

A telepathic dream is one in which you become aware of what someone else thinks, feels, or envisions. The messages you receive may not be in words; more likely, they are communicated in images such as a telephone, e-mail, advertisements—even letters scrawled on a sidewalk.

For more than 20 years, the International Association for the Study of Dreams (IASD) has held a dream telepathy contest at its annual conference. The contest was initiated in 1985 by Robert Van de Castle, a telepathic receiver who participated in studies conducted by Montague Ullman and Stanley Krippner at the Maimonides Dream Laboratory in Brooklyn, New York.

Conference participants are invited to submit images, and contest judges select four from this pool and seal them in envelopes. The judges then randomly choose a sender from the audience—that is, someone who will telepathically broadcast the image to others. The designated sender selects one of the envelopes, which he or she opens in privacy. During that night the sender transmits the image itself, as well as its cognitive and emotional content. The receivers then try to tune into this broadcast through their dreams and identify the image.

There are any number of ways to send an image; from simply staring at and studying the picture, to imagining one's self inside the image, interacting with the details and elements. For example, if the image is of a ballerina, the sender may visualize being a ballerina, imagining the costume and shoes, hearing the music, and feeling the graceful movements of the body.

The next morning, the participants write about or sketch their dreams (or what they received from the sender) and submit them for consideration. A prize is awarded to the person whose image most closely resembles the one communicated by the sender.

temperature

See **thermometer.**

temple

A temple represents the inner self or soul. If you are incubating dreams, this is a good sign that you are developing self-affirming skills. *See also* **abbey, church.**

tenderness

You are particularly sensitive at this time. Pay attention to what feels tender, as it can point to an underlying need for emotional or physical help. *See also* **illness, injury.**

tennis

Unless you feel especially competitive in a current situation, the constant back-and-forth will get you nowhere. *See also* **sports, table tennis.**

tent

As a temporary dwelling, does a tent provide a sense of security or independence? *See also* **apartment, camping.**

terror

Dream feelings of terror are often exaggerated expressions of everyday fears or anxieties. These are most typical among children, but some adults who are particularly creative or expressive also have them. *See also sidebar on page 194,* **nightmare.**

test

The common and universal dream of taking a test (exam) for which you are unprepared reflects similar waking-life anxieties over whether you deserve what you have achieved, or you may expect more recognition. Dreams that involve medical tests or exams can point to undisclosed health issues, whereas general diagnostic tests recommend maintenance or updates. *See also* **exam.**

theater

In a dream, what you see in a theater (or on a screen) often mirrors your life experiences. Does what you see on the stage

have resonance? Does it seem overly dramatic or true to life? Closely observe the set and characters. *See also* **audience, stage**.

thermometer

Thermometer readings represent emotions: Are you running hot, cold, or normal? If you are looking at an outdoor thermometer, does the reading determine how you will react to circumstances that day? In other words, will those you encounter receive a chilly reception or a warm welcome?

thief

This image doesn't necessarily represent something illegal—instead, you likely feel helpless or threatened by a potential loss. Or perhaps you have acquired something you don't think you deserve. *See also* **pickpocket, robbery.**

thimble

You are too tempermental or vulnerable right now to manage the small details of an important relationship or project. However, you will receive help from someone with thicker skin.

thirst

Thirst, like hunger, points to an emotional need or a longing for something. On the other hand, thirst is a sign that you are absorbing, or taking in, valuable information that will enhance your life now and in the long run. *See also* **drinking, hunger.**

thorn

Don't carry around old wounds, issues, or even people that present a burden. A thorn also represents annoyances or inconveniences that need to be removed before they grow into something bigger. *See also* **rose.**

All men whilst they are awake are in one common world: But each of them, when he is asleep, is in a world of his own.
—Plutarch

thread

Working with thread indicates that you are getting in touch with your creative side a little at a time. It is a delicate process, so be patient. If threads are hanging from your clothes, tend to loose ends.

throat

If your throat is sore, you are finding it hard to express your feelings. On the other hand, consider whether you find something difficult to swallow (e.g., ideas) or if you feel choked by something or someone. *See also* **neck.**

throne

See **pedestal.**

throwing

Do you feel like throwing in the towel? Alternately, throwing something away is a positive sign that you are ridding yourself of unwanted circumstances or affiliations. If you are throwing a ball, your target represents your immediate goals, so aim well! *See also* **ball, target.**

thumb

The meanings are varied, and the interpretation depends on the dream. Consider the colloquialisms: "thumbs-up" or "thumbs-down," "thumbing your nose at someone," being "under someone's thumb," and "sticking out like a sore thumb."

thunder

Like someone who is "all bark and no bite," thunder often predicts rumors that are meaningless. It can also represent someone who is boastful and seeks attention. Another interpretation is that thunder serves to draw your attention to something and perhaps warns of something foreboding. *See also* **lightning, storm.**

tiara

To see yourself wearing a tiara can be a cry for attention or a simple plea to be acknowledged for what you feel you have done well. *See also* **princess, royalty.**

ticket

A ticket can symbolize access or a penalty, so this image is particular to the dream itself. A missing or lost ticket signifies rejection. A lottery ticket can predict positive changes (not necessarily in terms of finances), but it can also warn against expenditures. *See also* **lottery.**

tickle

In terms of a physical sensation, some people enjoy being tickled, whereas others do not. Evaluate your own reaction. This dream feeling also reminds you to remain positive, to see the bright side of life.

tidal wave

See **tide, water, wave.**

tide

The tides represent life's ebb and flow and the power of your emotions. *See also* **ocean, water, wave.**

tiger

A tiger symbolizes power, strength, and energy. To be chased by a tiger reflects intimidation or vulnerability. Facing your attacker won't be as bad as you have imagined. *See also sidebar on page 54.*

tinsel

Tinsel is intended to draw attention to something. If the image isn't associated with the holidays, consider what is covered with tinsel.

tip

Tips symbolize giving and receiving. To receive a tip is a sign that you will benefit from

---

The Heart Is a Red, Red Rose

When author Mark Twain and his brother Henry worked on boats that traversed the Mississippi River, Mark recalled an eerie dream in which he saw Henry's corpse in a metal coffin in their sister's living room. The coffin was "magically" supported by two flimsy chairs, and on Henry's body lay a bouquet of flowers with one vivid red rose in the center.

A few weeks later, Henry was killed in a tragic accident on a riverboat. Attending his wake, Twain was shocked that the coffin was positioned just as it had been in his dream. Furthermore, as Twain stood over his brother's body, a woman approached and placed in the coffin a bouquet with a single crimson rose in the middle.

good advice. To give a tip implies that you want more of the good life.

tire

Unless you are concerned about a waking-life problem with a bicycle or vehicle tire, consider this symbol as a sign to tread lightly.

toilet

This is another common dream symbol, and there are a few interpretations. A toilet can represent a desire for privacy or a fear of being exposed. Alternately, it recommends that you release built-up tension or repressed feelings.

token

A token can be an expressed commitment, the degree of which depends on the context of the dream and what is offered. Is the token in the form of words, a trinket, or something that holds greater meaning? *See also* **promises**.

tomato

To dream of cultivating tomatoes means that you are facing a number of opportunities: Take your pick of the ripe ones! In general, a tomato symbolizes happiness, a full heart, and love. To eat a tomato predicts a passionate romance.

tomb

See **burial, casket, grave.**

tongue

A tongue is essential for verbal communication, but this dream symbol points out that you can be easily misunderstood. Consider idioms such as "tongue-tied," "tongue-in-cheek," and "tongue-lashing." *See also* **mouth, teeth.**

tools

This image reflects your capabilities and talents—and particularly the assistance you can offer to someone in need. Consider the types of tools in the dream and who might benefit most from them.

tooth

See **teeth.**

toothache

A toothache (or headache, heartache, or any other real or perceived ache) often reflects guilt or regret over harsh words, thoughts, or actions. The comfort you have is in knowing that the ache (for everyone involved) is temporary. *See also* **illness.**

topaz

Topaz symbolizes a calm, peaceful state of mind, but as a dream symbol, it warns of an imbalance: Don't let it push you over the edge.

topiary

This image has two entirely different interpretations: One is of manipulation. Regardless of how much you try, certain people or situations cannot be changed. At best, they can be made to look pretty, but any alteration is temporary. But topiary can also symbolize a transformation: If you are trying to change (or prune) yourself from within, you will see a gradual and positive change. *See also* **garden, landscape.**

torch

To light a torch is to clarify your own thoughts. Passing a torch is to provide others with your wisdom or experience. Also consider the idiom "to carry a torch": You have what it takes to ignite something. *See also* **fire.**

tornado

If you see a tornado, expect a domestic whirlwind (which won't necessarily be bad, just hectic). To be caught in a tornado represents emotional turmoil. *See also* **storm.**

torpedo

If you stay focused on what you want to achieve, you will make a big impact. A torpedo can also symbolize underlying aggression that could become explosive.

torture

This is often an exaggerated dream symbol that points to a guilty conscious. To witness torture in a dream implies that you view things with a very critical eye.

toupee

To wear a poorly matched or ill-fitting toupee indicates that something is out of place in your life. *See also* **hair, wig.**

towel

A towel is a symbol of resignation or surrender (consider the idiom "throw in the towel"). If you are drying your hands with a towel, a recent project will prove profitable. To fold towels predicts that you will be asked to bring order to a chaotic situation.

tower

Your ambitious goals are not easily attainable, but they are not totally out of reach. *See also* **tall.**

toy

This image can reflect childhood fun: Indulge yourself with a hobby. Alternately, a toy implies immaturity or ineffective manipulation (toying with someone). *See also* **childhood, playground.**

traction

Do you feel as if you are spinning your wheels? Or do you need to get a grip? To be in traction with an injury represents a stalemate.

trade

To trade or swap something in a dream implies that you have a covetous personality. Be grateful for your own possessions and resources. *See also* **market, shopping.**

traffic

Are you zooming through the express lane or stuck in traffic? This dream represents the style and speed at which you navigate through life. *See also* **car, highway.**

trailer

See **apartment, home, house.**

train

A train in motion is a sign that you are on the right track. Don't let yourself get distracted! A stalled train is a sign of hesitation or a warning to be more patient. *See also* **railroad.**

trance

If you dream of falling into a trance, you are detached from reality. If you are sitting or standing in a trance, you need to take a break from work and rejuvenate. If you are lying down in a trance, you may be in denial about a romantic relationship. *See also* **hypnosis.**

transformation

To witness something transforming, such as a

caterpillar into a butterfly, is an omen of positive changes to come. It can also represent a breakthrough in a personal matter.

trap

If you dream of falling into a trap, you are skeptical by nature and worried about being deceived by others. If you dream of setting a trap, you feel threatened by the success of someone else and secretly hope to see him or her fail.

trapeze

A trapeze is a symbol of a quick mind: You are someone who makes good decisions with little hesitation. It also highlights the fact that you can make intuitive connections between things when others cannot. *See also* **acrobat.**

travel

If you dream of travel, there is a literal interpretation—that you are about to embark on a trip. It may also indicate that you will take jaunts into new areas of interest and expertise, either through training, study, or simply trying new things.

tray

A tray suggests that you will get something effortlessly, as if handed to you on a silver platter. Be sure to examine its value.

treadmill

If not a literal hint to get more exercise, a treadmill can refer to dull, repetitive, or routine work. It can also represent energy that has been expended with minimal results. *See also* **running.**

Transforming Dreams

Renowned Taoist master Chuang Tzu once dreamed he was a butterfly unconcerned with a destination, or perhaps he was lost in flight. He recognized the symbolism of the dream after he recorded and reflected on it: "Was I before a man who dreamt about being a butterfly, or am I now a butterfly who dreams about being man?"

treasure

If you find treasure, you will receive an award—but you will be required to defend its worth. If you are treasure hunting, you are on a quest for recognition. *See also* **gold, pirate.**

tree house

To dream of living in a tree house reflects fantasy, escapism, or fond childhood memories. To build a tree house implies that you long for easier, less hectic times. This is a good time to take a relaxing vacation.

trees

A healthy tree is an omen of strength, endurance, prosperity, and growth. To dream of trimming or cutting down trees suggests that you are evaluating your roots or eliminating excess or negativity from your life. *See also individual tree listings,* **roots.**

trench

If you dream of being in a trench, consider what you are trying to hide from people and why. If there is water in the trench, you are concealing something for reasons of vanity and pride. To dig a trench is to set up barriers or to keep someone at arm's length. *See also* **burial, digging, hole.**

trespass

To purposely trespass in a dream indicates that you want to voice your opinions but feel they aren't welcome. Wait for a better opportunity before you offer suggestions. To trespass by accident implies that you are not aware of the feelings of others or that you have overstepped your boundaries.

triangle

A triangle is a symbol of power and harmony of body, mind, and spirit. It can also symbolize a romantic triangle. *See also sidebar on page 175.*

trigger

To pull a trigger is to make a decision or choice that cannot be reversed. To trigger a device (such as security lighting) is a hint to be alert for an unexpected event or news.

triplets

Triplets indicate unexpected surprises. They can also indicate that things will happen in threes. *See also* **baby, twins.**

trophy

To receive a trophy in a dream means you will finally achieve a long-standing goal. To give someone a trophy suggests that you look up to others without noticing your own worth. *See also* **medal.**

truck

A truck indicates that you are carrying a heavy burden. If the truck is in motion, the feelings may pass quickly. If the truck is parked, it may take a little while before the feelings pass. *See also* **car.**

trumpet

Dreaming of a trumpet is a reminder to promote your talents. There is a receptive audience waiting for you. *See also* **music.**

tugboat

A tugboat indicates that extra responsibilities may slow your pace. Be cautious when volunteering your time. *See also* **boats.**

tunnel

Dreaming of a tunnel means that you are going through a tense time, but it is almost over (look for the light). To emerge from a tunnel is assurance that your problems are solved.

turkey

A turkey symbolizes someone who speaks loudly and often but says little of value. *See also* **birds, food.**

turnstile

A turnstile indicates that your activities are being monitored or controlled. It also represents your need to keep a project moving at a regular, controlled pace.

turquoise

Turquoise is a symbol of spiritual and emotional healing. To wear turquoise is to benefit from wisdom.

turtle

Have patience. Dreaming of a turtle is a reminder that "slow and steady wins the race." *See also sidebar on page 54.*

tweezers

This dream symbol suggests that you rid yourself of useless thoughts or habits. To tweeze your eyebrows is a sign that your facial expressions have been misunderstood.

twins

A dream of twins is a reminder that there are two sides to every story. It also indicates that while two things may look the same on the exterior, they are often different inside. *See also* **baby, triplets.**

tying

The act of tying something, such as shoelaces, signifies completion. Also consider the relevance of idioms such as "tying the knot," "tying up loose ends," being "tied up," or "tied up in knots." *See also* **rope, string.**

typing

Typing a letter is a symbol of well-intended but ineffective communication. Typing can also warn against typecasting or stereotyping someone or something.

U

UFO

Prepare yourself: To dream of an unidentified flying object means you will meet an intriguing stranger, seemingly out of nowhere. To go onboard a UFO encourages you to explore the unknown or to go beyond your comfort zone. *See also* **aliens.**

ugliness

Pay attention to the details of this type of dream, because to perceive or judge something as ugly often reflects the way you feel about yourself. This image can also reflect a fear that a situation could get ugly unless cooler heads prevail.

umbrella

An umbrella can represent shelter: You will witness strife or arguments, but they won't involve you. However, to open an umbrella may imply that you are closing yourself off from others or that you are in a state of denial. It can also mean that you are trying to hide your feelings. To close an umbrella is an omen of reconciliation. *See also* **clothing, coat, disguise.**

umpire

An umpire represents a neutral party—someone outside a contentious situation that will help you settle the dispute. But if you are the umpire in a dream, make an effort to hear both sides of a story, and do your best to be objective. *See also* **referee.**

underbite

To dream that someone has an underbite signifies that information is being kept from you. If the image is of you, consider why you are holding back or being dishonest. *See also* **teeth.**

underdog

An underdog represents someone who appears to be mild-mannered and conservative but is in fact adventuresome and daring. Try things you've never done before, because this dream symbol also points to hidden talents.

underground

If your dream takes place underground, consider pursuing alternate routes to success. The image can also point to illegal behavior.

underneath

To be in this position suggests you have a hidden agenda, or perhaps you're looking for a way to get out from underneath something. Consider whether you feel trapped in a job or relationship.

understudy

If you dream of being an understudy, you have the ability to step into the spotlight when the opportunity arises,

---

A Dream with a Twist

Chemist Friedrich August Kekulé von Stradonitz, experiencing difficulty determining the molecular structure of benzene, fell asleep and dreamed of atoms in long chains, swirling and twisting in a snakelike fashion. Suddenly, one of the "snakes" bit its own tail and began to spin in a circle. This dream image inspired von Kekulé to formulate the groundbreaking theory that a benzene molecule is shaped like a ring.

but you also know when to step back and let others shine. Be prepared to do this soon. Also consider whether you are willing to settle for second best.

undertaker

This symbol suggests that you will take on an important but unpleasant assignment, which most likely requires you to clean up a complicated situation created by others.

undertow

On a positive note, you may soon be swept away in a passionate romance. Unfortunately, the image also suggests that you are getting in over your head. *See also* **drowning, swimming.**

underwater

If you are struggling underwater, you are under a great deal of pressure. If you are moving underwater with ease, you are able to adapt quickly to a new environment. If you are emerging from underwater, your difficulties are just about over.

underwear

To dream of being in your underwear in public points to guilt, shame, or an unreasonable fear of being embarrassed. *See also* **clothing, nudity.**

unemployment

This isn't always a literal symbol: To dream that you are unemployed (especially if you're not) indicates that you feel diminished or that you lack purpose. It can also signify a desire for more free time to pursue what really interests you. *See also* **job.**

unicorn

Traditionally, a unicorn symbolizes purity of heart, but it can also warn against selfish or one-sided thinking. To ride a unicorn is often a sign of spiritual growth.

unicycle

To ride a unicycle means you will soon tackle a challenge on your own—and you will do it well. *See also* **bicycle.**

uniform

Wearing a uniform signals a period in which you will feel powerless to make choices. To see someone else in uniform indicates the need for more discipline in your own life. *See also* **clothing.**

universe

If you dream of the universe, you are setting out on a quest for deeper knowledge and understanding of your purpose. *See also* **earth, space.**

university

A university represents your desire for knowledge and maturity of thought. To attend a university means you would like to know yourself better. To drop out of a university suggests that you need to devote more attention to everyday matters. *See also* **school.**

unkempt

Having an unkempt appearance in a dream is a sign that you are too distracted by work or other responsibilities in your waking life to attend to your basic physical and emotional needs. Alternately, this can symbolize depression or a low self-image.

unlock

If you unlock something in a dream, expect to be consulted for your wisdom and insight. It may also be a sign that you will discover hidden talents. *See also* **keys, lock.**

unplug

To unplug an electrical device suggests you are feeling disconnected from friends or family. To unplug a drain is to let go of old hurts and move toward forgiveness. *See also* **plug.**

unprepared

Depending upon the context of the dream, being unprepared has several meanings. It may just reflect waking-life worries, that you're not ready to embark on a plan, project, trip, etc. It may also mean that something is in the raw or early stages and is not yet ready or complete. Additionally, it could be a warning to get things in order before you try to go any further. Consider who or what was unprepared in the dream. *See also* **exam, school, test.**

unwrap

To unwrap something is to uncover the truth. It is an indication that you will find the information you seek. *See also* **gift.**

uproot

If you dream of being uprooted, you will soon acquire a better position in life or take on a new worldview. *See also* **moving.**

upstairs

A dream that takes place in an upstairs location predicts mental, emotional, or spiritual enlightenment. To climb the stairs to an upper floor is an omen of social advancement or a job promotion. *See also* **attic, basement.**

urgency

Feeling a sense of urgency is often a literal representation of panic or anxiety, but it can also warn you to take action or proceed with something as soon as possible. If you hesitate, you may later regret it.

utensils

As a dream symbol, cooking or eating utensils represent the practical skills or tools you need to proceed (and succeed) with regard to a personal or professional pursuit.

U-turn

Making a U-turn indicates that you will abruptly change your mind about an issue that you thought was settled. If someone else makes a U-turn in front of

> *Dreams are true while they last, and do we not live in dreams?*
> —Alfred, Lord Tennyson, "The Higher Pantheism"

you, expect plans to be altered or canceled. *See also* **car.**

V

vacancy

As a dream symbol, a vacancy sign can point to an opportunity for personal growth. If the image is that of neon motel lights that flash "vacancy," anticipate a negative change in your home life. If the sign flashes "no vacancy," you are doing what it takes to fulfill your needs and those of your family.

vacant

To differentiate from "vacancy," this image is usually that of a vacant lot, building, etc. The interpretations vary: You may desire a vacant space (that is, privacy, or a place that is yours alone when you need it), or you feel that something is missing from your life. Alternately, you may feel nothing at all—you are emotionally vacant. *See also* **empty.**

vacation

If you are dreaming about a vacation, chances are you need one. Are the images familiar and comforting (say, a family gathering or a pleasant place you have been to repeatedly with close friends)? Otherwise, try embarking on something new and extraordinary.

vaccination

A vaccination indicates that you will be strengthened during a trying time. *See also* **needle.**

vacuum

A vacuum represents a need or a void. If you are using a vacuum cleaner, what are you trying to take in or get rid of?

valedictorian

If you dream of being valedictorian, you are someone capable of leading or speaking on behalf of a group. If you dream of giving a valedictory speech, you have been given a great opportunity—be sure to take advantage of it. *See also* **graduation.**

valentine

Although the traditional image is one of admiration or love, this dream symbol doesn't usually correspond with an actual Valentine's Day (as designated on many calendars). The message is to take advantage of opportunities for romantic happiness whenever they present themselves. *See also* **heart.**

valley

In a biblical or spiritual sense, gazing into or walking through a valley indicates that you will feel protected from fears or the prospect of death. Walking into or out of a valley also represents the ups and downs of everyday life and indicates that you will survive the pitfalls that others succumb to. *See also* **canyon.**

valve

A valve points to opportunities that are either open or closed to you. It can also suggest that things are flowing smoothly in your work environment or in a personal relationship. Also note that even the most secure valve can succumb to extreme pressure. *See also* **pipes.**

vampire

The historic portrayal of a vampire is usually contradictory: It can be both attractive and repulsive. As a dream image, a vampire can warn against someone with a conflicting or inconsistent personality (someone who seems to change by day and night) or who feeds off the energy of others. Also, consider whether something (a burdensome career, an unhealthy relationship) is sucking the life out of you. *See also* **leeches.**

vanilla

To smell vanilla or use it as a flavoring is a sign of deception: What may seem enticing will prove to be disappointing and ordinary.

vanish

See **disappearance, magic.**

vanity

The word *vanity* means "empty" or "wane." To dream that someone appears vain indicates that you have a distorted perception of that person.

> *To believe in one's dreams is to spend all of one's life asleep.*
> —Chinese Proverb

Take a deeper look, and avoid superficial judgments.

vapor

To envision or be surrounded by vapor in a dream is a sign of support and protection, but realize that the image is only temporary. Ultimately, you will have to summon the strength to fend for yourself. Vapor can also represent a ghost from your past. Pay close attention to what is revealed if the vapor thins or fades. Finally, consider the adage "hysterical," as it was used in reference to women diagnosed with a nervous condition. *See also* **ghost, mist.**

varnish

Varnish represents a superficial gloss. Are you trying to make something look better than it is (perhaps yourself)? Also, consider whether there are issues at work or at home that have been glossed over on your behalf. *See also* **polishing.**

vase

Most vases are made to hold something: They can symbolize hope, plans, or potential. To dream of a vase filled with flowers suggests that your hard work will soon be acknowledged. A vase of flowers may also portend a secret admirer. An empty decorative vase could be a sign of hope or unused potential. *See also sidebar on page 115, individual flower listings,* **flowers.**

vault

If you dream of a vault, you should remember that personal matters are best kept private. To open a vault that belongs to another is to pry into someone else's affairs. To open a vault that you own is to place trust in a friend. If you dream of pole vaulting, you will more easily overcome difficult obstacles than you thought. *See also* **safe.**

vegetables

If not a literal hint to eat more vegetables, this symbol suggests that you place a high priority on maintaining better health. To do so will enable you to grow more resilient. *See also individual vegetables.*

vegetarian

Dreaming of a vegetarian lifestyle indicates that you should not waste the resources available to you, whether physical, emotional, or financial. It also suggests that you should be more self-sufficient.

vehicle

A vehicle represents how you think others view you. Are you a driver or a passenger? What condition is the vehicle in? Consider whether the model is new, old, or expensive: Is it a gas-guzzler or energy-efficient? All of these details provide clues that can help you achieve more self-awareness. *See also* **car, driving.**

veil

If you dream of someone wearing a veil over his or her face, you should be ready to safeguard another person's secret. If you are wearing a veil, you should avoid giving away too much information. Alternately, a veil can represent a form of disguise or concealment. Consider the term "thinly veiled secret." *See also* **disguise.**

veins

As vessels that carry blood to your heart, veins represent something on which your life depends. This dream image reminds you to pay attention to your health as well as your personal relationships (especially those of a romantic nature). And because a vein also refers to a distinctive quality or style (e.g., a particular vein of humor), this dream is complimenting you on your individuality. If you dream that your veins are unusually dark, protruding, or sore, you are wasting too much time under stressful conditions or spending too much time on the go. Take a rest!

velvet

Velvet can indicate pleasant indulgences, but it can also suggest that you "smooth out your rough edges."

venom
See **poison.**

vent

A vent can represent a need to get something off your chest. Is the vent open or closed? An open vent implies that speaking your mind will relieve guilt or regret. A closed vent warns you to be discerning about who you vent to.

ventilate

To ventilate a room is to get a breath of fresh air. New ideas or opportunities will soon perk up a seemingly unchanging or stale situation or relationship.

ventriloquist

This symbol indicates that someone is speaking on your behalf and doesn't have your story straight. Step in and speak your own mind before you are misjudged or taken for a fool. *See also* **dummy, mute.**

vertex

To dream of being at the vertex—or highest point of something (e.g., a pyramid)— suggests that you have set a high standard for yourself but will reach your goal with little difficulty. If viewing a vertex at a distance, your goals are within reach, but timing is important. *See also* **hill, mountain.**

vertigo

This time you may have gone too far. Experiencing vertigo in a dream can suggest that you are out of your comfort zone and are confused about where you are. Vertigo can also indicate that you are facing a dizzying array of choices. Take time to gather your thoughts before you make a decision. *See also* **dizziness.**

vest

A vest suggests shyness. If you are wearing a vest, you are uncomfortable expressing yourself to others. *See also* **clothing, coat.**

veteran

A veteran symbolizes struggle and survival. If you don't give up the fight, you will emerge a winner. *See also* **battle, war.**

veterinarian

If you dream that you are a vet, you have no problem expressing your affection and concern for animals but have

> *Dreams are, by definition, cursed with short life spans.*
> —Actor Candice Bergen

difficulty doing so with people. Try to be more expressive and compassionate toward those closest to you.

vibration

Unless you are sleeping in a vibrating bed, this dream feeling is trying to shake you out of a rut, whether that involves thought patterns or a sedentary or unproductive lifestyle. *See also* **alarm.**

victim

To feel like a victim in a dream warns against being too passive in trying to get what you want. You won't get a response or results unless you make your intent clear. To victimize others is to pass off obligations or responsibilities. That may work in the short term, but you will pay the price down the road.

victory

This image is often a goal among athletes or others who are about to compete in something. If you incubate a dream in which you are victorious or if you imagine yourself as a winner, chances are much better that you will be! *See also* **sports.**

vine

A vine represents your ability to reach out to others. Someone may be in need of help. Just be sure not to smother them or be overbearing in your assistance. Alternately, a vine can warn against clinging to others in a way that inhibits your personal growth. *See also* **ivy.**

vinegar

To use or smell vinegar foretells that a sweet romance will soon turn sour. Vinegar can also warn you of someone who has a sour disposition and will ruin a pleasant situation for everyone.

violence

See **aggression, hitting, kicking.**

violet

The color violet represents knowledge, enlightenment, wisdom, and spirituality. The flower recommends introspection and taking stock of your life. *See also sidebar on page 85,* **flowers.**

violin

A violin is a symbol of sympathy and compassion. To hear classical violin music can be an omen of either heartrending or troubling news. *See also* **fiddle, music.**

virginity

Outside of the sexual connotation, virginity as a dream symbol most often represents something that's pure or has never been explored. It can also symbolize aspects of your life in which you feel naïve or inexperienced, and it encourages you to develop those areas.

voices

Voices in a dream can be arbitrary and do not necessarily hold great meaning. The importance lies in what is being said and at what volume. A whispering voice can indicate that you are either secretive or considered a confidant. A booming voice suggests that you are someone who is hard to reach, either physically or emotionally. *See also* **talking.**

volcano

An erupting volcano foretells that you will soon unleash strong emotions. If you dream of a dormant volcano, you will keep your feelings bottled up. It's better to let people know what you are thinking and feeling. *See also* **explosion, lava.**

volunteer

To dream of volunteering your services can be an omen that recent good deeds will be recognized and rewarded. Alternately, consider whether you are giving away parts of yourself at the expense of your own happiness.

vomiting

If you dream of vomiting, you are trying to rid yourself of unpleasant memories. To observe another person doing so implies that you will help someone overcome a past hurt or wrongdoing.

voodoo

This dream image suggests that you are seeking an unorthodox or inappropriate way out of a troubling situation. To manipulate a voodoo doll points to an inability to confront the people who have hurt you.

voting

If you dream of voting, you feel pressured to make an important decision in your waking life. Alternately, it predicts that you will finally stand up for something in which you believe.

vows

Exchanging vows can foretell a wedding, but it more often represents the desire to make a commitment or to take an existing commitment more seriously. On the other hand, you may be ready to embark on a new life path or make a significant career change. For further clues, evaluate the specific words in the vow. *See also* **marriage, wedding.**

voyage

See **travel.**

vulture

Be wary of false friends. This symbol indicates that someone seeks to benefit from your loss. *See also* **leeches, vampire.**

W

wade

To wade through shallow water in a dream indicates that you have been reluctant about acknowledging something. Take comfort in the fact that you are finally ready to accept the truth. *See also* **ocean, swimming, water.**

waffles

Making or serving waffles points to indecision (that is, you are waffling or flip-flopping on an issue). Once you make your choice, though, everyone will accept it with thanks.

wagging

If someone is wagging a finger at you in a dream, you are feeling guilty about a recent word or action. If a dog is wagging its tail, you are feeling appreciated and admired. *See also* **fingers, pointing.**

wagon

To dream of traveling in a wagon indicates that you

possess the self-sufficiency that will enable you to adopt the simpler lifestyle you desire. *See also* **cabin, pioneer.**

wainscoting

Wainscoting indicates that you have not told the whole story. If the wainscoting is decorative and matches the rest of the room, you have hidden small details. If the wainscoting is unattractive and looks out of place, others will realize you have masked the truth.

waiting

Consider who is waiting in your dream. What is his or her mood? Waiting may symbolize patience or a lack thereof. It may also be a message to hold out for a better opportunity. To dream of being placed on a waiting list indicates that you need more practice in order to master a new skill.

wait staff

If you dream of waiting tables in any sort of restaurant, expect that you will soon juggle many tasks simultaneously, but you will do so with grace and ease. If you occasionally feel unappreciated for your efforts, don't let that stop you from striving for your goals. *See also* **baking, cooking.**

A Father and Son Guided by Dreams

Italian poet and playwright Dante Alighieri claimed that his classic work *The Divine Comedy* was told to him in a dream. After he died in 1321, a portion of the original manuscript went missing. Around that time, Alighieri's son Jacob dreamed that his father came to him and answered many of his questions concerning the afterlife. When Jacob asked about the missing pages of the manuscript, his father led him to a room in which he often slept when alive. Alighieri touched one of the walls and said, "What you have sought is here." Then he disappeared. When Jacob woke, he found the missing pages behind the wall, just where his father had indicated.

wake

To dream that you are caught in the wake of a boat or ship foretells a struggle that will require you to ask for help from someone who is currently more grounded. To attend the wake of someone who has died is to recall fond memories of someone you have lost touch with. Reach out to that person before it's too late. Finally, to feel that you have awakened while you sleep indicates that you are dreaming lucidly—you are a lucky person who will gain a lot from this ability! *See also Chapter 5, pages 37–46.*

walking

A dream in which you are walking can be interpreted by your pace and overall emotion while doing so. Are you walking intently toward someone or something, or are you out for a leisurely stroll, taking in and appreciating all that you encounter? Do you feel that you are going in the right direction, or do you feel lost? A dream in which you are trying to walk but can't move your feet represents extreme frustration in your waking life. *See also* **immobility, running.**

wall

A wall is a classic dream symbol: It can mark an obstruction or obstacle—essentially, a predicament—that you have to overcome. Whether the wall is solid (made of bricks) or flimsy (made of plywood) indicates how easily you will get through this period. A wall can also mean that you are ensconced in your own reality or that you have put up walls around you, distancing yourself from friends, family, or an uncomfortable situation. Don't dismiss the idea the someone might be driving you up a wall! *See also* **door, obstacles.**

wallet

This image represents your confidence and sense of identity. What is the condition of the wallet? Does it contain money or personal identification, or is it empty? These observations will provide you with an idea of the value you place on your opinions or in your ability to provide for yourself or your family. To dream of losing a wallet represents financial worries that will prove problematic. *See also* **money, purse.**

wallpaper

Wallpaper (especially if you find a pattern or color displeasing) can indicate deception: Someone is trying to hide something shameful from you. But to apply wallpaper can suggest that you will soon undergo a change in appearance that will provide you with a new lease on life and give a greater sense of self-worth. *See also* **painting, renovate, wainscoting.**

walnut

This nut generally represents an unforeseen abundance in your personal or professional life. Cracking open a walnut in a dream means you will soon solve a perplexing problem. Whole walnuts reflect barriers that may prove hard to crack.

walrus

In some cultures, a walrus represents strength and self-sufficiency. This dream image can also warn against barking out orders or displaying false bravado: The person who calls you out on such behavior will be much more nimble, both physically and intellectually. A walrus can also predict that you will need to be thick-skinned with regard to forthcoming comments or accusations.

waltz

A dream in which you are waltzing with someone reflects that you are in step with your current partner. To waltz alone, however, is a sign that your tendency to breeze through life with little effort will get you nowhere. *See also* **dance.**

wand

Waving a magic wand points to your ability to persuade or control others. Be warned that your influence is temporary at best. A wand also serves to remind you that you have to actually work for what you want. *See also* **magic, magician.**

wander

This isn't necessarily a negative dream image: Although wandering can suggest aimlessness or a lack of motivation, it more often indicates that you are in a life phase that will bring you clarity and direction. The fact that you are wandering rather than remaining stagnant means you will soon acquire the self-awareness that you have been missing. *See also* **journey, quest, walking.**

want

Try to distinguish this common dream feeling from an actual need. What do you want and why? Frequently, to dream that you want something points to what you feel you are lacking emotionally. For example, if you dream that you want a new house, you should consider whether you are content with your family life. *See also* **need, yearning.**

war

Not usually a literal symbol, war can point to any impending or ongoing argument. And, as with any other type of confrontation, the war often centers on a conflict you are having with yourself. Focus on the issues that initiated the war or that keep it going. In most cases, you are the only one who can resolve things peacefully. *See also* **argument, battle.**

warehouse

A warehouse represents the vast resources you have at your disposal. Although you have been unaware of them, they are yours for the taking.

warmth

This dream feeling often reflects a need for security and acceptance. If you feel comfortably warm, expect to be welcomed into a new social or professional situation. However, there is a fine line between feeling warm and *too* warm: Pay attention to this symbolism. *See also* **thermometer.**

warning

To feel that you are being warned in a dream is a message to pay closer attention to important matters in your waking life. The clues lie in the specific images, objects, and people in the dream. To send out a warning is a cry for help— you can no longer manage a problematic situation on your own. *See also* **alarm.**

In dreams begins responsibility.
—William Butler Yeats

---

warts

To envision yourself with warts (whether or not you have them) indicates that you are unhappy with your appearance—to the point of obsession. Realize that most people take little notice of your perceived imperfections. To notice warts on others warns against making superficial judgments. An alternate interpretation is that you will soon encounter a less-than-favorable situation or a persistently difficult person.

washing

Washing anything indicates a desire to cleanse, purify, or rid yourself of unwanted things, whether they are possessions, habits, or relationships. If the washing is difficult (e.g., stains are hard to remove), you may have a guilty conscience and should come clean. *See also* **bath, clean, shower.**

waste

See **garbage, litter.**

watch

If the image is of a timepiece, check the time or how fast it's moving for clues to its meaning. This dream image carries similar significance with regard to your recognition of the passing of time (or life) in general. Are you aware of its pace? Does it seem to move slow or too fast? Alternately, do you feel you are being watched or monitored? If so, adjust your behavior appropriately. Consider idiomatic uses of the word, such "watch yourself," "stand watch," and "watch out." *See also* **clock, witness.**

water

Water is an extremely common symbol that can represent anything from actual physical thirst to the way in which your life plan is flowing. First, consider the body of water in your dream: Is it large and deep like an ocean (or sea) or relatively small and shallow like a pond? Also note the conditions of the water: Is it clean, murky, smooth, or choppy? Are you ready to jump in or do you have fears? The answers to these questions will offer insight as to how you might change aspects

of yourself or your life. *See also* **lake, ocean, pond, swimming.**

waterfall

A waterfall indicates a need for an outpouring of emotion. Don't hold back!

wave

Waving your hand denotes that you are ready to dismiss or embrace someone or something. Waving an object such as a flag can be a sign of support or surrender. Waves in a body of water reflect emotions that seem to be ever-changing: Whether the waves are gentle or crashing determines a period of relaxation or turmoil. Also consider the movement of water as it relates to tides. *See also* **ocean, tide, water.**

wax

To dream of wax dripping from a candle is a sign that a relationship is running out of air. To wax something such as a car or furniture reflects a need to polish your skills. *See also* **candle, polishing.**

weakness

Feeling weak in a dream is most often an indication that you are feeling run-down. Consider whether you have taken on too many responsibilities, and then decide what really requires your attention.

wealth

To dream of being or becoming wealthy is a sign that you are lacking something emotionally that can't be filled with money. You will gain insight into a perplexing issue. *See also* **affluence, poverty.**

weasel

Be warned of an untrustworthy person who doesn't play by the rules. If you dream of a weasel, you may have trust issues.

weather

Weather represents your emotions, and dreams of certain weather conditions will influence your mood the following morning. *See also* *individual weather conditions.*

wedding

A wedding represents cooperation. It doesn't have to be a literal symbol but instead can indicate a union or commitment of any sort, such as a business venture or a political or community effort. Alternately, if you feel wed to a particular idea, does it ultimately benefit you? *See also* **marriage.**

weeds

Weeds represent bad habits that can interfere with your goals. To weed a lawn or garden is a sign that you are looking after your health. *See also* **garden.**

weight

See **heavy.**

welcome

A dream in which you are welcomed into an event or party reflects a positive self-image. If you welcome people into your home, your gracious hospitality will be appreciated and acknowledged. However, if you dream of a welcome mat, beware of people who will take advantage of your generous spirit.

well

A well represents the depth of your knowledge. Someone will soon contact you in an attempt to draw from your wisdom.

wet

Do you feel like a fish out of water? If you dream of being wet in an environment where

---

It's Raining Bullets

Scottish inventor James Watt dreamed of being bombarded with tiny round pellets of lead as he walked through a storm. Upon waking and considering this dream, Watt had an idea that perhaps if molten lead were dropped from a great height into water, it would form small spheres, like the pellets in his dream. He successfully tested his theory by dropping molten lead from a church tower into water below. Watt's dream provided a simpler, more efficient way to produce lead shot, a process that had always proved time-consuming and laborious.

you should be dry, you are fixated on how others perceive you. If you dream of watering plants, you need to nurture someone before it is too late. *See also* **garden, plants, water.**

whale

Dreams that feature a whale serve to reassure you that what has seemed overwhelming will begin to proceed smoothly. There's no more need to wail about it.

wheel

A wheel indicates cycles and patterns. Be aware of falling back into old habits. Exercise self-control. *See also* **circles.**

wheelbarrow

Using a wheelbarrow assures you that the strength and confidence you are gaining through physical labor will pay off financially. However, be wary of someone who asks you to carry his or her burden.

whip

If you dream of a whip, you have an irrational fear of communication and are afraid of anyone who might lash out at you. Instead, use the metaphorical whip to confront a crisis and make yourself heard. Also consider whether the idiom "whipped" (as in someone who is easily manipulated) applies to you.

whirlwind

See **hurricane, tornado, wind.**

whisper

To whisper in a dream implies that you have revealed secrets or information that should have been kept confidential. To hear whispers could point to a new relationship: Someone may soon be whispering sweet nothings in your ear, but consider the value of nothings. *See also* **voices.**

whistle

The sound of a whistle or whistling warns that your time may be running out to tell someone the truth. To blow a whistle is to put an end to idle speculation or gossip. *See also* **alarm, horn.**

white

The color white can represent purity of heart and clarity of mind, but if your dream images are only white, you need to expand your horizons and appreciate the beauty life has to offer. *See also sidebar on page 85.*

widow/widower

Whether or not your spouse has died, this feeling can reflect abandonment, loneliness, or neglect. *See also* **death.**

wife

As an archetypal figure, a wife can represent a female mate, partner, or friend in a relationship that is personal or related to business. *See also individual familiy members,* **family.**

wig

If you don't usually wear a wig, to dream of wearing one suggests that you feel a need to disguise yourself. Is there something you are ashamed of or are trying to conceal? Wearing a wig can also point to fears of growing old or appearing older than you are. *See also* **hair, toupee.**

wiggle

This dream feeling indicates that you are caught in a situation you can't wiggle out of. Wiggling suggests that you are in an uncomfortable position in your career or

friendship. Best to speak up about it.

wild/wilderness

Anything referred to as wild typically can't be cultivated, tamed, or owned. To dream that you are a wild person suggests that you loosen your bond with conventional thoughts and ideals—a little freedom will do you a world of good. To dream that you are wandering through or lost in the wilderness reflects a quest for solitude and reinforces your ability to live on your own. *See also* **forest, woods.**

willow tree

Dreams that feature a willow tree signify that you will be acknowledged as someone who is flexible in your attitudes and beliefs. If you dream of sitting under a willow tree, you seek the company of more open-minded people. Alternately, you may be shy or incapable of speaking up for yourself. *See also* **trees.**

wilt

You shouldn't necessarily worry if you feel faint or droopy: Consider it a price paid for an extraordinary effort! If this interpretation doesn't apply, do you tend to wilt under work-related pressure or other heated circumstances? The cause can be attributed to low self-esteem or a bout of sadness or fatigue due to an underlying health issue. *See also* **wither.**

win

To win something in a dream means that through a hardship, you will gain wisdom and a new perspective. Use that confidence to pursue your goals. *See also* **lottery, victory.**

wind

As a dream symbol, wind traditionally represents the impression you leave on the people you meet for the first time. Do you appear as a sudden gust, only to leave just as quickly? In the meantime, what have you stirred up? Another interpretation is that you are in a relationship that is in transition. Things are subject to change without notice, but remember to listen to what's blowing in the wind. *See also* **weather, wind chimes, windmill.**

wind chimes

This dream image serves to remind you of the beauty and harmony in your life. Enjoy the tranquility while it lasts.

windmill

You are trying to motivate or energize others to tackle or complete a task, most likely at work. Have no fear: You have a sensible, alternative approach that no one else has considered.

window

A window reflects your personal or professional opportunities. Is the window open or closed? If you can see your reflection in the window, is the image accurate or distorted? A window can also symbolize a last-ditch way to escape a stifling relationship. *See also* **door, mirror.**

wine

Wine can reflect your appreciation for indulgences

that you may or may not feel you deserve. If you dream of drinking wine or making a toast, you will soon have the opportunity to engage in something pleasurable. A different interpretation points to the word "whine." *See also* **alcohol, thirst.**

wings

Wings symbolize protection and security. In what ways does someone shelter you under his or her wing, and what is your response to that? Of course, a wing is also a symbol of flight. You should expect to go beyond what you perceive as your limitations. *See also* **birds, flying.**

wink

If you dream of receiving a wink, expect flirtation or even a romance to arise from unusual circumstances. At the same time, don't put a lot of hope into the longevity of the encounter.

winter

This season represents a period of slow or minimal growth. Take advantage of the time and reflect or concentrate on what you want to achieve.

wise old man/ wise old woman

These archetypes draw attention to human wisdom and intuition. If you dream of talking to such figures, pay

The Turtle Boat

Admiral Yi Sun-shin, commander of the Korean navy in the late 16th century, was growing increasingly concerned about the invasion of Japanese forces. One night he dreamed that a huge turtle rose from the sea with fire shooting out of its mouth. When the admiral awakened, he immediately began drawing design plans for the world's first ironclad battle-ship, referred to as a *kobukson,* or turtle boat. The *kobukson* had a closed roof that resembled a turtle's back and a bow fashioned in the shape of a dragon's head, covered with iron spikes. The crew, hidden inside, fired cannonballs through the mouth of the dragon, which made it appear that the dragon was spewing smoke. Admiral Yi and his men would proceed to use the *kobukson* to successfully fight off Japanese fleets.

attention to their messages. In doing so, you will realize that they are sent from your subconscious mind. *See also* **guru.**

wishbone

A wishbone is an omen of good luck. Expect a long-held wish to come true!

witch

There are various ways to interpret this symbol (which includes the image of a warlock), but it most often reflects issues of empowerment. If you dream of the traditional images of the evil or good witch, you either feel suspicious of or antagonistic toward someone, or you see yourself as above others and will take advantage of this perception whenever possible. If you dream of a pagan witch, you long to get back to nature and reconnect with the inner self. To dream that you are performing witchcraft—that is, you can conjure spells or summon supernatural powers—means that you feel insignificant or ignored in your waking life. *See also* **magic.**

withdrawal

Making a monetary withdrawal from a bank means you are feeling positive and have plenty of physical and emotional energy to expend. But withdrawal has negative implications as well. If you dream of withdrawing from people or situations, your energy has been depleted. Take this as a suggestion to care for yourself and refuel. To dream that you are going through withdrawal from a substance, (alcohol or drugs) is often a direct reflection of what you are experiencing or need to experience in real life.

wither

Something that withers (such as a flower) can reflect deep disappointment or feelings of neglect. Alternately, it warns that you will have to rise to the occasion to meet your goals or what other people expect of you. In other words, don't give in to pressure! *See also* **wilt.**

witness

Have you inadvertently seen something that is causing you anxiety? Perhaps you feel scrutinized and worry what others may think.

wizard

You will soon meet someone who may appear outwardly strange or eccentric but who will give you indispensable advice. Heed it!

wolf

A wolf can symbolize survival, solitude, or predation. If you dream of a lone wolf, you will face a trying situation and will have to rely on your own strength to get through it. If you dream of a pack of wolves, look for help from your family and friends to tackle a crisis. If you dream of being chased by a wolf, you will soon be contacted by an old acquaintance. Be warned, however: That person has less-than-honorable intentions. *See also sidebar on page 54.*

wood/woods

Traditionally, wood (as a product of trees) is lauded for its strength, stability, and potential for growth. If you dream of working with pieces of wood, are you whittling them (which implies either overanalysis or distraction), or are you carving a larger piece (reflecting creativity and concentration)? To walk through a wooded area points to a need for self-reflection. You likely feel confused or lost in your waking life, but if you actually look at and appreciate what surrounds you (that is, the gifts you have), you will gain a more positive perspective. *See also* **forest, nature, trees.**

woodpecker

The symbolism of this bird serves to remind you of the importance of fortitude and perseverance. To hear the repetitious sound of a woodpecker is a sign that you have forgotten to do something. Remember your commitments, because others are relying on you.

worm

Are you trying to worm your way into or out of a situation? A worm can represent an intrusive person or someone who manages to become involved in other people's business. To dream of putting a worm on a hook (as bait) suggests enticement or a desire to catch someone's eye.

worship

To worship in a dream indicates that you are intimidated by the accomplishments of others. Don't be quick to put anyone on a pedestal. The dream symbol can also indicate that you hold yourself to impossibly high standards. *See also* **pedestal, praying.**

wound

An open wound is a sign of unfinished business. To apply a bandage to a wound is a sign of denial. A healing wound signifies that difficult times are almost over because you have offered forgiveness. *See also* **bandage, injury.**

wreath

A wreath made of laurel means that you will soon complete a difficult task. If you dream of a Christmas (or other holiday) wreath, long-held hopes will be realized but quickly dashed. A funeral wreath foretells the end

of a negative state of mind.

wrestle

If you dream of wrestling, you are trying to choose your options. However, realize that the fight is one that you are having with your conscience or subconscious. The important point: Listen to your intuition. *See also* **argument.**

wrinkles

A wrinkled face can represent wisdom and the passage of time. The fear of having wrinkles suggests that you have an immature view of life or that you don't appreciate the wisdom of your elders. If you dream of wrinkled fabric, you need to iron out kinks in a project or relationship before it can proceed to the next stage. *See also* **iron, old.**

> *Only the dreamer shall understand realities, though, in truth, his dreaming must not be out of proportion to his waking!*
>
> —Margaret Fuller,
> *Summer on the Lakes*

wrist

Your wrist reflects your strength and flexibility in the face of adverse conditions. A sprained wrist is a sign of indecision, and a broken wrist foretells broken promises.

writing

If you dream of writing, you desire to express long-suppressed opinions. You may need to get something off your chest. Pay attention to the symbolism in what you have written. *See also* **diary, letter.**

X

x

The letter "X" translates numerically as "10," which implies perfectionism (a goal that is, of course, unrealistic). Also consider these diverse and often contradictory idiomatic references: "X" marks the spot, "X" warns of an intersection (or a point of indecision), and "X" is a mathematical term that means an unknown quantity. What's more, it is universally acceptable to use the letter "X" in place of a signature.

x-ray

Dreams that focus on X-rays usually highlight your keen intuition and recommend that you use it to identify someone with a transparent character. Alternately, this dream symbol can reflect that you are being scrutinized by someone. Be sure of the image you want to project. *See also* **radiation.**

xylophone

To play a xylophone foretells a confusing situation with many possible solutions. Consider all of them and then choose the one that sounds right to you.

Y

yacht

A dream of owning a yacht reflects your desire for a lifestyle that seems unattainable but is, in fact, realistic if you are patient and stay focused on your goals. *See also* **boats.**

yams

Yams signify self-sufficiency, creativity, and good health. If this vegetable isn't part of your usual diet, its symbolism suggests that you change a bland routine.

yard

A front yard represents the person you are in public. A backyard represents your personal, private side. Is your yard well-maintained (that is, you try hard to keep up appearances) or unkempt (you don't care about how others view you)? Do you believe in the adage "the grass is greener on the other side of the fence"? *See also* **grass, lawn.**

yardstick

Don't be so quick to measure each new experience based on those in your past. Recognize and embrace every moment as unique.

yarn

Tangled yarn represents gossip and hurt feelings over a misunderstanding. To unravel tangled yarn is to get to the bottom of a story. To create something with yarn foretells a celebration with family and friends. *See also* **knit, sewing.**

yawn

Physiologically, yawning while you think you are dreaming suggests that you are not getting enough REM (or restful) sleep. As an actual dream symbol, a yawn can represent hesitation or a pause in thought. Perhaps you are reevaluating a business negotiation or the quality of a personal relationship. Alternately, a yawn can

---

Tuning into Dreams

Comedian and songwriter Steve Allen woke from a dream in which he heard the music and lyrics for a song. He immediately played the notes on his piano, wrote down the lyrics, and completed the tune. The song "This Could Be the Start of Something Big" was featured in the 1950s musical hit *The Bachelor.* Allen claimed that he often heard music in his dreams and even titled another dreamed-up tune "I Had a Dream Last Night About My Old Piano."

reflect how you feel your life is progressing. Apparently, it's time to pick up the pace.

yearning

To yearn for something in a dream is different from wanting in the intensity or immediacy of what is desired. The key is in the objects or symbols in the particular dream sequence. *See also* **need, want.**

yeast

The smell of yeast suggests that your emotions, if they go unchecked, may soon get out of control. It can also be a sign that someone needs you to fill a void in his or her life. *See also* **baking, bread.**

yell

As with any other loud expression, yelling is your dream self's attempt to make you aware that something or someone requires your attention. The same interpretation applies if someone is yelling at you.

yellow

The color yellow represents clear thinking, logic, and intellect. To wear yellow or see someone wearing yellow is an indication of neutral feelings. *See also sidebar on page 85.*

yenta

This symbol can reflect your attempt to pass along important information. Unfortunately, the meaning of your words was confusing or lost in translation. On the other hand, you may have misread well-intended advice. Give the source another chance.

yield

If you yield to someone or something in a dream, you will soon receive recognition for a charitable act. To graciously yield to someone foretells a harmonious personal or business relationship. However, if you yield begrudgingly or against your will, prepare to defend yourself in a formidable argument.

Dreams are faithful interpreters of our inclinations; but there is art required to sort and understand them.
—French essayist Michel de Montaigne

yodel

Someone is calling out to you. Pay attention to the words rather than the way they are delivered. This dream symbol can also mean that you will renew an old friendship. *See also* **singing, voices.**

yoga

To dream of practicing yoga indicates that if you are put in a stressful situation, patience and flexibility will bring you relief.

yoke

To wear a yoke reflects the fact that you have been carrying a hidden burden for far too long. Now is the time to let it go. *See also* **saddle.**

yolk

An egg yolk refers to beginnings or possibilities. It can also represent someone who is shy or introverted. If that description doesn't pertain to you but you know such a person, help draw him or her out of that shell. *See also* **egg.**

youthfulness

If you dream of being youthful, expect to experience a resurgence of energy or an increased enthusiasm for life in general. Alternately, youthfulness implies naïvete or inexperience. *See also* **age.**

yo-yo

This dream symbol indicates that someone seemingly close to you will renege on a promise. A yo-yo can also point out a period of indecision or inconsistent thoughts or actions. Take time to get your bearings.

Z

zebra

To dream of a zebra is a reminder that the truth can be murky—in other words, not everything is either black or white. Be willing to compromise.

zero

This dream image can have different meanings. You may have hit a low point and are ready to start over. Or you may feel empty because someone or something is no longer in your life. If may also be a sign that you are zeroing in on something or getting closer to realizing a goal. *See also sidebar on page 175.*

zigzag

To see a zigzag pattern indicates that information you have received can be interpreted in several ways. If you feel confused or unsure, straighten out the situation yourself.

zinc

In general, zinc is a symbol that you will soon heal from a long-held wound. What's more, this element indicates that you will also enjoy improved mental and physical health.

zipper

If you dream of a zipper, you should remember to hold your tongue when you feel the urge to gossip. If not, you will later get caught and regret what you've said. *See also* **gossip, mouth.**

zircon

Don't be fooled by outward appearances or get taken in by flashy ads. Something seems too good to be true—and that's exactly what it is.

zodiac

The astrological zodiac indicates that you place too much emphasis on fate—in other words, what is "meant to be" or what's "in the stars."

zombie

Feeling listless? Tired of routine? A zombie implies that something in your life has become monotonous and a change is needed. It can also represent someone who is uncomfortable making decisions and prefers things to stay as they are.

zoo

A zoo can represent excitement, chaos (this place is a zoo), or oppression and confinement. Consider the interpretation that best applies to you.

Appendix
LET YOUR JOURNEY BEGIN!

As you begin to record and interpret your dreams, the messages will be more meaningful if you include as many details as possible (title, reminder phrase, emotions, characters, etc.). Using this sample journal entry as a guide, write your own dream journal entry in the space provided. Consider this your first step in mastering the art of dream interpretation—and be prepared to live a richer, more purposeful life!

Sample Dream Journal Entry

Dream Title: Trying to Meet Mom for Lunch

Overall Theme: Motherhood

Notes About the Day: It has been hectic all morning at home, but Mom wants to meet me downtown for lunch—just the two of us. I know that, once again, she'll want to talk about how I (being an older and newly divorced mother) plan to support my child and myself. In the meantime, the baby is teething and has been fussy, and the sitter arrived late. I am unusually tired and barely have the energy to take a shower before running out the door. I feel guilty as I leave and hear the baby crying.

Reminder Phrase: I remember my dreams easily.

Dream Content: I have a lunch date with Mom, but as usual, I'm running late. It's a cloudy, misty day as I walk downtown to our favorite restaurant. In the distance, I see Mom standing under an archway. I quicken my pace, but I don't seem to get any closer to her. I am slowed by the cumbersome package I'm carrying. The next time I look ahead, I see Mom standing under a different type of arch. I keep walking toward her, but I'm distracted while trying to figure out why what I'm carrying seems so heavy. Suddenly, a man steps in front of me and tries to sell me a

---

Sample Dream Journal Entry *continued*

watch. I don't want it. He keeps saying, "Take it! Take it!" I walk away, grumbling angrily to myself. I don't feel well, but then I remember that I have to get to Mom, so I rush toward the restaurant. Before I reach it, I awaken, feeling frustrated.

Emotions: Frustration, anxiety, confusion, guilt, anger

Weather: Cloudy, misty

Location: Downtown

Characters: My baby, me, the sitter, my mother, and the strange man

Objects: Arch (over Mom); package (in my hands); watch (in man's hands)

Personal Observations: In the dream, I feel anxious, ill, guilty, and easily distracted. What's more, I can't believe I've forgotten my intent to meet Mom.

The General Interpretation

This dream self uses "arch" in reference to "archetype." Her mother, who stands under different arches, represents the archetypal mother, or the part of the personality that nurtures. The fact that she isn't able to get to her mother as her mother waits under the arches suggests that their relationship is at a standstill.

The interesting conflict centers on nurturing and motherhood: The dreamer is distracted because she is concerned about her baby, but at the same time, she forgets her commitment to her own mother. She feels weighed down by the package she is carrying: The package could represent her baby at home, but because this dreamer mentions that she feels ill, the package likely represents a pregnancy she's not yet aware of. The strange man could represent an authority figure who is trying to give her advice. He repeats himself, indicating that his message is important. The watch he is selling could represent the passage of time, referring, perhaps, to a "biological clock" or an urgency to have more children.

DREAM JOURNAL

_____

_____

_____

_____

_____

_____

_____

_____

_____

_____

_____

_____

_____

_____

_____

_____

_____

_____

_____

_____

_____

_____

_____

_____

_____

_____

_____

_____

_____

_____

_____

_____

_____

_____

_____

_____

_____

_____

_____

_____

_____

_____

_____

_____

_____

_____

_____

_____

_____

_____

_____

_____

_____

_____

_____

_____

_____

*I've dreamt in my life dreams that
have stayed with me ever after,
and changed my ideas; they've gone
through and through me,
like wine through water, and altered
the colour of my mind.*

—Emily Brontë